Developing College Reading

Second Edition

Lee A. Jacobus

University of Connecticut

Harcourt Brace Jovanovich, Inc.

New York San Diego Chicago San Francisco Atlanta

ISBN: 0-15-517602-1
Library of Congress Catalog Card Number: 78-71194
Printed in the United States of America

Preface

Developing College Reading, Second Edition—like its companion, *Improving College Reading*—contains significant material of particular interest to the young adult reader. The method of organization (proceeding from relatively simple to more difficult selections) has proved successful in the first edition of this book and in the three editions of its companion volume. Instructors who have used the books have repeatedly indicated that the method stimulates their students to measurable progress.

This volume contains passages by some of our finest writers: Katherine Anne Porter, Reinhold Niebuhr, Shirley Jackson, Robert Frost, Rachel Carson, Arthur Koestler, Aldous Huxley, Joseph Wood Krutch, Francis Steegmuller, and Loren Eiseley. Subjects range from new developments in psychology to reflections on anthropology, from the history of the written word to the romance of the roller coaster, and from reminiscences of Hollywood's golden days to memories of slavery. Paul Theroux brings us to the frontiers of India for a glimpse of a legendary railroad; a young Chinese-American, Leslie Wong, experiences an uneasy return to his roots; Vine Deloria calls Hollywood up short for its portrayal of American Indians; Alvin Toffler reveals something of the changes in language in his speculations on Shakespeare; Lawrence F. Peter and Raymond Hull discuss the Peter

Principle and its influence on our lives; the implications for the future are explored in David Sheridan's predictions about a second coal age; Andrew Cockburn alerts us to an unspoken nuclear disaster that has already occurred; fear of aging is the subject of Albert Rosenfeld's frank study of our attitudes toward the old; and the impact of computers (which have brought their own revolution into our lives) is the concern of the editors of *Time* magazine. The poetry selections—Amy Lowell's "Patterns" and Robert Service's delightful "The Cremation of Sam McGee," for example—offer a special kind of pleasure and challenge to the careful reader.

Students will most likely progress straight through the book from beginning to end as the readings and testing material become gradually more difficult. Or they may, if the instructor chooses, work on selected readings within the five sections rather than proceeding in any strict order. All the selections are new to this edition, and the readings in each section are relatively equal in their level of difficulty.

This Second Edition features a more direct and simplified testing apparatus of a kind that is familiar to most students. The exercises following each selection are designed to help students develop concentration, locate important ideas or concepts, retain detail, and—above all—build their vocabularies. Each of the major sections begins with a Vocabulary Preview that defines the more difficult words in the section and tests students' retention of them. The reading progress charts at the back of the book enable students to evaluate their own progress. Reading speed is not emphasized in the tests that accompany the selections, but by using the appropriate chart a student can calculate his or her own speed and establish an individual index of reading efficiency.

I want to thank Sharon Jacobus, who helped in the research and secretarial chores for this book. And I wish to dedicate the book to all instructors of reading development.

Lee A. Jacobus

Contents

SECTION 5

SECTION 1

Vocabulary Preview

The following words come from the seven reading selections in Section 1. Study the list carefully, pronouncing the words aloud if possible. Conceal the definitions with a card or your hand and test your command of the meanings of the words.

apathy, *noun* lack of interest
apparatus, *noun* device used for a particular purpose
belie, *verb* to give a false impression
benison, *noun* a blessing
climatic, *adj.* having to do with weather conditions
connoisseur, *noun* an expert qualified to judge in some field of art or taste
conspicuously, *adv.* in a manner attracting attention; strikingly
diverge, *verb* to move in different directions starting from the same point; to differ
elliptical, *adj.* oval-shaped
entomology, *noun* the study of insects
expendable, *adj.* disposable
exploitation, *noun* unjust or improper use of someone or something
fervor, *noun* enthusiasm; excitement
forte, *noun* one's strong point; something at which a person excels
horrendous, *adj.* dreadful
inaudible, *adj.* not able to be heard
incinerated, *verb* burnt to ashes
incompetence, *noun* inability to act effectively
indolent, *adj.* lazy; slow
inextricably, *adv.* tangled inseparably
inherent, *adj.* an essential characteristic of something
inundate, *verb* to overwhelm; to flood
ironically, *adv.* expressing the opposite of what is really meant
leviathan, *noun* something formidable
liabilities, *noun* financial debts; disadvantages
luminous, *adj.* giving off light
maneuverable, *adj.* able to be moved
mastodons, *noun* extinct, elephantlike animals
multiethnic, *adj.* of a variety of ethnic backgrounds

obsolete, *adj.* outmoded; no longer in use
parabola, *noun* a kind of curve
ponderous, *adj.* heavy
precariously, *adv.* unstably; subject to chance
resilient, *adj.* springing back; recovering readily from misfortune
savannas, *noun* broad, open plains
servility, *noun* a state of slavish submission
shrouded, *verb* screened from view
tubular, *adj.* shaped like a tube
undulating, *adj.* wavelike
vogue, *noun* fashion, fad

Choose the word or phrase that best defines the vocabulary item:

1. ____ exploitation: (a) damning (b) harmful (c) unfair use (d) sudden eruption (e) careful examination

2. ____ savanna: (a) southern exposure (b) copper mine (c) playing field (d) plains (e) deforestation

3. ____ belies: (a) fakes (b) is truthful (c) inconsequential (d) indolent (e) lazy

4. ____ inundate: (a) refrain from (b) flood (c) cool (d) timeless (e) portentous

5. ____ ponderous: (a) weighty (b) thoughtful (c) meditative (d) hesitant (e) enormous

6. ____ diverge: (a) separate from (b) hesitate (c) storm (d) precise (e) unreflective

7. ____ resilient: (a) silent (b) subtle (c) elastic (d) explicit (e) smooth, silky

8. ____ undulating: (a) soothing (b) sexy (c) wavy (d) thoughtful (e) pleasing

9. ____ entomology: (a) grave digging (b) bird watching (c) insect study (d) philosophy of environment (e) science of fish

10. ____ servility: (a) good service (b) submissiveness (c) courage (d) rage (e) anguish

11. ____ conspicuously: (a) obviously (b) silently (c) without being noticed (d) by means of direct action (e) astonishingly

12. ____ inextricably: (a) intinately (b) fallaciously (c) cautiously (d) stolidly (e) inseparably

13. ____ apathy: (a) without interest (b) quickness (c) alarm (d) school spirit (e) a kind of illness

14. ____ indolent: (a) industry (b) excitement (c) lazy (d) redeeming (e) dull

15. ____ inherent: (a) essential; within (b) genetic; the family (c) referring to skin (d) meaningful, serious (e) regardful

1

Roots in China

Leslie Wong

Even Americans of Chinese ancestry may feel "culture shock" at seeing their relatives in China. When Leslie Wong visited his grandparents and cousins, he didn't know what to expect. His surprises were numerous.

When most visitors go to the People's Republic of China, they see factories, communes and schools. Near Peking they see the Great Wall, the Ming Tombs and the Summer Palace. On a recent trip I saw all these but also saw something else, something that few go to China to see: their own family.

Each year, some persons whom the Chinese consider to be "overseas Chinese" are permitted to enter the People's Republic and visit relatives. Until recently, most of the overseas Chinese came from places in the Orient: Hong Kong, Macao and Singapore, for example. But since the recent decrease in tension in Sino-American relations, some Americans of Chinese descent are being allowed to visit their relatives in China. My mother, Sophia Wong, and I were granted visas for this reason.

My grandfather, my maternal aunts, uncles and cousins all live in China. In 1946 my mother immigrated to the United States. She had not seen any members of her family since. For her, the trip would be a return to her native country and to her family after 30 years of absence. I viewed the visit as a unique opportunity to meet relatives whom I had never known before.

I may look Chinese. Certainly, the roots of my ancestry are in China. My father was born in Hong Kong, my mother in Shanghai. I was born in Oakland, California, and spent most of my life there until college. Even though the political fervor and increased ethnic consciousness that I found in college may have made me more aware of my ancestry, I am still conspicuously American in culture—a result of growing up in a middle-class, multi-ethnic neighborhood.

My friends envied me in being able to go to China to get a firsthand look at "my" culture. But my friends were wrong. I found, after my 30-day visit, that despite the fact I look Chinese, know how to use chopsticks and cook a few Chinese dishes, I felt unconnected with the flow of life in China. My culture wasn't in China, of course. My culture is the one in which I grew up. What China was like had always been a mystery to me. I still had little knowledge of China when I walked across the border at Shumchim, near Hong Kong. I had deliberately refrained from doing any extensive research so that I could form my own conclusions from experience and observations. But walking across the border seemed to instill a new feeling of excitement and anticipation.

Most of my relatives live in Shanghai. The patriarch is my 93-year-old grandfather, Chang Tat-seung. Others include an uncle who is a factory superintendent and mechanical engineer; another uncle who is an assembler in an automobile factory; an aunt who is a retired librarian; and another aunt, a medical book illustrator, who arrived from Hankow with her daughter especially for this family reunion.

My grandfather lives with his second wife near the end of a lane. The three-story building has one family to a floor and all share a single bathroom on the second floor. The entrance is dimly lit by a bare bulb. Each time my mother and I visited my grandfather, an old woman who lives on the ground floor opened the door for us and greeted us. Each time we walked up the twisting stairs that led to his studio, we wondered, because of my grandfather's age, whether he shouldn't have an apartment on a lower floor. When we asked my step-grandmother about this, she told us the government had once offered him a ground-floor apartment but grandfather had turned it down. He said it was good exercise walking up and down stairs.

After the first night of meeting my family at grandfather's apartment, I came away not having a clear picture of exactly who each person was. After seeing various members of my family every day for a week, I was finally able to recognize them and call them by name. One evening, at an elaborate dinner at grandfather's apartment, I took a thoughtful look at my family. I knew a little bit about each one and I was beginning to acquire images of how my cousins were living their lives. Owing to the language problem, I could not communicate directly with them; I realized that I didn't really know them and I felt half-a-world apart from them. Being with my relatives for a week counted for very little. They were really still strangers to me, and if someone had walked in off the street and introduced himself to me as being still another relative, I would have believed him.

After a little while, however, I did begin to learn more. For example, my 15-year-old cousin, Chou Hsiao-mi, probably will work in a factory next year after she finishes high school. She likes to read fiction and studies trigonometry, geometry, physical education, English, music and industry basics. She will also study health and chemistry in her next school term. She is a member of the Red Guard, which was fascinating to me when I recalled the role of the Red Guard during the Cultural Revolution of the 1960s, before her time. Through her mother, she explained her activities as a Red Guard member. She will work on a farm, put up political posters and attend political meetings. She is in the Red Guard, she says, because she is a better student than most in her class.

The longer I am in China, the more curious I get about the lives my relatives are living. On the other hand, my relatives do not seem to be curious about my life in the United States. On few occasions did any of them ask us about our lives at home in our own country. One aunt, the librarian, asked us about the treatment of blacks in the United States. She then discussed the difficulty of changing one's thinking and attitudes and feelings: "Very slowly the changes come . . . looking back over the years since the revolution, I see that I have wiped out the old thinking."

Most of the conversations that I have with my relatives are in English, which most of my aunts and uncles speak. When I speak to my cousins, who do not speak English, my grandfather or my mother translates. I begin to see the ridiculousness of the barriers when I draw on my three years of high school French to talk to one of my cousins. When we had ended our brief conversation, my uncle joked: "It is good that you have finished talking. You have used up all the French words Leslie knows."

I respect my grandfather for his great age and for much more. When he was a 23-year-old student attaché, he arrived in the United States to study agriculture. He visited a number of states, including Washington and Mississippi, before enrolling in Yale University's Sheffield Scientific School in the fall of 1906. He graduated in 1909 with a degree in engineering. It is my grandfather who is telling me these things about himself. He is a man who has lived through three periods of contemporary Chinese history, from the Boxer Rebellion to the formation of the Republic of China in 1912 to the declaration of the People's Republic of China in 1949.

After Yale, he went to France to do graduate work. After a second trip to the United States, he returned home again through France, sailing from Marseilles. On board his ship he met Dr. Sun Yat-sen and spent the next 30 days with him. When they reached Shanghai, grandfather went back to his family and Dr. Sun continued on to Peking, where some months later he helped father the revolution that formed the Republic of China.

At first, grandfather worked as an engineer at the Anyuan coal mines in 1913.

Later he went to Peking and became a professor of physics at Peking University, a job he held until 1930. Returning to Shanghai, he served in the municipal government and later with the People's Republic until he retired in 1956 at 73.

He still does translation work (he is fluent in English, Russian, French and Chinese), reads everything he can get his hands on and takes a daily walk. The last day of our visit in Shanghai, we went for a walk together to a nearby park that he says he normally never goes to "because there are too many old people there" for his comfort.

One of my aunts was curious to know why I didn't speak Chinese. My mother told her that she had tried to teach me when I was a child, but one day when I was playing in front of our house with some friends, an airplane roared over our heads. I shouted with excitement, using the Chinese word for airplane, *fei chi*. When I realized that my friends didn't understand what I was saying, I didn't want to speak Chinese anymore, at all.

My initial reluctance to speak with my cousins began to fade. Somehow we sensed the desire to communicate with each other, so everybody worked harder at it. Sometimes it became embarrassing. One of my cousins had prepared a few words of greeting for us; when I pressed her to say them she blushed and shyly demurred. She then agreed to say the words but only if I said something in Chinese first. I never did hear the greeting. . . .

On the evening before we left Shanghai to return home, my mother and I saw our family once again at grandfather's home. After dinner, grandfather gave me gifts to take back to America: some stamps for my father, a map of China and a capsule biography of himself which he had compiled. It begins in 1883, the year of his birth, listing years and corresponding world events up to the year 1983. He intends to live to be 100 years old and doesn't project beyond that. (I think that, considering his current health and level of activity, he will live to be even older than 100.)

Three cousins ride with us to the train station. They ask when we will come to see them again. We tell them that it is expensive but that we will try to come soon. Other uncles, aunts and cousins are at the station to see us off. The train is steam-powered and when we aren't moving fast, the steam drifts off to the side and makes the landscape appear misty.

I realize, after being stared at by curious Chinese, that China is a foreign place to me and that I have few things in common with it. I doubt that I have realized the full implications of my visit and I don't know if I ever will. I would like to return and get to know my family in China as well as I know my family in the United States. I did find that while the roots of my ancestry were Chinese, they have been lost. My visit suggested that there once was something there, but today my life is inextricably rooted in America.

LENGTH: 1670 WORDS

Name ____ Class ____ Date ____

1 Roots in China

SCORING: Reading time: ____	Rate from chart: ____ W.P.M.		
RETENTION	number right ____	× 4 equals ____	points
INFERENCES	number right ____	× 2 equals ____	points
COMPLETION	number right ____	× 4 equals ____	points
VOCABULARY	number right ____	× 3 equals ____	points
	(Total points: 100)	**Total** ____	points

RETENTION Based on the passage, which of the following statements are True (T), False (F), or Not answerable (N)?

1. ____ The author does not look Chinese.
2. ____ One of Leslie's cousins speaks French.
3. ____ Chang Tat-seung is 93 years old.
4. ____ Actually, Leslie Wong was somewhat ashamed of his grandfather.
5. ____ Leslie's grandfather went to Yale.
6. ____ The University of Peking was disbanded.
7. ____ None of the Wongs remember China before the revolution.
8. ____ One relative expected Leslie Wong to speak Chinese.
9. ____ Leslie Wong felt that his roots are inextricably in Shanghai.
10. ____ The patriarch of the family speaks only Chinese.

INFERENCES Which three of the following eight statements, based on the passage, are most likely true? ____; ____; and ____

1. Sun Yat-sen was known as the Father of the Revolution.
2. People in China are quite oppressed by the Communist regime.
3. Leslie Wong feels he is American first and Chinese second.
4. The Wongs were not "loose" enough to make jokes.
5. Most of Leslie's relatives were not curious about America.
6. As an American, Leslie frightened his cousins.

7. Most of the Wongs in China have specific jobs and careers.

8. China is trying to improve its housing facilities.

COMPLETION Choose the best answer for each question:

1. ____ Leslie's 15-year-old cousin is in the Red Guard because she: (a) speaks French. (b) is a good student. (c) needs the money. (d) is a soldier.

2. ____ Leslie's grandfather trained to be: (a) an accountant. (b) a mathematician. (c) an airplane pilot. (d) an ingineer.

3. ____ One language not referred to in the article is: (a) Russian. (b) English. (c) Pekingese. (d) Spanish.

4. ____ The People's Republic of China was declared in: (a) 1906. (b) 1923. (c) 1949. (d) the 1960's.

5. ____ One of the gifts Leslie received was a capsule history of: (a) the family. (b) the Chinese revolution. (c) his grandfather. (d) stamp collecting.

6. ____ Leslie's grandfather lives with: (a) his wife. (b) a 15-year-old dog. (c) one of the student cousins. (d) a government official.

VOCABULARY Choose the word or phrase that best defines the vocabulary item:

1. ____ reluctance: (a) hurt (b) repugnance (c) unwillingness (d) idea (e) feeling

2. ____ contemporary: (a) unimportant (b) personal (c) current (d) cross (e) torrid

3. ____ fluent: (a) wet (b) capable (c) stuck (d) awash (e) sensible

4. ____ foreign: (a) hostile (b) distant (c) lost (d) dangerous (e) unfamiliar

5. ____ inextricably: (a) deeply (b) unwillingly (c) impossibly (d) slowly (e) slyly

6. ____ unique: (a) good (b) heavy (c) singular (d) solicited (e) unsanctioned

7. ____ fervor: (a) sickness (b) pride (c) love (d) excitement (e) redness

8. ____ ethnic: (a) being Chinese (b) concerning regionalism (c) of a shared culture (d) relating to origins (e) sensing differences

9. ____ extensive: (a) broad (b) narrow (c) sudden (d) tense (e) meaningful

10. ____ anticipation: (a) worry (b) delight (c) corroboration (d) speculation (e) previous participation

2

The Other Road

Rachel Carson

The food supply of the earth is limited. Insects tend to reduce it by infesting grains and soils. One solution–using pesticides–may poison the earth. In this passage, Rachel Carson, a noted writer on ecology, suggests that there may be another solution.

We stand now where two roads diverge. But unlike the roads in Robert Frost's familiar poem, they are not equally fair. The road we have long been traveling is deceptively easy, a smooth superhighway on which we progress with great speed, but at its end lies disaster. The other fork of the road—the one "less traveled by"—offers our last, our only chance to reach a destination that assures the preservation of our earth.

The choice, after all, is ours to make. If, having endured much, we have at last asserted our "right to know," and if, knowing, we have concluded that we are being asked to take senseless and frightening risks, then we should no longer accept the counsel of those who tell us that we must fill our world with poisonous chemicals; we should look about and see what other course is open to us.

A truly extraordinary variety of alternatives to the chemical control of insects is available. Some are already in use and have achieved brilliant success. Others are in the stage of laboratory testing. Still others are little more than ideas in the minds of imaginative scientists, waiting for the opportunity to put them to the test. All have this in common: they are *biological* solutions, based on understanding of the living organisms they seek to control, and of the whole fabric of life to which these organisms belong. Specialists representing various areas of the vast field of biology are contributing—entomologists, pathologists, geneticists, physiologists, biochemists, ecologists—all pouring their knowledge and their creative inspirations into the formation of a new science of biotic controls.

Through all these new, imaginative, and creative approaches to the problem of sharing our earth with other creatures there runs a constant theme, the awareness that we are dealing with life—with living populations and all their pressures and counterpressures, their surges and recessions. Only by taking account of such life forces and by cautiously seeking to guide them into channels favorable to ourselves can we hope to achieve a reasonable accommodation between the insect hordes and ourselves.

The current vogue for poisons has failed utterly to take into account these most fundamental considerations. As crude a weapon as the cave man's club, the chemical barrage has been hurled against the fabric of life—a fabric on the one hand delicate and destructible, on the other miraculously tough and resilient, and capable of striking back in unexpected ways. These extraordinary capacities of life have been ignored by the practitioners of chemical control who have brought to their task no "high-minded orientation," no humility before the vast forces with which they tamper.

The "control of nature" is a phrase conceived in arrogance, born of the Neanderthal age of biology and philosophy, when it was supposed that nature exists for the convenience of man. The concepts and practices of applied entomology for the most part date from that Stone Age of science. It is our alarming misfortune that so primitive a science has armed itself with the most modern and terrible weapons, and that in turning them against the insects it has also turned them against the earth.

LENGTH: 583 WORDS

2 The Other Road

SCORING: Reading time: _____ Rate from chart: _____ W.P.M.				
RETENTION	number right _____	× 4 equals _____	points
INFERENCES	number right _____	× 2 equals _____	points
COMPLETION	number right _____	× 4 equals _____	points
VOCABULARY	number right _____	× 3 equals _____	points
	(Total points: 100)	**Total** _____	points

RETENTION Based on the passage, which of the following statements are True (T), False (F), or Not answerable (N)?

1. ____ Sharing the earth with other creatures is a problem.
2. ____ Insects are part of a whole fabric of life.
3. ____ DDT presents more risks than we at first suspected.
4. ____ Only one of the "roads" assures preservation of the earth.
5. ____ The choice of roads is not ours to make.
6. ____ The road we have been following is like a superhighway.
7. ____ Scientists have been developing biological solutions to insect control.
8. ____ Rachel Carson favors the term "control of nature."
9. ____ Basically, chemical controls are poisons.
10. ____ Robert Frost is a poet.

INFERENCES Which three of the following eight statements, based on the passage, are most likely true? ____; ____; and ____

1. There are few alternatives to chemical control of insects.
2. Entomology is a relatively primitive science.
3. The Stone Age of science has only just ended.
4. Poets seem more interested in this problem than scientists.
5. Chemical solutions actually attack life.
6. Only a few scientists are contributing to solving these problems.

7. Pathologists have made many of the most important contributions.

8. Biological solutions can really be very successful in controlling insects.

COMPLETION Choose the best answer for each question:

1. ____ Biological solutions seek to: (a) recall (b) astonish (c) control (d) destroy living organisms.

2. ____ Many scientists are working together to form a new science to be known as: (a) poison controls. (b) deadly controls. (c) flight controls. (d) biotic controls.

3. ____ At the end of our current "smooth superhighway" of progress lies: (a) pain. (b) plenty. (c) a deceptive divergence. (d) disaster.

4. ____ Biological solutions have: (a) been in limited use. (b) never been in use. (c) been ridiculed as ineffective. (d) Stone Age precedents.

5. ____ Chemical practitioners have ignored life's capacity to: (a) spread out. (b) fight back. (c) surge and recede. (d) turn against the earth.

6. ____ Rachel Carson is worried about filling our world with: (a) insects. (b) more scientists. (c) poisonous chemicals. (d) frightening risks.

VOCABULARY Choose the word or phrase that best defines the vocabulary item:

1. ____ diverge: (a) tell (b) send off (c) separate (d) deepen (e) respond to

2. ____ surge: (a) sound (b) rise (c) fall (d) distinguish (e) alleviate

3. ____ primitive: (a) sudden (b) vicious (c) dangerous (d) early (e) primarily

4. ____ barrage: (a) assault (b) defense (c) attempt (d) denials (e) suspense

5. ____ arrogance: (a) ambition (b) anger (c) pride (d) sorrow (e) confidence

6. ____ accommodation: (a) fear (b) arrangement (c) skill (d) home (e) living space

7. ____ vogue: (a) space (b) harm (c) skill (d) mirage (e) fad

8. ____ resilient: (a) stiff (b) soft (c) flexible (d) brilliant (e) resistance

9. ____ tamper: (a) sink in (b) touch (c) flood (d) water (e) alter

10. ____ vast: (a) slow (b) heavy (c) wasteland (d) enormous (e) worst

3

Out of This World

Editors of American Legion

Very soon the space shuttle will make it practical to maintain and visit large space platforms. The shuttle may not literally be able to take us out of this world, but it can lift us to staging points that can. If the shuttle lives up to its promise, the era of space travel may be at hand.

Wintertime is vacation time in Florida and this year you can plan one of those out-of-this-world trips . . . literally . . . for your destination is straight up—a huge resort hotel orbiting hundreds of miles above the Earth.

With visions of zero-gravity games and shuttle flights to the Moon dancing through your head, you're off to the airport. The moment you arrive your journey takes on the air of a Jules Verne fantasy. Poised restlessly at the end of a concrete ribbon is your waiting spaceplane—a gleaming, stubby-winged leviathan of the heavens.

You board the sprawling space giant and take a seat among the other passengers, ranging from fellow tourists to working scientists. As you fumble with the safety harness, the pilot's voice fills the cabin. "Takeoff in one minute!" A moment later, rocket engines deep within the bowels of the metal bird begin to pulsate with a quickening rhythm. You stiffen. The great adventure is about to begin.

Takeoff comes with an unnerving suddenness. You explode down the runway at

---

a dizzying speed. In seconds you are airborne, climbing steeply . . . endlessly. The soft contour seat becomes a man-eater as acceleration forces hammer your body downward. Your weight increases two . . . three times. You want to look out of the window but it is an effort merely to turn your head. Yet, there is no discomfort. The pressure of acceleration, the overwhelming thunder of the rockets combine to produce a pleasant euphoria.

Soon you are hurtling over Africa, the Eurasian land mass, into night, and emerging into a crimson new dawn. Abruptly, the muted roar of the spaceliner's engines drops to an audible rumble . . . then a hiss . . . then silence. A new sensation. Your body rises gently against restraining harness. The centrifugal force that comes from being whirled about your world at nearly 18,000 mph . . . like a ball on the end of a cord . . . has cancelled gravity. You are in space.

As you toy with the delights of weightlessness, your spaceliner begins to move up and down, back and forth, in gentle swaying motions.

The end of the fantastic voyage comes with the softest of thuds. You have arrived—300 miles above the Earth. In the process, you circled the globe—and in less time than it takes to fly the Atlantic.

A 21st century happening? Surprisingly, outings in orbit may be practical a lot sooner than you think. The reason? Emergence of the reusable Space Shuttle, a startling innovation of the Space Age that makes commercial exploitation of the heavens a possible reality.

The first Space Shuttle rolled from its assembly plant late last year. Landing tests were scheduled for 1977 and the first orbital flight will be conducted later. Soon the Space Shuttle will begin operational missions from the Kennedy Space Center in Florida.

The Shuttle will solve a nagging and often embarrassing problem for the National Aeronautics and Space Administration—the astronomical cost of doing business in space. In fact, NASA has designed its programs for the next two decades around this versatile space commuter. As a roving work platform in space, it will be used to launch, repair and replace expensive satellite systems, and to serve as a manned space laboratory for periods of up to 30 days duration. Later it is ticketed to serve as a sort of space taxi for ferrying men and supplies to and from orbiting space stations, and as an emergency ambulance service in space to rescue injured and stranded astronauts.

An Interim Upper Stage (IUS) being developed by the Department of Defense will be used for missions requiring orbits higher than 500 miles—the Shuttle's operational limit—and to inject payloads into escape trajectories to the moon and the planets.

Ironically, the development of the Space Shuttle parallels the development of the large rocket boosters that opened the era of space exploration. The story begins in the late 1950's, when spacecraft designers wrestled with the problem of how to bring back returning spacemen without burning them to cinders.

When a spacecraft slices into Earth's air ocean, it is traveling at speeds up to 25,000 mph. Resulting air friction creates temperatures of around 5,000 degrees. The spacecraft's angle of reentry must be precise. Even a small error can throw it thousands of miles off course with disastrous consequences. As the late astronaut Gus Grissom once said: "We literally explode a man into space, then bring him back like a meteor."

Apollo astronauts referred to their reentry procedure as "sliding down the stove pipe." Their bell-shaped craft, only slightly more maneuverable than a descending rifle bullet, had to be guided with unerring accuracy through an invisible "window" in the atmosphere 300 miles wide and 40 miles deep. Not an easy feat considering they had to take aim from thousands of miles out in space.

If they barreled in too steeply, they would be crushed and incinerated by the thickening air mass. If they came in too shallow, they would bounce off the Earth's blanket of air and become aimless wanderers in space. Their final descent to an ocean landing was controlled by what veteran spaceman Tom Stafford once described as the most gratifying sight in the world to a returning astronaut, "those big, beautiful, landing 'chutes."

Even as the Apollo program was taking initial form, designers knew there had to be a better way to move in and out of space. Huge rockets, such as the 363-foot-tall Apollo/Saturn V, then on the drawing boards, would be intricate and costly to build and launch. Moreover, they would be totally expendable . . . each complete vehicle a one-shot investment. Only the Command Module, or crew compartment, of the huge moon rocket would return safely to Earth.

Researchers hit pay dirt in late 1961. An unusual, wingless shape emerged from wind tunnels at NASA's Langley Research Center in Virginia. It wasn't much to look at, resembling a halved apple—rounded on the bottom and flat on top. But tests proved it to be airworthy, and with the addition of small fins and rudders it could be maneuvered with relative ease. Elated designers dubbed their newest creation the "lifting body."

The first lifting body was flight tested in 1962, the same year that astronaut John Glenn (now a U.S. Senator from Ohio) became the first American to orbit the Earth. The M2F1, a fragile craft constructed of plywood and tubular steel, was towed to a height of 10,000 feet and glided to safe landing near Edwards, CA. Test pilot Milton Thompson, who once jockeyed the needle-nosed X-15 rocket plane to an altitude of 211,000 feet and a speed of 3,700 mph, called the flight the most unique of his career.

"It was an odd feeling to gaze from the canopy and not see any wings," he said.

By 1968, advanced lifting body designs had been piloted to heights approaching 100,000 feet and speeds beyond sound. Unmanned versions were lofted into space by rockets, rammed back through the atmosphere at extreme velocities and guided by radio control to safe landings in the ocean. A year before Apollo 11 began its historic journey to the surface of the Moon, designers were convinced that the stubby, wedge-shaped lifting body was indeed the shape of tomorrow. . . .

Unlike the futuristic version described at the beginning of the story, present technical restraints require that the Space Shuttle be launched vertically like a conventional rocket. At liftoff, the Orbiter's three main engines and the two solid booster rockets are ignited. At an altitude of about 25 miles, the two solids shut down, pop off automatically and parachute into the ocean off Cape Canaveral. The boosters, located by built-in homing devices, are recovered and returned to the Cape for refurbishing and reuse.

Shortly after Orbiter is inserted into orbit, the external belly tank runs dry and the Orbiter's main engines shut down. They will not be used again during the mission. The belly tank is jettisoned and pointed back towards Earth by a small deorbit motor. It is the only piece of the Shuttle package which is expendable.

When the Orbiter completes its mission, it returns to Earth, zips through the atmosphere like any other aircraft and glides to a landing on an ordinary runway.

The actual landing—to a commercial airlines passenger—would be somewhat of a "grabber." It will be a computer controlled and accomplished "dead stick"—without power.

The glide slope will be a steep 24 degrees, compared to the two and a half to three degrees for a commercial airliner on a landing approach.

NASA says the Space Shuttle will open an era of economical space activity. The cost of launching a conventional rocket carrying an unmanned payload runs from about $10 million to $15 million, depending upon the launch vehicle used. The manned moon missions, using the massive Saturn V, cost $400 million. In contrast, the average Space Shuttle launch will average $10.5 million, and it can loft as many as three satellites at a time.

Currently, the overall cost of delivering a pound of payload into Earth orbit runs from $600 to $1,700. The Shuttle is expected to reduce the pound-in-orbit cost to approximately $160.

Additional savings will be achieved by the Shuttle's ability to retrieve and repair ailing satellites that otherwise might have to be replaced entirely. For example, two days after launch in April 1966, the battery aboard the $50 million Orbiting Astronomical Observatory-1 failed, dooming the mission to failure. Had the Space Shuttle been available, the defective satellite could have been rescued and repaired at a cost of a Shuttle launch—$10.5 million—roughly one-fifth of the satellite's replacement cost.

LENGTH: 1985 WORDS

3 Out of This World

SCORING: Reading time: ____ Rate from chart: ____ W.P.M.			
RETENTION	number right ____	× 4 equals ____	points
INFERENCES	number right ____	× 2 equals ____	points
COMPLETION	number right ____	× 4 equals ____	points
VOCABULARY	number right ____	× 3 equals ____	points
	(Total points: 100)	**Total** ____	points

RETENTION Based on the passage, which of the following statements are True (T), False (F), or Not answerable (N)?

1. ____ A space shuttle launch will cost about 10 million dollars.
2. ____ Thirty years ago no one would have thought the shuttle could work.
3. ____ The era of space exploration began in the 1950's.
4. ____ The shuttle's angle of descent is gentler than that of a jetliner.
5. ____ The lifting body looked a bit like a halved apple.
6. ____ Air can cause re-entry burning.
7. ____ The space shuttle is 100% reusable.
8. ____ There is no experience of weightlessness with the shuttle.
9. ____ The first wingless lifting body was developed in 1961.
10. ____ Apollo 11 made it to the surface of the moon.

INFERENCES Which three of the following eight statements, based on the passage, are most likely true? ____; ____; and ____

1. The space shuttle means important savings in space research.
2. We have gone about as far as we can go in space exploration.
3. Space stations are most practical right now as ambulances.
4. Gus Grissom is envious of those astronauts who will use the shuttle.
5. The wingless lifting body surprised even the veteran test pilots.
6. NASA has not been active in planning space exploration for the 1980's.
7. The first shuttle will plant the American flag in space.
8. The Orbiter will use an ordinary runway for landings.

COMPLETION Choose the best answer for each question:

1. ____ Langley is a: (a) space station. (b) research center. (c) moon base for Apollo 11. (d) pilot who first tested the lifting body.

2. ____ The problem with the giant Saturn V was that it was: (a) inaccurate. (b) slow. (c) never fully operational. (d) totally expendable.

3. ____ NASA says Orbiter opens the era of: (a) economical (b) military (c) peaceful (d) conventional space exploration.

4. ____ Orbiter's booster rockets: (a) are expendable. (b) parachute into the ocean. (c) are the only solid substances on it. (d) are used for re-entry, too.

5. ____ The Orbiting Astronomical Observatory had a failure in its: (a) rockets. (b) automatic sensors. (c) solar orientation feeder. (d) battery.

6. ____ Orbiter will reduce the cost of one pound of payload to: (a) $4.50. (b) $10.5 million. (c) $160. (d) $1,700.

VOCABULARY Choose the word or phrase that best defines the vocabulary item:

1. ____ defective: (a) useful (b) trying (c) flawed (d) policeman (e) sensor

2. ____ refurbish: (a) fix (b) use again (c) recommend (d) plush (e) eclectic

3. ____ expendable: (a) important (b) reusable (c) disposable (d) very costly (e) flown

4. ____ halved: (a) exploded (b) discarded (c) possessed (d) had (e) split

5. ____ velocities: (a) speeds (b) ascents (c) bicycles (d) times (e) re-entries

6. ____ jettisoned: (a) maintained (b) dropped off (c) upheld (d) in deep (e) tied on

7. ____ payload: (a) hardware (b) boosters (c) orbiters (d) cost factor (e) cargo

8. ____ euphoria: (a) fear (b) happiness (c) depression (d) anxiety (e) elation

9. ____ versatile: (a) steady (b) unbounded (c) flexible (d) unturned (e) twisted

10. ____ intricate: (a) delicate (b) complex (c) altitudinal (d) slow (e) scientific

4

Narrative of an American Slave

Frederick Douglass

Because slaveowners frowned on their learning to read and write, firsthand narratives of American slaves' experiences are few. One of the most powerful that was written is by Frederick Douglass, an escaped slave who became a leading Abolitionist. The description of his transformation from a self-respecting person into a brute is a moving indictment of slavery.

I left Master Thomas's house, and went to live with Mr. Covey, on the 1st of January, 1833. I was now, for the first time in my life, a field hand. In my new employment, I found myself even more awkward than a country boy appeared to be in a large city. I had been at my new home but one week before Mr. Covey gave me a very severe whipping, cutting my back, causing the blood to run, and raising ridges on my flesh as large as my little finger. The details of this affair are as follows: Mr. Covey sent me, very early in the morning of one of our coldest days in the month of January, to the woods, to get a load of wood. He gave me a team of unbroken oxen. He told me which was the in-hand ox, and which the off-hand one. He then tied the end of a large rope around the horns of the in-hand ox, and gave me the other end of it, and told me, if the oxen started to run, that I must hold on upon the rope. I had never driven oxen before, and of course I was very awkward. I, however, succeeded in getting to the edge of the woods with little difficulty; but I had got a very few rods into the woods, when the oxen took fright, and started full tilt, carrying the cart against trees, and over

NARRATIVE OF AN AMERICAN SLAVE From *Narrative of the Life of Frederick Douglass, an American Slave* (1845).

stumps, in the most frightful manner. I expected every moment that my brains would be dashed out against the trees. After running thus for a considerable distance, they finally upset the cart, dashing it with great force against a tree, and threw themselves into a dense thicket. How I escaped death, I do not know. There I was, entirely alone, in a thick wood, in a place new to me. My cart was upset and shattered, my oxen were entangled among the young trees, and there was none to help me. After a long spell of effort, I succeeded in getting my cart righted, my oxen disentangled, and again yoked to the cart. I now proceeded with my team to the place where I had, the day before, been chopping wood, and loaded my cart pretty heavily, thinking in this way to tame my oxen. I then proceeded on my way home. I had now consumed one half of the day. I got out of the woods safely, and now felt out of danger. I stopped my oxen to open the woods gate; and just as I did so, before I could get hold of my ox-rope, the oxen again started, rushed through the gate, catching it between the wheel and the body of the cart, tearing it to pieces, and coming within a few inches of crushing me against the gate-post. Thus twice, in one short day, I escaped death by the merest chance. On my return, I told Mr. Covey what had happened, and how it happened. He ordered me to return to the woods again immediately. I did so, and he followed on after me. Just as I got into the woods, he came up and told me to stop my cart, and that he would teach me how to trifle away my time, and break gates. He then went to a large gum-tree, and with his axe cut three large switches, and, after trimming them up neatly with his pocket-knife, he ordered me to take off my clothes. I made him no answer, but stood with my clothes on. He repeated his order. I still made him no answer, nor did I move to strip myself. Upon this he rushed at me with the fierceness of a tiger, tore off my clothes, and lashed me till he had worn out his switches, cutting me so savagely as to leave the marks visible for a long time after. This whipping was the first of a number just like it, and for similar offences.

I lived with Mr. Covey one year. During the first six months, of that year, scarce a week passed without his whipping me. I was seldom free from a sore back. My awkwardness was almost always his excuse for whipping me. We were worked fully up to the point of endurance. Long before day we were up, our horses fed, and by the first approach of day we were off to the field with our hoes and ploughing teams. Mr. Covey gave us enough to eat, but scarce time to eat it. We were often less than five minutes taking our meals. We were often in the field from the first approach of day till its last lingering ray had left us; and at saving-fodder time, midnight often caught us in the field binding blades.

Covey would be out with us. The way he used to stand it, was this. He would spend the most of his afternoons in bed. He would then come out fresh in the evening, ready to urge us on with his words, example, and frequently with the whip. Mr. Covey was one of the few slaveholders who could and did work with his hands. He was a hard-working man. He knew by himself just what a man or a boy could do. There was no deceiving him. His work went on in his absence almost as well as in his presence; and he had the faculty of making us feel that he was ever present with us. This he did by surprising us. He seldom approached the spot where we were at work openly, if he could do it secretly. He always aimed at taking us by surprise. Such was his cunning, that we used to call him, among ourselves, "the snake." When we were at work in the cornfield, he would sometimes crawl on his hands and knees to avoid detection, and all at once he would rise nearly in our midst, and scream out, "Ha, ha! Come, come! Dash on, dash on!" This being his mode of attack, it was never safe to stop a single minute. His comings were like a thief in the night. He appeared to us as being ever at hand. He was under every tree, behind every stump, in every bush, and at every window, on the plantation. He would sometimes mount his horse, as if bound to St. Michael's, a distance of seven miles, and in half an hour afterwards you would see him coiled up in the corner of the wood-fence, watching every motion of the slaves. He would, for this purpose, leave his horse tied up in the woods. Again, he would sometimes walk up to us, and give us orders as though he was upon the point of starting on a long journey, turn his back upon us, and make as though he was going to the house to get ready; and, before he would get half way thither, he would turn short and crawl into a fence-corner, or behind some tree, and there watch us till the going down of the sun.

Mr. Covey's *forte* consisted in his power to deceive. His life was devoted to planning and perpetrating the grossest deceptions. Every thing he possessed in the shape of learning or religion, he made conform to his disposition to deceive. He seemed to think himself equal to deceiving the Almighty. He would make a short prayer in the morning, and a long prayer at night; and, strange as it may seem, few men would at times appear more devotional than he. The exercises of his family devotions were always commenced with singing; and, as he was a very poor singer himself, the duty of raising the hymn generally came upon me. He would read his hymn, and nod at me to commence. I would at times do so; at others, I would not. My noncompliance would almost always produce much confusion. To show himself independent of me, he would start and stagger through with his hymn in the most discordant manner. In this state of mind, he prayed with more than ordinary spirit. Poor man! such was his disposition, and success at deceiving, I do verily believe that he sometimes deceived himself into the solemn belief, that he was a sincere worshipper of the most high God; and this, too, at a time when he may be said to have been guilty of compelling his woman slave to commit the sin of adultery. The facts in the case are these: Mr. Covey was a poor man; he was just commencing in life; he was only able to buy one slave; and, shocking as is the fact, he bought her, as he said, for *a breeder*. This woman was named Caroline. Mr. Covey bought her from Mr. Thomas Lowe, about six miles from St. Michael's. She was a large, able-bodied woman, about twenty years old. She had already given birth to one child, which proved her to be just what he wanted. After buying her, he hired a married man of Mr. Samuel Harrison, to live with him one year; and him he used to fasten up with her every night! The result was, that, at the end of the year, the miserable woman gave birth to twins. At this result Mr. Covey seemed to be highly pleased, both with the man and the wretched woman. Such was his joy, and that of his wife, that nothing they could do for Caroline during her confinement was too good, or too hard, to be done. The children were regarded as being quite an addition to his wealth.

If at any one time of my life more than another, I was made to drink the bitterest dregs of slavery, that time was during the first six months of my stay with Mr. Covey. We were worked in all weathers. It was never too hot or too cold; it could never rain, blow, hail, or snow, too hard for us to work in the field. Work, work, work, was scarcely more the order of the day than of the night. The longest days were too short for him, and the shortest nights too long for him. I was somewhat unmanageable when I first went there, but a few months of this discipline tamed me. Mr. Covey succeeded in breaking me. I was broken in body, soul, and spirit. My natural elasticity was crushed, my intellect languished, the disposition to read departed, the cheerful spark that lingered about my eye died; the dark night of slavery closed in upon me; and behold a man transformed into a brute!

LENGTH: 2660 WORDS

Name Class Date

4 Narrative of an American Slave

SCORING: Reading time: _____ Rate from chart: _____ W.P.M.				
RETENTION	number right _____	× 4 equals _____	points
INFERENCES	number right _____	× 4 equals _____	points
COMPLETION	number right _____	× 2 equals _____	points
VOCABULARY	number right _____	× 3 equals _____	points
	(Total points: 100)	**Total** _____	points

RETENTION Based on the passage, which of the following statements are True (T), False (F), or Not answerable (N)?

1. _____ Before coming to Covey's, Douglass had not done field work.
2. _____ Covey could not work in the fields himself.
3. _____ Covey never said his prayers.
4. _____ Douglass and Covey did not work together at any time.
5. _____ Douglass always obeyed Covey instantly.
6. _____ Covey took great care in administering beatings.
7. _____ Fortunately, Douglass was beaten only once or twice by Covey.
8. _____ The rope was tied to the horns of the in-hand ox.
9. _____ Local slaveowners thought Covey was too harsh.
10. _____ Douglass joined Covey's slaves on January 1, 1933.

INFERENCES Which three of the following eight statements, based on the passage, are most likely true? _____; _____; and _____

1. Douglass and Covey attended the same religious services.
2. Beatings were very rarely administered to slaves.
3. The slaves and the Coveys were really part of a contented "family."
4. Covey's cruelty and discipline broke Douglass's spirit.
5. The slaves did not have to work when it snowed.
6. The slaves had a remarkable capacity for hard work.

7. Douglass stayed at Covey's for the rest of his life.

8. Slaveowners seemed to operate very differently from one another.

COMPLETION Choose the best answer for each question:

1. ____ The slaves' nickname for Mr. Covey was: (a) the rat. (b) the sneak. (c) the man. (d) the snake.

2. ____ Mr. Covey's *forte* consisted in his power to: (a) work. (b) sleep. (c) feel pity and devotion. (d) deceive.

3. ____ One of the nearest towns was: (a) St. Michael's. (b) Owensboro. (c) Atlanta. (d) Woodsboro.

4. ____ Douglass's previous slavemaster was named: (a) Covey. (b) Thomas. (c) Tiger. (d) Harriman.

5. ____ Caroline was purchased to be used as a: (a) cook. (b) housemaid. (c) breeder. (d) fieldhand.

6. ____ Covey's plantation was near a: (a) town. (b) commercial river. (c) main highway to Atlanta. (d) woods.

VOCABULARY Choose the word or phrase that best defines the vocabulary item:

1. ____ noncompliance: (a) lying (b) resistance (c) sulking (d) fear (e) ingratitude

2. ____ perpetrating: (a) saving (b) continuing (c) sensing (d) committing (e) being

3. ____ consume: (a) save (b) spend (c) use (d) allow (e) inflate

4. ____ yoke: (a) join (b) bear (c) pull (d) center (e) split

5. ____ cunning: (a) spirit (b) imagination (c) slyness (d) sense (e) deceit

6. ____ grossest: (a) dirtiest (b) greatest (c) best (d) least (e) worst

7. ____ conform: (a) like (b) shape (c) tense (d) beguile (e) agree

8. ____ faculty: (a) capacity (b) sight (c) friends (d) learning (e) desire

9. ____ wretched: (a) poor (b) weak (c) senseless (d) miserable (e) sad

10. ____ disposition: (a) capacity (b) inclination (c) inspiration (d) need (e) finality

5

Roller Coaster: King of the Park

Robert Cartmell

Amusement parks have long promised excitement, especially in the form of "thrills and spills." Traditionally, it is the roller coaster that has threatened the most spills and offered the most thrills. In this article, Robert Cartmell traces its origins, describes its glorious past, and offers some thoughts about the future.

In quieter days, two steamboats, *Americana* and *Canadiana,* used to cross Lake Erie between Buffalo and Crystal Beach on the Canadian side. It was a tranquil ride, and the park at Crystal Beach became a favorite picnic ground for western New Yorkers.

The peace was shattered in 1927. Crystal Beach opened a horrendous roller coaster called the "Cyclone." Designed by Harry Guy Traver, it was billed as "The Most Fearsome Coaster Ever Built." Some 75,000 people came to its opening day and knocked down railings to get a good look. The vice president of Crystal Beach recalls that "the 'Cyclone' was a wicked ride. Before the last cars left the top of the first hill, the front car had already started on a bank. Every turn was twisted sharply and there was a figure eight which the cars ran at top speed. The 'Cyclone' is the only coaster that I have heard of that had a nurse manning a first-aid station."

Riders often fainted, and broken ribs from flying elbows were not unusual. People came from all over the world to watch; some dared to ride. (Even now,

---

Hollywood is capitalizing on these reactions with *Rollercoaster,* in something called "Sensurround.")

Palisades Park, located on the Hudson across from Manhattan, watched the "Cyclone's" opening with interest. They needed something to rival the roller coasters out at Brooklyn's Coney Island. They ordered an identical monster from Harry Traver. The new "Cyclone" opened in 1928 and Robert Garland reported on it in an editorial for *The New York Telegram:* "As a connoisseur of roller coasters, I advise you to consult a doctor before you climb aboard the new 'Cyclone' at Palisades Park . . . That 'Cyclone' doesn't play fair. It drags you up an incline, tosses you down the other side, turns you over this way, turns you over that way, and before you can remember what comes after 'Thy kingdom come,' shoots you to stars again."

Then the Depression hit. The next 30 years saw 1,300 roller coasters ground under by bulldozers or left to decay. Even Harry Traver's "Cyclones" were leveled—not an easy job, since wrecker's ball, weather, bulldozers and dynamite barely budged them. Crystal Beach finally decided to use some of the structuring and wooden parts in a new, mostly steel, coaster. The wood and steel remains have become a shrine for roller coaster buffs.

Amusement parks remained in the doldrums until the early Fifties. Walt Disney found them "dirty and unpleasant" but gambled on the idea and built Disneyland. Instead of a scattering of rides, his park was like a preplanned movie set with every part related. This idea of a "theme park" rejuvenated the industry. The response through the Sixties and Seventies has been tremendous. Walt Disney World in Florida, for example, had more than 13 million visitors last year.

Where did the undisputed king of the amusement park get its start? The answer: Russia. Not long ago, a Soviet track team was eager to ride the "Rebel Yell" at Kings Dominion, the new theme park outside Richmond, Virginia. During the ride they kept chanting "Russian Mountains" (a European term for roller coaster), although they did not speak English. Their guide later explained to them that roller coasters originated as ice slides built on a solid framework of wood in St. Petersburg during the 17th century. Passengers sat in a guide's lap—both precariously balanced on a two-foot sled. They then shot down a 70-foot high, 50-degree slope at dizzying speeds. This inspired the name "Russian Mountains."

The French prolonged the coaster-riding season by establishing the first wheeled coaster in Paris in 1804. The name "Russian Mountains" was used. In 1817, the famous "Aerial Walk" opened at nearby Beaujon Garden. Its many improvements and safety devices soon made the 1804 ride obsolete.

The first roller coaster in the United States was an inclined railway used to carry coal down to Mauch Chunk, Pennsylvania. In 1870 it was converted to haul passengers to the top of Mt. Pisgah, then drop them at a rate of 60 feet to the mile. A slow pace, but the ride through the mountains was magnificent.

It took the engineering skills of LaMarcus A. Thompson to made a device like the Mauch Chunk Railway work at an amusement park. He became known as the "Father of Gravity"—and an inventor of the commercial roller coaster. Thompson installed a primitive device called "The Switchback Railway" at Brooklyn's Coney Island in 1884. Cars ran down an undulating track, seldom exceeding six miles an hour; attendants then pushed the cars up the next hill for a return ride. It was crude but immensely popular. A day's receipts totalled $700 (at five cents a ride), and Thompson was overwhelmed with orders.

On the same beach, Captain Paul Boyton installed a bizarre apparatus called the "Beecher" or "Flip Flap Coaster." On this rickety nightmare, cars performed a 360-degree somersault. Only the blessings of centrifugal force clamped the cars to the tracks—and the passengers to their seats. Frequent complaints of an uncomfortable strain on the neck caused a decline in patronage, and the ride was soon dismantled.

In 1901, Edward Prescott's "Loop-the-Loop" became the talk of Coney Island. Instead of the Flip-Flap's true circle, the new ride successfully used an elliptical track and removed those "uncomfortable strains." The success was short-lived. Many remained skeptical though a glass of water, on test runs, failed to spill a drop.

The Roaring Twenties saw Coney Island boom, and Riverview Park in Chicago operated six coasters. Pioneers of aviation, including the Wright Brothers, admired the speed, curves and drops. Charles Lindbergh (who once worked in an amusement park) reportedly said that Coney Island's 1927 "Cyclone" was a greater thrill than flying an airplane at top speed.

Working with Frank Church, Harry Traver assembled a masterpiece at Playland park at Rye beach, New York. Aptly named the "Aero-Coaster," it was the greatest body-wringer and the most violent ride ever built. It was not only 90 feet high but had its first drop ten feet below ground. It looped continually and never stopped grinding until it reached the platform.

How do the rides of today compare with these legendary coasters? Many will say the rides built in the 1960s and '70s make the older coasters look like child's play. Others will tell you that it's financially impossible to equal the thrills, ingenuity and craftsmanship of the older rides. One yardstick exists. The 1927 "Cyclone" still stands on Surf Avenue at Coney Island. By any measure—including today's wax-smooth rides—it is a masterpiece. It is 80-foot proof that the coasters of the Twenties were the finest ever made.

Prominent among today's coaster designers is John Allen, formerly of the Philadelphia Toboggan Company. His masterpiece is probably the "Mister Twister" at Elitch's Gardens in Denver. Ninety-six feet high, it is crammed with treacherous hills and curves and has the best tunnel ride in existence. Many list it as the finest roller coaster standing today.

The Associated Press lists the "Texas Cyclone" at Astroworld in Houston as the ultimate roller coaster. A close second is the "Thunderbolt" at Kennywood

Park near Pittsburgh. It uses a natural valley to hide the most frightening parts of the ride. The final drops of 80 and 90 feet make its finish the most devastating in the world.

Yet it's not the finish, nor the first drop, nor the curves that distinguish a great roller coaster. It's the pacing—the way the speed, hills, curves, tunnels and finish are combined. A good roller coaster is as theatrically contrived as a Broadway play. ''We build in psychology,'' says designer John Allen. ''Part of the appeal is the imagined danger. That's why riders start screaming before the car even takes off.''

The ride up the first hill is intentionally slow; the car is allowed to dangle at the top so that you can contemplate the view—for miles—and savor the supposed terrors ahead. Then down it goes. The thrill comes not from the speed but from accelerating in seconds from 5 mph to 60 mph and into a state of weightlessness. That's the glory—or horror.

Every effort is made to make a roller coaster seem terrifying, yet the ride is among the safest at an amusement park. The fear that cars will jump the track and that the passengers will be thrown out is unfounded. The cars cannot jump the track because undertrack wheels prevent their flying upward, and side friction wheels keep them on course. An iron bar locked across the passenger's lap can be released only by an attendant or by a device.

Despite all precautions, major accidents do occur. Passengers change seats in mid-ride; they stand; they perform balancing acts on sharp curves. ''All patrons are possessed with an old suicidal instinct and the wisest operator devises means to prevent them from doing away with themselves. We just have to figure the customer as an accident, looking for a place to happen,'' says a former Coney Island operator.

At the old Glen Echo Park in Washington, D.C., a fully loaded coaster car started up the first hill with a young couple in the front seat. He foolishly attempted to stand at the top and was thrown to the pavement below and instantly killed. The ride had to finish but it took two interminable minutes. All the passengers had seen the accident, since it happened in front of them. The young lady whose escort had just been killed stepped out. The other 12 passengers stayed on!

At Conneaut Lake in western Pennsylvania, the coaster entered a dark tunnel midway through the ride. Nightmarish screams could be heard for miles as the cars echoed through the dark recesses. The screams continued until the train reached the unloading platform. Passengers flew off the cars, stumbling, arms flying, gasping for breath. The front car had hit a skunk.

Most mishaps involve belongings: wallets, wigs, hats and keys are often lost. Operators say they find enough loose change under the tracks to keep them going into the winter months. A bra and false teeth were found under the ''Cyclone'' at Coney Island. LeSourdsville Lake Park outside Cincinnati had a girl wearing a paper dress on their "Space Rocket." She returned, says the maintenance crew, stark naked.

Has the Ultimate Roller Coaster been built? No. Is there a limit to what the designers have planned for our minds and bodies? No again. Walt Disney World opened its 175-foot high "Space Mountain" in 1975 at a cost that was more than that of Disneyland in 1955. James Irwin, lunar module pilot of Apollo 15, calls it rougher than Saturn V.

Knotts Berry Farm in California has premiered its "Corkscrew Coaster." Based on the 1901 "Loop-the-Loop," it drops passengers off a 75-foot precipice into two 360-degree somersaults. Nearby, at Magic Mountain, "The Great American Revolution" coaster features a ghastly vertical loop 70 feet high.

In a recent "Ultimate Roller Coaster" competition, three Fairchild test engineers submitted the KC-135 research plane (affectionately labeled the "Vomit Comet") as their candidate. It won hands down. Height: start at 25,000, peak at 35,000 feet; distance: 9 miles horizontally in 70 seconds for each parabola. These statistics were shown to a coaster designer. He roared, then headed for the drawing board.

LENGTH: 1790 WORDS

Name *Class* *Date*

5 Roller Coaster: King of the Park

SCORING: Reading time: ____	Rate from chart: ____ W.P.M.		
RETENTION	number right ____	× 4 equals ____	points
INFERENCES	number right ____	× 2 equals ____	points
COMPLETION	number right ____	× 4 equals ____	points
VOCABULARY	number right ____	× 3 equals ____	points
	(Total points: 100)	**Total** ____	points

RETENTION Based on the passage, which of the following statements are True (T), False (F), or Not answerable (N)?

1. ____ Roller coasters started on the Canadian/American border.
2. ____ "Theme parks" revived the amusement park industry.
3. ____ The origin of roller coasters dates back to the seventeenth century.
4. ____ The space program used roller coasters for training.
5. ____ The highest coaster ride mentioned is 225 feet.
6. ____ Walt Disney always thought amusement parks were delightful.
7. ____ Many roller coasters were dismantled after the Depression.
8. ____ The coaster's thrill comes from speed, not acceleration.
9. ____ The passenger never experiences weightlessness.
10. ____ The 360° loop has never actually been achieved.

INFERENCES Which three of the following eight statements, based on the passage, are most likely true? ____; ____; and ____

1. Coasters succeed regardless of the state of the economy.
2. People are willing to pay to be terrified.
3. The St. Petersburg ice "mountains" have never really been topped.
4. Even accidents do not frighten passengers off the coaster.
5. The military applications of the coaster are extensive.
6. The old coasters were good, but not as good as the modern ones.
7. Russians are particularly fearful of coasters.
8. The 1927 "Cyclone" is a landmark in coaster design.

COMPLETION Choose the best answer for each question:

1. ____ Walt Disney's "Space Mountain" cost more than the 1955: (a) World Series. (b) Space program. (c) Disneyland. (d) Coney Island "Cyclone."

2. ____ The roller coaster ride is among the: (a) worst (b) smoothest (c) most sudden (d) safest in the amusement park.

3. ____ One coaster operator thinks patrons have: (a) unlimited funds. (b) suicidal instinct. (c) very little brains. (d) pure nostalgia.

4. ____ An early American coaster was built from: (a) scrap wood and steel. (b) a disused geyser. (c) a mining railroad. (d) stolen plans.

5. ____ The 1927 Coney Island "Cyclone" is considered to be: (a) a yardstick. (b) more frightening than ever. (c) a death-trap. (d) "Mister Twister."

6. ____ One designer explained that he builds: (a) terror (b) uncertainty (c) psychology (d) total discomfort into his coasters.

VOCABULARY Choose the word or phrase that best defines the vocabulary item:

1. ____ tranquil: (a) restful (b) scary (c) foreign (d) moving (e) in love

2. ____ contrived: (a) concealed (b) driven (c) made (d) elaborated (e) feared

3. ____ intentionally: (a) surely (b) carefully (c) quickly (d) purposefully (e) with little effort

4. ____ obsolete: (a) recent (b) complete (c) stubborn (d) worthless (e) undone

5. ____ decline: (a) reduction (b) deduction (c) hill (d) lay out (e) sudden fall

6. ____ interminable: (a) soon (b) unmentionable (c) without end (d) late (e) fearful

7. ____ unfounded: (a) broken (b) wrong (c) true (d) still standing (e) imagined

8. ____ precautions: (a) signs (b) drops (c) medical aids (d) means (e) safety aids

9. ____ savor: (a) sense (b) mumble (c) bewilder (d) have (e) enjoy

10. ____ mishaps: (a) trials (b) accidents (c) new plans (d) misfortune (e) loops

6

The Peter Principle

Lawrence F. Peter and Raymond Hull

In any organization in which employees rise to higher and higher levels, the Peter Principle is at work. It states, simply, that people rise until they reach a level at which they are incompetent. As long as they display competence, they will be promoted. But the minute they do not display competence, they must stay where they are.

When I was a boy I was taught that the men upstairs knew what they were doing. I was told, "Peter, the more you know, the further you go." So I stayed in school until I graduated from college and then went forth into the world clutching firmly these ideas and my new teaching certificate. During the first year of teaching I was upset to find that a number of teachers, school principals, supervisors and superintendents appeared to be unaware of their professional responsibilities and incompetent in executing their duties. For example my principal's main concerns were that all window shades be at the same level, that classrooms should be quiet and that no one step on or near the rose beds. The superintendent's main concerns were that no minority group, no matter how fanatical, should ever be offended and that all official forms be submitted on time. The children's education appeared farthest from the administrator mind.

At first I thought this was a special weakness of the school system in which I taught so I applied for certification in another province. I filled out the special forms, enclosed the required documents and complied willingly with all the red tape. Several weeks later, back came my application and all the documents!

No, there was nothing wrong with my credentials; the forms were correctly filled out; an official departmental stamp showed that they had been received in good order. But an accompanying letter said, "The new regulations require that such forms cannot be accepted by the Department of Education unless they have been registered at the Post Office to ensure safe delivery. Will you please remail the forms to the Department, making sure to register them this time?"

I began to suspect that the local school system did not have a monopoly on incompetence.

As I looked further afield, I saw that every organization contained a number of persons who could not do their jobs.

A Universal Phenomenon

Occupational incompetence is everywhere. Have you noticed it? Probably we all have noticed it.

We see indecisive politicians posing as resolute statesmen and the "authoritative source" who blames his misinformation on "situational imponderables." Limitless are the public servants who are indolent and insolent; military commanders whose behavioral timidity belies their dreadnaught rhetoric, and governors whose innate servility prevents their actually governing. In our sophistication, we virtually shrug aside the immoral cleric, corrupt judge, incoherent attorney, author who cannot write and English teacher who cannot spell. At universities we see proclamations authored by administrators whose own office communications are hopelessly muddled; and droning lectures from inaudible or incomprehensible instructors.

Seeing incompetence at all levels of every hierarchy—political, legal, educational and industrial—I hypothesized that the cause was some inherent feature of the rules governing the placement of employees. Thus began my serious study of the ways in which employees move upward through a hierarchy, and of what happens to them after promotion.

For my scientific data hundreds of case histories were collected. Here are three typical examples.

MUNICIPAL GOVERNMENT FILE, CASE NO. 17 J. S. Minion* was a maintenance foreman in the public works department of Excelsior City. He was a favorite of the senior officials at City Hall. They all praised his unfailing affability.

"I like Minion," said the superintendent of works. "He has good judgment and is always pleasant and agreeable."

*Some names have been changed, in order to protect the guilty.

This behavior was appropriate for Minion's position: he was not supposed to make policy, so he had no need to disagree with his superiors.

The superintendent of works retired and Minion succeeded him. Minion continued to agree with everyone. He passed to his foreman every suggestion that came from above. The resulting conflicts in policy, and the continual changing of plans; soon demoralized the department. Complaints poured in from the Mayor and other officials, from taxpayers and from the maintenance-workers' union.

Minion still says "Yes" to everyone, and carries messages briskly back and forth between his superiors and his subordinates. Nominally a superintendent, he actually does the work of a messenger. The maintenance department regularly exceeds its budget, yet fails to fulfill its program of work. In short, Minion, a competent foreman, became an incompetent superintendent.

SERVICE INDUSTRIES FILE, CASE NO. 3 E. Tinker was exceptionally zealous and intelligent as an apprentice at G. Reece Auto Repair Inc., and soon rose to journeyman mechanic. In this job he showed outstanding ability in diagnosing obscure faults, and endless patience in correcting them. He was promoted to foreman of the repair shop.

But here his love of things mechanical and his perfectionism become liabilities. He will undertake any job that he thinks looks interesting, no matter how busy the shop may be. "We'll work it in somehow," he says.

He will not let a job go until he is fully satisfied with it.

He meddles constantly. He is seldom to be found at his desk. He is usually up to his elbows in a dismantled motor and while the man who should be doing the work stands watching, other workmen sit around waiting to be assigned new tasks. As a result the shop is always overcrowded with work, always in a muddle, and delivery times are often missed.

Tinker cannot understand that the average customer cares little about perfection—he wants his car back on time! He cannot understand that most of his men are less interested in motors than in their pay checks. So Tinker cannot get on with his customers or with his subordinates. He was a competent mechanic, but is now an incompetent foreman.

MILITARY FILE, CASE NO. 8 Consider the case of the late renowned General A. Goodwin. His hearty, informal manner, his racy style of speech, his scorn for petty regulations and his undoubted personal bravery made him the idol of his men. He led them to many well-deserved victories.

When Goodwin was promoted to field marshal he had to deal, not with ordinary soldiers, but with politicians and allied generalissimos.

He would not conform to the necessary protocol. He could not turn his tongue to the conventional courtesies and flatteries. He quarreled with all the dignitaries and took to lying for days at a time, drunk and sulking, in his trailer. The conduct of the war slipped out of his hands into those of his subordinates. He had been promoted to a position that he was incompetent to fill.

An Important Clue!

In time I saw that all such cases had a common feature. The employee had been promoted from a position of competence to a position of incompetence. I saw that, sooner or later, this could happen to every employee in every hierarchy.

HYPOTHETICAL CASE FILE, CASE NO. 1 Suppose you own a pill-rolling factory, Perfect Pill Incorporated. Your foreman-pill roller dies of a perforated ulcer. You need a replacement. You naturally look among your rank-and-file pill rollers.

Miss Oval, Mrs. Cylinder, Mr. Ellipse and Mr. Cube all show various degrees of incompetence. They will naturally be ineligible for promotion. You will choose—other things being equal—your most competent pill roller, Mr. Sphere, and promote him to foreman.

Now suppose Mr. Sphere proves competent as foreman. Later, when your general foreman, Legree, moves up to Works Manager, Sphere will be eligible to take his place.

If, on the other hand, Sphere is an incompetent foreman, he will get no more promotion. He has reached what I call his "level of incompetence." He will stay there till the end of his career.

Some employees, like Ellipse and Cube, reach a level of incompetence in the lowest grade and are never promoted. Some, like Sphere (assuming he is not a satisfactory foreman), reach it after one promotion.

E. Tinker, the automobile repair-shop foreman, reached his level of incompetence on the third stage of the hierarchy. General Goodwin reached his level of incompetence at the very top of the hierarchy.

So my analysis of hundreds of cases of occupational incompetence led me on to formulate *The Peter Principle:*

In a Hierarchy Every Employee Tends
to Rise to His Level of Incompetence

A New Science!

Having formulated the Principle, I discovered that I had inadvertently founded a new science, hierarchiology, the study of hierarchies.

The term "hierarchy" was originally used to describe the system of church government by priests graded into ranks. The contemporary meaning includes any organization whose members or employees are arranged in order of rank, grade or class.

Hierarchiology, although a relatively recent discipline, appears to have great applicability to the fields of public and private administration.

This Means You!

My Principle is the key to an understanding of all hierarchal systems, and therefore to an understanding of the whole structure of civilization. A few eccentrics try to avoid getting involved with hierarchies, but everyone in business, industry, trade-unionism, politics, government, the armed forces, religion and education is so involved. All of them are controlled by the Peter Principle.

Many of them, to be sure, may win a promotion or two, moving from one level of competence to a higher level of competence. But competence in that new position qualifies them for still another promotion. For each individual, for *you,* for *me,* the final promotion is from a level of competence to a level of incompetence.

So, given enough time—and assuming the existence of enough ranks in the hierarchy—each employee rises to, and remains at, his level of incompetence. Peter's Corollary states:

In time, every post tends to be occupied by an employee who is incompetent to carry out its duties.

Who Turns the Wheels?

You will rarely find, of course, a system in which *every* employee has reached his level of incompetence. In most instances, something is being done to further the ostensible purposes for which the hierarchy exists.

Work is accomplished by those employees who have not yet reached their level of incompetence.

LENGTH: 1665 WORDS

6 The Peter Principle

SCORING: Reading time: _____ Rate from chart: _____ W.P.M.				
RETENTION	number right _____	× 4 equals _____	points
INFERENCES	number right _____	× 2 equals _____	points
COMPLETION	number right _____	× 4 equals _____	points
VOCABULARY	number right _____	× 3 equals _____	points
	(Total points: 100)	**Total** _____	points

RETENTION Based on the passage, which of the following statements are True (T), False (F), or Not answerable (N)?

1. ____ The Peter Principle is supposed to apply to all hierarchies.
2. ____ Perfectionism became one mechanic's shortcoming.
3. ____ Once promoted, General Goodwin dealt better with politicians than soldiers.
4. ____ The author was once a teacher.
5. ____ The Peter Principle has been accepted by the Academy of Sciences.
6. ____ Occupational incompetence is found everywhere.
7. ____ Peter admits to having no data on which to base his theories.
8. ____ The Peter Principle does not apply to every employee in every hierarchy.
9. ____ Peter felt he had inadvertently founded a new science.
10. ____ Not everyone is involved with hierarchies.

INFERENCES Which three of the following eight statements, based on the passage, are most likely true? ____; ____; and ____

1. Peter is himself a victim of his own principle.
2. It is clear that Peter is deadly serious in this article.
3. Labor unions are particularly susceptible to the Peter Principle.
4. The first Peter Principle was head of a school.
5. The Peter Principle was formulated upon observed experience.

6. Once having formulated the principle, Peter lost his job.

7. Competent people are doing the work of the world.

8. There is a great deal of visible incompetence.

COMPLETION Choose the best answer for each question:

1. ____ Peter had his credentials returned so that the post office would: (a) send them. (b) lose them. (c) register them. (d) interrogate him.

2. ____ Sphere was a foreman in a: (a) post office. (b) public works department. (c) protocol agency. (d) pill-rolling factory.

3. ____ The case names were changed in order to protect: (a) Peter himself. (b) the guilty. (c) the systems analyst. (d) innocent people.

4. ____ Peter saw that the cases he'd collected had a: (a) problem for solving. (b) common feature. (c) resolution if he could find it. (d) flaw.

5. ____ When he was a boy, Peter accepted the emphasis on: (a) work. (b) speed. (c) personal discipline. (d) knowledge.

6. ____ The Peter Principle states that, given time, every employee rises to his level of: (a) competence. (b) skill. (c) incompetence. (d) impotence.

VOCABULARY Choose the word or phrase that best defines the vocabulary item:

1. ____ dismantled: (a) assorted (b) unbuilt (c) destroyed (d) disassembled (e) lost

2. ____ ostensible: (a) apparent (b) silly (c) obvious (d) showy (e) ridiculous

3. ____ protocol: (a) news (b) procedure (c) productivity (d) flare (e) signal

4. ____ resolute: (a) assured (b) cool (c) deeply aware (d) sore (e) resultant

5. ____ hypothesize: (a) know (b) sense (c) figure out (d) say (e) assume

6. ____ affability: (a) good naturedness (b) quietness (c) pliable qualities (d) desire for personal pleasure (e) imaginative capacity

7. ____ indolent: (a) surly (b) lazy (c) mean (d) alarmed (e) pacified

8. ____ innate: (a) unknown (b) inherent (c) indecent (d) innocuous (e) very mad

9. ____ diagnose: (a) imagine (b) have (c) recognize (d) complain (e) smell

10. ____ incomprehensible: (a) incompetent (b) unclear (c) interrupting (d) indefensible (e) limiting

7

Africa

Anne Morrow Lindbergh

A well-known poet describes the timelessness of Africa. Anne Morrow Lindbergh watches the wildlife roam the vast savannas of Kenya. She sees the mountains, the green hillsides, the predators and the prey. She hears sounds older than mankind and sees beings that remind her of prehistory.

Africa, as one is always told, is a country of violent contrasts. Even the climatic contrasts within a single day in the highlands of Kenya or Tanzania are breathtaking. At midday the thin air trills with a dry heat. Bare hills burn in the copper dust. Quivering heat waves run like brush fire on the horizon. Eyes rest in relief on anything green—a line of flat-topped acacia trees floating like clouds on the airless savannas, or the four gentle peaks of the Ngong Hills. If one is out on the road, one counts the hours till sundown. In camp, shaded by trees, one faces the faint breeze and sits quite comfortably listening to continuous bird chatter. There are not only sounds one recognizes—monotonous tolling doves, whistling starlings, squawking hornbills—but a constant babble of unfamiliar noises: birds that sound like water bubbling from a bottle, birds that sound like tailors' scissors and mechanical toys, birds that endlessly repeat "hic-haec-hoc" or, more currently, just "ye-ye." One sits and waits for evening.

It comes swiftly, with the delicious balm of water after thirst. One is released from apathy, full of energy. The heat and dust of noon are forgotten. The air clears and is still; vistas expand between trees; one could advance unhindered to any horizon.

At our camp near Kimana in Kenya, we can see a distant line of ragged purple mountains to the north. To the south, Kilimanjaro's white top, cloud-covered all day, looms up enormous, gleaming, benign as the full moon. The savannas turn golden; acacia shadows lengthen to dark pools across the grass. Flocks of gazelle, cropping in the sun's late rays, are white as narcissus.

Night is again violent—cool, even cold on the high plateau. There is a sudden change of tension, a heightened quality of awareness. The mass of stars overhead beat down like rain. The profound mystery of darkness inundates the world.

A flood of sights, smells, noises, all alien to day, roll in at dusk. The earth vibrates with sounds as the sky vibrates with stars—crickets answering constellations. Against a curtain of insect-drone, one hears the rumble of lion, the eerie cry of hyena, sharp zebra barks braying gnu, shrieking baboons, and a thousand unexplained hoots, snorts, and thuds.

One listens like a dog on the watch—as primitive man once listened, in mystery and apprehension. It is safe in the tent—a lantern hung on the ridgepole, the fire flickering outside; and yet, one listens—one listens.

With predawn comes the benison of small-bird song, innocent twittering in the trees overhead, announcing to the world that night is over, that day has returned, and those who have survived can greet the morning, radiant and cool. The mountain reappears, newly capped with snow. The prairie shimmers with a hint of dew. Zebras move slowly through vistas of trees, cropping the silver grass like animals of paradise.

But it is not paradise, nor the peaceable kingdom. Lions made their kills last night, or at dawn; and now, gorged, are asleep under trees. Hyenas have found the carcass. Vultures circle overhead.

Another violent contrast; another turn of life's wheel; another face of the wilderness to accept. For Africa embraces both the bright and the dark, the benign and the cruel, the fleeting and the timeless, the swift and the ponderous—the impala and the elephant.

We see elephants in the evening on approaching our first campsite beside a dry riverbed. The pale dusty track angles in on our right, a luminous stream of sand pockmarked by animal hooves. Leaving our Land-Rover on a bank, we walk out onto the dry bed. We look both ways, and stop. Downriver stands a cliff of elephants—dark, enormous, motionless, their tree-sized legs rooted in sand, their ears widespread, great trunks facing us, white tusks gleaming in the dusk. They sway now, and blow dust from their sinuous trunks, huge ears flapping gently as palm fronds. They begin to move in single file along the bank, great shadows melting in and out of trees. In no hurry, they move deliberately, picking up one muffled foot after another with noiseless grace. We stand silently mid-river and watch the procession march in solemn rhythm, as if keeping time to inaudible drums.

Late in the evening, we hear them at the muddy pool across the river from our tent. They are pawing at the ground with ponderous feet to reach new water. They slosh in the mud and spray each other with their trunks. In the moonlight we can dimly see their hulking shapes; as we hear the water on their dusty hides, we feel ourselves a part of their joy.

Elephants, browsing through trees as lesser animals through bushes, give one not only another dimension of size and space, but another dimension of time. Their mammoth forms hark back to the world of mastodons. The slow, even rhythm of their march makes one feel they are moving to another time than man's. They have come from ages before us and are going somewhere we will never reach. Grizzled and wrinkled as old trees, they seem even older—old as hills or rocks, carved out of earth and imperishable as earth. The memory returns of the Indian myth about Brahma creating the first elephants, "the elephants of the directions of space," to support the universe.

LENGTH: 1020 WORDS

Name _______________ *Class* _______________ *Date* _______________

7 Africa

SCORING: Reading time: _____ Rate from chart: _____ W.P.M.			
RETENTION	number right _____	× 4 equals _____	points
INFERENCES	number right _____	× 2 equals _____	points
COMPLETION	number right _____	× 4 equals _____	points
VOCABULARY	number right _____	× 3 equals _____	points
	(Total points: 100)	**Total** _____	points

RETENTION Based on the passage, which of the following statements are True (T), False (F), or Not answerable (N)?

1. ____ The savannas are airless in the daytime.
2. ____ The acacia trees have flat tops.
3. ____ The elephants dowse themselves at night.
4. ____ The elephants marched up the riverbed to the campsite.
5. ____ Mt. Kilimanjaro has snow on it.
6. ____ No zebras showed up on the prairie.
7. ____ Anne Lindbergh's campsite is in Kenya.
8. ____ Anne Lindbergh made her observations on foot because she had no vehicle.
9. ____ The evenings were as hot and stuffy as the days.
10. ____ The elephants were described as being a "cliff."

INFERENCES Which three of the following eight statements, based on the passage, are most likely true? ____; ____) and ____

1. Things are not like this anymore in Africa.
2. Africa's contrasts help make it fascinating.
3. No one knows how Africa's animals can live in peace.
4. Anne Morrow Lindbergh was in Africa to hunt elephant.
5. Some of the rivers nearby had served as canals in the past.
6. This was the dry season.

7. Anne Morrow Lindbergh was not full of energy during the day.

8. African governments had tried to stop this safari.

COMPLETION Choose the best answer for each question:

1. ____ One of the birds mentioned is: (a) the pelican. (b) a mourning dove. (c) the whooping crane. (d) the starling.

2. ____ The hills with "gentle peaks" are the: (a) Kilimanjaros. (b) Ngongs. (c) Tanzanian steppes. (d) Tailors' Scissors.

3. ____ The lions, hyenas, and vultures remind us this is not: (a) Europe. (b) northern Africa. (c) the Peaceable Kingdom. (d) a mere dream.

4. ____ The gnus make a: (a) barking (b) hooting (c) braying (d) thudding sound.

5. ____ The elephants marched as if: (a) drunk. (b) frightened. (c) they moved through history. (d) keeping time.

6. ____ Brahma created the first elephants to: (a) please man. (b) remind us of mastodons. (c) support the universe. (d) pack the earth together.

VOCABULARY Choose the word or phrase that best defines the vocabulary item:

1. ____ shimmer: (a) glow (b) listen (c) slip away (d) seem (e) illuminate

2. ____ balm: (a) relief (b) pain (c) boredom (d) care (e) talk

3. ____ vistas: (a) cars (b) lines (c) fields (d) views (e) passports

4. ____ apprehension: (a) uncertainty (b) depression (c) sense (d) purport (e) resistance

5. ____ inundate: (a) seem (b) harm (c) flood (d) hinder (e) refuse

6. ____ imperishable: (a) sound (b) unstable (c) senseless (d) lost (e) lasting

7. ____ luminous: (a) shadowy (b) flimsy (c) glowing (d) apparent (e) unsought

8. ____ hark back to: (a) repent (b) recall (c) return (d) rescind (e) follow back

9. ____ inaudible: (a) loud (b) soft (c) big (d) weird (e) silent

10. ____ apathy: (a) low regard (b) senselessness (c) state of uncaring (d) being drawn into a reverie (e) avoiding clear responsibility

SECTION 2

Vocabulary Preview

The following words come from the eight reading selections in Section 2. Study the list carefully, pronouncing the words aloud if possible. Conceal the definitions with a card or your hand and test your command of the meanings of the words.

aquatic, *adj.* living in water; performed in water
beneficial, *adj.* helpful
bonafide, *adj.* genuine
classic, *adj.* a model of its sort; of permanent value
conduits, *noun* channels
confiscate, *verb* seize; take over
countenance, *noun* mood or character; facial expression
demeanor, *noun* conduct; manner
denizens, *noun* inhabitants
derelict, *noun* abandoned property; outcast
durability, *noun* ability to last or endure
emissions, *noun* something given off; waste
ensconced, *adj.* securely surrounded
epidemiological, *adj.* pertaining to epidemics
epitomize, *verb* to be the embodiment of
espionage, *noun* the art of spying
extradite, *verb* surrender a criminal to another authority for trial
fraught, *adj.* full of
genial, *adj.* pleasant; polite
hostelry, *noun* an inn or hotel
ideological, *adj.* having to do with a consistent set of political or social beliefs
impromptu, *adj.* spontaneous; on the spur of the moment
infiltrate, *verb* to penetrate
inscrutable, *adj.* not understandable
interned, *adj.* confined; jailed
inquisitor, *noun* one who questions; investigator
irretrievably, *adv.* permanently; beyond the point of bringing back
just, *adj.* lawful, fair
luminaries, *noun* famous people
maimed, *adj.* mutilated; disfigured

mammoth, *adj.* enormous
phraseology, *noun* a way of saying something; choice of words
raconteur, *noun* a storyteller
renegades, *noun* traitors; outlaws
rubbernecking, *adj.* turning one's head to view a spectacle
sluicing, *verb* to flush
somnolent, *adj.* sleepy
succor, *noun* aid or help
surreptitious, *adj.* secret
tertiary, *adj.* of third importance
toxic, *adj.* poisonous
tranquil, *adj.* peaceful
transient, *noun* someone who is in a place temporarily
unabashed, *adj.* not ashamed or embarrassed
unscathed, *adj.* unharmed
witticism, *noun* a witty remark

Choose the word or phrase that best defines the vocabulary item:

1. ____ sluicing: (a) damming (b) cutting (c) flushing (d) plunging (e) running
2. ____ inscrutable: (a) unintelligible (b) simple (c) evil (d) ineluctable (e) fine
3. ____ epitomize: (a) scarify (b) sum up (c) be an example of (d) try (e) clarify
4. ____ tertiary: (a) third (b) alarmingly (c) tall (d) simplify (e) finalize
5. ____ extradite: (a) cozy (b) take over (c) superfluous (d) give to another authority (e) write more than would be necessary
6. ____ raconteur: (a) gangster (b) simpleton (c) storyteller (d) friend (e) foe
7. ____ infiltrate: (a) seep into (b) stem from (c) move over (d) stymie (e) clever
8. ____ just: (a) some (b) have correct (c) lawful (d) courage (e) fright
9. ____ somnolent: (a) alert (b) alarmed (c) sleepy (d) tight (e) drunk
10. ____ demeanor: (a) manner (b) harmful (c) the manor house (d) slouch (e) style
11. ____ ensconced: (a) founded (b) secure (c) everywhere (d) revised (e) enjambed
12. ____ succor: (a) desire (b) fool (c) impertinence (d) priority (e) aid
13. ____ irretrievably: (a) lastly (b) formerly (c) slowly (d) permanently (e) slyly
14. ____ surreptitiously: (a) flawlessly (b) in secret (c) apart (d) firstly (e) lately
15. ____ emissions: (a) waste (b) smoke (c) sounds (d) faults (e) causes
16. ____ conduits: (a) sewers (b) silver (c) mansions (d) channels (e) terms
17. ____ fraught: (a) tense (b) alarmed (c) subtle (d) filled (e) cowardly
18. ____ unabashed: (a) naked (b) without shame (c) witty (d) slovenly (e) genuine

19. ____ epidemiological: (a) stuffy (b) detained (c) epidemic (d) ecologic (e) logical

20. ____ inquisitor: (a) friend (b) host (c) questioner (d) of high rank (e) lictor

8

Our First Car

Shirley Jackson

Getting one's first car is something like a rite of passage in America. For those of us who know a great deal about cars, the problem of getting one is not frightening. But for those, like Shirley Jackson, who know little about cars, it can be an eye-opening experience.

The man from the driving school was named Eric, and he was about eighteen years old and undisguisedly amused at meeting anyone who could not drive a car. When I told him sharply that in his business he must meet quite a few people who could not drive a car he laughed and said that usually people my age did not try to learn new tricks. I eyed the dual-control car he had parked in our driveway and said falsely that I might surprise him by learning faster than he expected. He patted me on the shoulder and said, "That's my girl."

Laurie and Jannie and my husband holding the baby stood on the front porch cheering and waving as I rode off with Eric, crushed into a corner of the seat to avoid touching any of the dual controls, and desperately afraid that if I did the car would go out of control and rocket madly off the road, no doubt killing other innocent people and very probably ending my driving lessons. Laurie and Jannie and my husband holding the baby were again on the front porch cheering, two hours later, when I came back with Eric, dismayed and bewildered and not pre-

---

pared to take levelly any childish prattle about how we would drive around when we had a car.

I took ten lessons from Eric, including lessons in stopping and starting, making a U turn—that was how I got the dent in the back of the car, but Eric said they were insured against that kind of thing—making right turns and left turns, shifting gears, backing and filling, allemande left, and reeling and writhing and fainting in coils. He neglected to teach me how to turn on the lights and what to do when a funny little noise started somewhere inside. Every time I got out of his car in front of my own house, weak-kneed and with my hands stiffened into a permanent grasp on a steering wheel, I was greeted with cheers and friendly criticism by my faithful family. I completely captivated one of Laurie's friends—a young gentleman from Cub Scouts whose mother and father both know how to drive, and have for years—by running smack into the stone wall at the foot of our garden, something no one else has so far been able to do, since the wall is set approximately seven feet from the driveway and is clearly visible. Evenings, I studied a little book Eric had sold me, which told in graphic detail what to do in case the car skidded out of control, what to do in case the steering wheel came off in my hands (from this I got the vivid impression of running the car like a bobsled, and steering by leaning from side to side), and how to bandage a compound fracture.

My test, which I shall always believe was supposed to be a test of whether or not I could drive a car, I passed seemingly without effort, and with only one bad moment when, told to stop completely halfway up a hill which may well have been Mount Everest, I realized that the head inquisitor assumed with infinite amusement that I would be able to start again. He was a very patient man, and waited for several minutes, tapping his fingers gently against the window while I scoured my mind for Eric's directions on starting a car on a hill. (Swing your wheel sharp? Turn down your lights? Keep one foot on the clutch and one foot on the brake and one foot on the starter . . .?") "Well?" said the inquisitor, looking at me evilly.

I gestured competently with one hand, keeping the other one locked to the wheel in some obscure belief that only my grip on the wheel kept the car from rolling back down the hill. "State law," I said carelessly. "Child coming, can't start."

He glanced at me briefly and then craned his neck out of the window to see where a boy about twenty was sauntering down the sidewalk. I had hoped to distract his attention, and did, but I then discovered that it is not possible to be surreptitious about starting a stalled car on a hill. I firmly believe that the inquisitor gave me a license only because he was sure I could never start a car and so could never become a substantial menace on the highways.

Meanwhile, it had been decided who was to ride in front (Baby), I had learned to drive, the lessons had been paid for, and I had a little piece of official paper saying that I knew how to drive. We lacked only a car. This was adjusted by a gentleman who, saying he acted only from pure friendship, sold us one of *his* cars. He said he was very reluctant to part with it, particularly at that price, he said it was a better car than any of the new ones on the market, he praised its spark plugs and its birdlike appetite for oil.

"The cigarette lighter doesn't work," I pointed out in a spirit of pure critical inquiry.

"Neither does the clock," said my husband.

"And the fender is sort of caved in," I added.

"Tell you what I'll do," the man said. "I'll pay for the license plates."

"Better get that cigarette lighter fixed right away," my husband told me, as we surveyed our new car. "And the clock. Best to be on the safe side."

"I'll have to find a place to get them fixed," I said.

"Can't be too careful," my husband said.

I got into the car and reasoned out how to start it and drove with great caution, in the middle of the road, to a garage that could be reached without a left turn, and there I talked for quite a while with a young man covered with grease and oil who had "Tony" written across the front of him in big red letters. "Got a nice car there," he said, after I had told him we had just bought it, and what we paid for it, and had added trustingly that I had just learned to drive and had never before owned a car and knew nothing about cars or motors or, as a matter of fact, driving. "You're even going to have to tell me what gas to use," I added laughingly.

Tony nodded soberly. "But you got a real nice car there," he insisted, "for the price you paid, you couldn't get a better one. Needs a little attention, of course." He laughed. "Wouldn't be a car if it didn't," he told me.

"Yes, I know," I said. "The cigarette lighter—"

"You take that clutch, for instance," Tony said. He opened the door and pushed the pedal up and down reflectively. "Now I guess you don't know anything about the clutch, do you?" he asked. I shook my head, and he went on, "Well, it's a funny thing about the clutch. You go along for maybe one, two thousand miles and then all of a sudden . . ." He shrugged expressively. "You got a repair job costs you maybe two, three hundred dollars. Always better to get the clutch fixed in time, saves you money, expense, wear and tear."

"You mean I have to get something fixed?"

He shrugged again. "You don't *need* to, of course," he said. "But you got to look at it this way. You got small children, you're driving them around in the car, you're not going to take chances with *them.*"

Nervously I agreed that I was not going to take chances with my small children.

"Well, then," said Tony. "Now brakes are important, too." He pushed the brake pedal down and shook his head sadly. "That guy sold you this car," he said.

"Is this going to be very expensive?" I asked.

"Well, now," Tony said, and laughed. "But let's look it over and see just exactly what you need. No sense getting something you don't *need,*'' he said jovially.

From then on, as nearly as I can remember, it was wheel alignment and something called camber or clamber or clabber, and wheel work was always expensive because every single car in the world except the make and model I owned had little adjustable pegs which could be fixed for next to nothing, but when Tony had to work with nonadjustable pegs, well, peg work was always expensive. Body work, too, would always set you back plenty, but it was the lives of my children I was taking in my hands if I let the fenders go.

''You got to regard this as an *investment,*'' Tony said earnestly. ''Now, I wouldn't be treating you fair if I let those spark plugs go, for instance. You'd say I played you a pretty dirty trick if you had to come back a month from now for a big repair bill, you'd say to me, 'Tony, why didn't you fix those spark plugs a long time ago before I had to pay this big repair bill?' You see, it's an investment *now* so's it won't cost you so much *later*. Now take the muffler.''

''Muffler,'' I said. Tony pointed to something under the car which I could not see.

''You see that?'' he said. ''I guess you didn't notice it before or you would of called it to my attention sooner. Lucky thing I saw it in time, I wasn't looking for anything like *that.*''

''What would have happened?'' I asked him nervously.

He shook his head. ''Can't ever tell,'' he said ''*Nothing* might have happened—for a while. And then one day you're going up a hill, car full of children . . .'' He shook his head again. ''And the brake lining,'' he said. ''*And* the ignition system.''

I then made one of the bigger mistakes of my life. ''How are the tires?'' I asked.

Tony laughed. ''You call those *tires?*'' he demanded. ''Why, let me tell you, one day I saw a guy, had his two little children with him, and I said to him—''

LENGTH: 1890 WORDS

8 Our First Car

SCORING: Reading time: _____	Rate from chart: _____ W.P.M.	
RETENTION	number right _____ × 4 equals _____	points
INFERENCES	number right _____ × 3 equals _____	points
COMPLETION	number right _____ × 3 equals _____	points
VOCABULARY	number right _____ × 3 equals _____	points
	(Total points: 100) **Total** _____	points

RETENTION Based on the passage, which statements are True (T), False (F), or Not answerable (N)?

1. _____ Eric's car had only one set of controls.
2. _____ Tony sold the author her car.
3. _____ Shirley Jackson took ten lessons from Eric.
4. _____ The car dealer cheated Shirley Jackson.
5. _____ Shirley Jackson failed her driving test the first time.
6. _____ Starting on a hill baffled Shirley Jackson.
7. _____ Tony, the garageman, did not know about Shirley Jackson's children.
8. _____ Shirley Jackson refused to tell Tony the price of the car.
9. _____ The car salesman offered to pay for the license plates.
10. _____ Shirley Jackson bought the car before she had her license.

INFERENCES

1. _____ Which of the following statements, based on the passage, is most likely accurate?
   (a) Mr. Jackson had probably been driving for years.
   (b) Eric did not take Mrs. Jackson riding at night.
   (c) Laurie and Jannie are nearby friends of the family.
2. _____ Which of the following statements is most likely inaccurate?
   (a) Shirley Jackson felt thoroughly confident about learning to drive.
   (b) After her first lesson, Mrs. Jackson feared she might never drive.
   (c) Buying a car turned out to be easier than the Jacksons thought.

COMPLETION Choose the best answer for each question:

1. ____ The first problem Mrs. Jackson spotted in her car was with the: (a) lights. (b) horn. (c) cigarette lighter. (d) rearview mirror.

2. ____ The car salesman said he acted out of: (a) Los Angeles. (b) pure friendship. (c) serious concern. (d) the highest motives.

3. ____ Shirley Jackson was sure the inspector gave her a license because she: (a) could not start the car. (b) smiled nicely. (c) had a baby. (d) drove so well.

4. ____ The Cub Scout knew: (a) how to drive. (b) nothing. (c) Laurie. (d) Eric.

5. ____ When Shirley Jackson got out of Eric's car in front of her house she was greeted with: (a) jeers. (b) Jannie. (c) cheers. (d) uncertainty.

6. ____ One part of the car not mentioned in the article is the: (a) fender. (b) headlight. (c) clutch. (d) choke.

7. ____ The man from the driving school was: (a) irritating. (b) undisguisedly amused. (c) surprisingly thoughtful. (d) a friend of the car salesman.

8. ____ Tony tried to make Mrs. Jackson regard her car as: (a) a series of problems. (b) a tired old friend. (c) an investment. (d) a big mistake.

VOCABULARY Choose the best definition for each vocabulary entry:

1. ____ soberly: (a) drily (b) wholly (c) slowly (d) seriously (e) laughingly
2. ____ adjustable: (a) fixable (b) changeable (c) fixed (d) smooth (e) flexible
3. ____ jovial: (a) serious (b) funny (c) suspicious (d) godlike (e) impressive
4. ____ reflectively: (a) thoughtfully (b) glowingly (c) lowly (d) fully (e) lovely
5. ____ infinite: (a) shot (b) long (c) heavily (d) not good (e) endless
6. ____ obscure: (a) unclear (b) foreign (c) impotent (d) frightful (e) unsought
7. ____ inquiry: (a) trial (b) sentiment (c) fear (d) questioning (e) requirement
8. ____ crane: (a) stretch (b) feed (c) birdlike (d) appetite (e) lift
9. ____ menace: (a) anti-female (b) search (c) threat (d) point (e) fear
10. ____ surreptitious: (a) open (b) secret (c) harmful (d) funny (e) not alive

9

The Cremation of Sam McGee

Robert Service

"The Cremation of Sam McGee" *is the tale of two adventurers in the Yukon, described realistically, but with compassion and humor. It is a testament to the fidelity of those who shared "the trail" in the gold rush of '49.*

There are strange things done in the midnight sun
By the men who moil for gold;
The Arctic trails have their secret tales
That would make your blood run cold;
The Northern Lights have seen queer sights,
But the queerest they ever did see
Was that night on the marge of Lake Lebarge
I cremated Sam McGee.

Now Sam McGee was from Tennessee, where the cotton blooms and blows.
Why he left his home in the South to roam 'round the Pole, God only knows.
He was always cold, but the land of gold seemed to hold him like a spell;
Though he'd often say in his homely way that "he'd sooner live in hell."

THE CREMATION OF SAM MCGEE From *The Collected Poems of Robert Service,* Reprinted by permission of Dodd, Mead & Company, New York, and McGraw-Hill Ryerson Limited, Scarborough, Ont.

On a Christmas Day we were mushing our way over the Dawson trail.
Talk of your cold! through the parka's fold it stabbed like a driven nail.
If our eyes we'd close, then the lashes froze till sometimes we couldn't see;
It wasn't much fun, but the only one to whimper was Sam McGee.

And that very night, as we lay packed tight in our robes beneath the snow,
And the dogs were fed, and the stars o'erhead were dancing heel and toe,
He turned to me, and "Cap," says he, "I'll cash in this trip, I guess;
And if I do, I'm asking that you won't refuse my last request."

Well, he seemed so low that I couldn't say no; then he says with a sort of moan:
"It's the cursèd cold, and it's got right hold till I'm chilled clean through to the bone.
Yet 'tain't being dead—it's my awful dread of the icy grave that pains;
So I want you to swear that, foul or fair, you'll cremate my last remains."

A pal's last need is a thing to heed, so I swore I would not fail;
And we started on at the streak of dawn; but God! he looked ghastly pale.
He crouched on the sleigh, and he raved all day of his home in Tennessee;
And before nightfall a corpse was all that was left of Sam McGee.

There wasn't a breath in that land of death, and I hurried, horror-driven,
With a corpse half hid that I couldn't get rid, because of a promise given;
It was lashed to the sleigh, and it seemed to say: "You may tax your brawn and brains,
But you promised true, and it's up to you to cremate those last remains."

Now a promise made is a debt unpaid, and the trail has its own stern code.
In the days to come, though my lips were dumb, in my heart how I cursed that load.
In the long, long night, by the lone firelight, while the huskies, round in a ring,
Howled out their woes to the homeless snows— O God! how I loathed the thing.

And every day that quiet clay seemed to heavy and heavier grow;
And now I went, though the dogs were spent and the grub was getting low;

The trail was bad, and I felt half mad, but I swore I would not give in;
And I'd often sing to the hateful thing, and it hearkened with a grin.

Till I came to the marge of Lake Lebarge, and a derelict there lay;
It was jammed in the ice, but I saw in a trice it was called the "Alice May."
And I looked at it, and I thought a bit, and I looked at my frozen chum;
Then "Here," said I, with a sudden cry, "is my cre-ma-tor-eum."

Some planks I tore from the cabin floor, and I lit the boiler fire;
Some coal I found that was lying around, and I heaped the fuel higher;
The flames just soared, and the furnace roared—such a blaze you seldom see;
And I burrowed a hole in the glowing coal, and I stuffed in Sam McGee.

Then I made a hike, for I didn't like to hear him sizzle so;
And the heavens scowled, and the huskies howled, and the wind began to blow.
It was icy cold, but the hot sweat rolled down my cheeks, and I don't know why;
And the greasy smoke in an inky cloak went streaking down the sky.

I do not know how long in the snow I wrestled with grisly fear;
But the stars came out and they danced about ere again I ventured near;
I was sick with dread, but I bravely said: "I'll just take a peep inside.
I guess he's cooked, and it's time I looked"; . . . then the door I opened wide.

And there sat Sam, looking cool and calm, in the heart of the furnace roar;
And he wore a smile you could see a mile, and he said: "Please close that door.
It's fine in here, but I greatly fear you'll let in the cold and storm—
Since I left Plumtree, down in Tennessee, it's the first time I've been warm."

There are strange things done in the midnight sun
By the men who moil for gold;
The Arctic trails have their secret tales
That would make your blood run cold;
The Northern Lights have seen queer sights,
But the queerest they ever did see
Was that night on the marge of Lake Lebarge
I cremated Sam McGee.

9 The Cremation of Sam McGee

SCORING: Reading time: _____ Rate from chart: _____ W.P.M.				
RETENTION	number right _____	× 4 equals _____	points
INFERENCES	number right _____	× 3 equals _____	points
COMPLETION	number right _____	× 3 equals _____	points
VOCABULARY	number right _____	× 3 equals _____	points
	(Total points: 100)	**Total** _____	points

RETENTION Based on the passage, which statements are True (T), False (F), or Not answerable (N)?

1. ____ Cap and Sam were heading out for gold.
2. ____ Cap and Sam were on the Dawson trail.
3. ____ They began several days away from Lake Lebarge.
4. ____ Arctic trails apparently have secret tales.
5. ____ Cap remained true to his oath.
6. ____ The trail was good just before he got to Lake Lebarge.
7. ____ Cap kept driving the dogs without rest, day and night.
8. ____ Cap was sweating when Sam was being cremated.
9. ____ The Northern Lights are visible from Lake Lebarge.
10. ____ Sam McGee died during the day.

INFERENCES

1. ____ Which of the following statements is most likely accurate?
   (a) Sam McGee was in the Arctic only because of the gold.
   (b) Sam McGee never complained about the bitter cold.
   (c) Sam McGee left behind a rich life in Tennessee.
2. ____ Which of the following statements is most likely inaccurate?
   (a) Sam seemed to have a premonition of his death.
   (b) Cap was not happy to carry out his promise.
   (c) The story is told by Sam McGee.

COMPLETION Choose the best answer for each question:

1. ____ Sam McGee was cremated on the: (a) barge (b) marge (c) sarge (d) large of Lake Lebarge.
2. ____ Sam McGee came from: (a) Primrose. (b) Dawson. (c) Hunger. (d) Plumtree.
3. ____ Cap referred to Sam's corpse as: (a) a debt unpaid. (b) a promise given. (c) clay. (d) brawn and brains.
4. ____ The derelict was: (a) lost. (b) a boat. (c) stolen. (d) forlorn.
5. ____ Sam McGee was cremated in a: (a) boiler. (b) hurry. (c) blizzard. (d) solemn ceremony.
6. ____ One thing Sam McGee dreaded was: (a) the howling of the huskies. (b) a cold northern wind. (c) an icy grave. (d) a friend who let you down.
7. ____ When Cap opened the furnace door he saw: (a) nothing at first. (b) the simple coals. (c) the past and the future. (d) Sam smiling.
8. ____ Cap drove: (a) the "Alice May." (b) a sleigh. (c) from day to day. (d) only half the way.

VOCABULARY Choose the best definition for each vocabulary entry:

1. ____ dread: (a) illness (b) joy (c) fear (d) insufficiency (e) food
2. ____ moil: (a) boil (b) soil (c) foil (d) toil (e) roil
3. ____ stern: (a) alive (b) severe (c) strong (d) maddened (e) tender
4. ____ burrow: (a) hide (b) make (c) did (d) cover (e) dig
5. ____ grisly: (a) awful (b) gear (c) huge (d) mad (e) alarming
6. ____ grub: (a) insecticide (b) tube (c) comestibles (d) luck (e) feather
7. ____ heed: (a) have (b) understand (c) cold rain (d) light (e) need
8. ____ mushing: (a) going (b) sensing (c) crushing (d) furrowing (e) priming
9. ____ derelict: (a) ships (b) abandoned (c) lazy (d) stupid (e) resistant
10. ____ loathe: (a) love (b) see (c) tolerate (d) imagine (e) hate

10

The Great Spy Escape

Donald McCormick

We all know that spies do get caught and that countries often agree to exchange them. Spies rarely escape from custody, but when they do their means of escape may be dramatic and thrilling. The escape of George Blake, master spy, from an English prison is a masterpiece of intrigue, cleverness, and derring-do.

The classic example of the carefully organised escape of a spy from prison in modern times is that of George Blake, who got away from Wormwood Scrubs Jail in London and found his way to Russia.

Blake, the son of an Egyptian Jew married to a Dutchwoman, joined the Dutch Resistance movement as a youth during the German occupation of Holland in World War II. He escaped to Britain, joined the Royal Navy as an ordinary seaman and eventually became an officer. His knowledge of languages impressed the authorities and he was later employed on intelligence work. After the war he became a senior agent of the British Secret Service in Germany.

In 1948 he was appointed as a vice-consul in Korea, but still continued with his work as an agent, which was unusual because the general rule is that a member of the Diplomatic Service does not mix in espionage.

Then, for three years, Blake was interned by the North Koreans and subjected to brain-washing. On his release from captivity when the Korean War ended in 1953, Blake rejoined the British Secret Service and was sent, to Berlin with instructions to infiltrate the Soviet network and to pose as a double-agent.

THE GREAT SPY ESCAPE From *The Master Book of Spies* by Donald McCormick. Reprinted by permission of the publisher, Sir Joseph Causton & Sons Ltd.

There is still an element of mystery about Blake's next moves. To play the highly dangerous game of a double-agent even in the cause of one's own country (Blake was a British subject because his father had a British passport) is fraught with grave risks for any spy. Effectively to pose as a double-agent one must pass on at least some useful information to the enemy. At some point or other the question is bound to arise: is he telling the enemy too much?

The charge against Blake ultimately was that he had passed on too much information to the Russians and that he had not merely posed as a Soviet agent, but actually joined their ranks. A German informer warned the British Secret Service that their man in Berlin had betrayed several Western agents, both British and American, to the Russians and consequently sent some of them to their death.

Blake was told by the British Foreign Office to report to London. When he did so he was arrested and in May, 1961, sentenced to 42 years' imprisonment for betraying secrets to the Russians. Astonishingly, Blake admitted the charges, made no excuse for his conduct and actually pleaded guilty. What is more he stated at his trial that he had decided 'to join the Communist side to establish a balanced and more just society'.

No doubt the Russians made various attempts to have Blake exchanged for one of their prisoners. Such a plan was almost certainly rejected by the British on the grounds that his release would further endanger their networks. Somehow the information that an exchange was ruled out, but that an attempt at a rescue would be made was passed to Blake in prison.

Late on Saturday night, 22 October, 1966, it was announced that George Blake had escaped from Wormwood Scrubs Prison. A nation-wide alert operation was set in motion and a watch kept at all British airports. Yet at this very moment Blake was hiding out in an apartment only a short distance from the prison. A few months later he was in Moscow.

The secret of Blake's escape and how it was organised has been carefully kept. Neither the Russians, nor the British will tell exactly what happened. But it is clear that the KGB [the Russian intelligence agency] went to great lengths to plan this operation over a long period.

One interesting fact emerged which suggested the British had been singularly careless in their security arrangements: for a short period Blake and Konon Molody were in the same prison. It is possible, therefore, that they could have communicated with one another.

The key man in Blake's escape, on his own admission, was Sean Bourke, an Irishman who had been a fellow-prisoner in Wormwood Scrubs. Bourke has since asserted that Blake asked him to help in his rescue and that the whole affair was done solely on his own initiative.

When Bourke was released from prison he started to plan the escape operation. Miniature radio equipment was smuggled into Blake at Wormwood Scrubs so that he was able to talk to Bourke by radio. Nobody appears to have monitored those conversations.

Bourke himself operated his radio at a site quite close to the prison walls. Every detail of the escape plan was passed by radio so that, when the moment arrived, Blake was able to take full advantage of all the local knowledge of movements of prison officers.

At 5.30 pm on the night of his escape Blake was watching television with other prisoners. He left the room and told two prison officers he was going back to his cell to read. Instead he went up to the landing on the second floor to a window, of which he had already loosened one of the bars. It is now thought that he had already broken the bar, then replaced it and held it in position with some adhesive tape blackened by boot polish.

Blake got through the window, lowered himself on to the roof of a covered passage below and had only a drop of about five feet to the ground. It was now six o'clock and raining fairly steadily. Timing the movements of the prison officers who patrolled the walls of the jail, Blake made his way to the wall where on the inside a rope ladder had already been thrown over by Bourke.

In a matter of minutes Blake was over the wall, jumping the twenty feet to the ground where Bourke was waiting with a car in the roadway. This was the worst part of the escape and Bourke said afterwards, when interviewed in a television programme, that Blake 'knocked himself unconscious when he jumped and badly twisted his wrist'.

Bourke dragged Blake into the car and drove off to the nearby apartment where he was to lie low until the hue and cry for him had ceased.

After Blake's escape to Russia Bourke joined him over there. But Bourke was no starry-eyed admirer of the Soviet regime and he found that, now the escape had been successfully negotiated, neither Blake nor the KGB had any use for him. He was regarded as somewhat of a nuisance. So Bourke went back to Ireland where he was immediately faced with extradition proceedings with a view to his being sent back to Britain to be charged with aiding Blake's escape.

When the case was heard Bourke declared: 'I have never been a Communist . . . I sprang Blake from a slow, lingering death', meaning that he did this on humanitarian grounds and not because of ideological sympathies. Ordered to be extradited, he appealed against this decision and won his case. Thus it is that the only detailed account we have of Blake's escape is that of Sean Bourke himself.

LENGTH: 1107 WORDS

10 The Great Spy Escape

SCORING: Reading time: _____	Rate from chart: _____ W.P.M.			
RETENTION	number right _____	× 4 equals _____	points	
INFERENCES	number right _____	× 3 equals _____	points	
COMPLETION	number right _____	× 3 equals _____	points	
VOCABULARY	number right _____	× 3 equals _____	points	
	(Total points: 100)	**Total** _____	points	

RETENTION Based on the passage, which statements are True (T), False (F), or Not answerable (N)?

1. ____ Blake's escape was organized from abroad by the Russians.
2. ____ Actually, Blake was innocent of the charges against him.
3. ____ The prison wall was twenty feet high.
4. ____ Wormwood Scrubs is out in the English countryside.
5. ____ Sean Bourke was a Russian agent planted in the prison.
6. ____ Blake's nationality was Egyptian.
7. ____ Konon Molody was the brains behind the entire escape.
8. ____ Blake hid out in London before escaping to Russia.
9. ____ Blake and Bourke communicated by radio.
10. ____ The British never formally admitted Blake had escaped.

INFERENCES

1. ____ Which of the following statements is most likely accurate?
   (a) Blake's brainwashing caused him to become a Communist.
   (b) The rope ladder proved more important than the loose bar.
   (c) Blake acted on ideological, not humanitarian grounds.
2. ____ Which of the following statements is most likely inaccurate?
   (a) Various spy agencies have contact with one another.
   (b) Blake had enormous trouble posing as a double agent.
   (c) Several agents died because Blake exposed them.

COMPLETION Choose the best answer for each question:

1. ____ When he fell, Blake: (a) alarmed the guards. (b) twisted his wrist. (c) sprained an ankle. (d) hit the covered passage below.
2. ____ Blake actually: (a) is a double agent now. (b) wanted to go to Egypt. (c) disliked Bourke. (d) pleaded guilty.
3. ____ For his part in the escape, Bourke: (a) did time. (b) was extradited. (c) never repented. (d) was sent to Siberia.
4. ____ The person interviewed on television was: (a) Konon Molody. (b) George Blake. (c) Sean Bourke. (d) the author.
5. ____ The British almost certainly rejected a plan for: (a) radio monitoring. (b) freeing Blake. (c) chaining their prisoner. (d) prisoner exchange.
6. ____ Bourke said the entire escape was done on his: (a) free time. (b) one day off. (c) own initiative. (d) Boy Scout word of honor.
7. ____ The author says the British were: (a) unorthodox (b) careless (c) overly cautious (d) quite irregular in their security arrangements.
8. ____ After the war, Blake's instructions were to infiltrate the: (a) Soviet (b) Korean (c) German (d) Irish spy network.

VOCABULARY Choose the best definition for each vocabulary entry:

1. ____ ideological: (a) thoughtful (b) political (c) personal (d) pertaining to espionage (e) without personal honor
2. ____ singularly: (a) slowly (b) purely (c) only (d) wholly (e) particularly
3. ____ admission: (a) going to (b) application (c) confession (d) escape (e) effort
4. ____ just: (a) good (b) bad (c) a mere (d) slow (e) fair
5. ____ classic: (a) old (b) fine (c) stylish (d) social (e) model
6. ____ infiltrate: (a) decimate (b) penetrate (c) modulate (d) elate (e) berate
7. ____ fraught: (a) filled (b) empty (c) captured (d) scared (e) mired
8. ____ interned: (a) imprisoned (b) hospitalized (c) taught (d) educated (e) affrighted
9. ____ grave: (a) dead (b) low (c) serious (d) meaningful (e) funny
10. ____ hue and cry: (a) moaning (b) propaganda (c) message (d) dares (e) alarms

11

Dirty Water in the Bulrushes

Kathryn W. Burkhart

The industrial progress of our time has brought with it various kinds of pollution. One of the most serious is the pollution of our water. In attempting to control it, we have used chemicals such as chlorine to kill bacteria. However, scientists are now finding that natural methods, such as filtration through fields of bulrushes, are even more effective and may provide our best hope for water purification.

In the Sudan, women walk to the Blue Nile, the White Nile or the River Nile every morning and evening carrying leather bags or large clay pots. They fill them with about 20 liters of water, put them on their heads and carry them home. There they add seeds or leaves, bits of bark or root to the muddied water they have collected. Within two to three hours the dirty brown water is clear and drinkable. Chemical tests show that after 12 hours it is totally pure. Somehow nature's simple old tools have eaten every drop of dirt and bacteria that had polluted the water. It is an ancient, seemingly magic ritual that continues to purify drinking water for Sudanese families every day.

"There is danger for the Sudanese in collecting water," says Dr. Samia Al Asharia Jahn, a faculty member at the University of Khartoum who for five years has been collecting data on the native methods of water purification and the effectiveness of those methods. But the danger to which Dr. Jahn is referring is not pollution. "The danger is . . . crocodiles. Especially during the flood season, the crocodiles are abundant. Since we have the dam it is not such a big problem, but the small crocodiles still come over the dam and they are very deadly when they come to the edge of the water.''

Taking water from a faucet as we do seems much safer than gathering water in a dirty, crocodile infested river. But recent reports warn us that the risk we take drinking water from the tap ultimately may be just as dangerous. Despite mechanical and chemical depolluting schemes that are far more sophisticated than those used by the Sudanese, including sand filtration, permanganate oxidation and chlorination, the water we drink may nevertheless contain many more potentially dangerous pollutants and contaminants than the water drunk in the Sudan.

We have serious, urgent water problems relatively new to mankind as a result of industrialization and expanding population. Most of our current water treatment methods have been around, without major improvement, for 60 years. They were designed to eliminate harmful waterborn disease bacteria, such as typhoid and dysentery bacilli and cholera. They do little to detect or fight more insidious contaminants whose effects on users and the balance of life may not show up for decades.

Purifying our drinking water becomes more difficult as time passes. Scientists explain that we are inventing dangerous chemicals faster than we can deal with them: even faster than we can determine their effect on human beings. Every year our industries are originating at least 500 new chemicals—pesticides, synthetics, adhesives, surface coatings and solvents—and are releasing them into our surface and groundwater supplies. Any community that gets its public water supply from a river containing any industrial discharge or runoff from agricultural areas using pesticides and herbicides may be dangerously affected by these contaminants—even if it has an elaborate purification plant. The plant was not built to cope with such new problems.

Once contaminants get into any of the water around us, it is likely to get into our drinking water as well. ''Water is a system,'' says Dr. Robert Pierson, a research biochemist and environmentalist at the University of Pennsylvania. ''Whatever we do to one part affects the other parts. Substances washed into our waterways, lead leached by pipes, industrial discharges into rivers, toxic residue from pesticides in the soil, which get into fresh water bodies and kill or damage marine life—all these things threaten life support systems on the face of the earth. Life came to terms with itself over millions of years, Dr. Pierson says. ''In that biochemical evolution, life has found certain chemicals useful, but it has taken millions of years to make its decisions. Here we are now releasing 500 new chemicals every year! Life doesn't know how to deal with them, and we run serious risk of fouling up that fine, highly molecular machine by adding all these new molecules. It is something like trying to adjust a very fine Swiss watch by opening it up, turning your head and sticking in a screwdriver.''

Studies by the Environmental Protection Agency and the Environmental Defense Fund released in 1974 revealed that 66 dangerous chemicals, ''carcinogens'' all potentially able to cause or promote cancer, had been found in the drinking water of New Orleans. EDF suggested that New Orleans has a 40 percent higher incidence of cancer than the national average in part because of the presence of carcinogenic substances in the public water supply drawn from the Mississippi River.

Dr. Robert H. Harris of the EDF and Dr. Samuel S. Epstein of Case Western Reserve, who conducted the EDF study, believe the carcinogens they found are residuals of industrial wastes dumped into the Mississippi upstream. They found that the local water treatment processes failed to detect or remove many of the waste substances from the public water supply. Moreover they concluded that chlorination of the water for the purposes of purifying it actually converted many harmless chemicals into dangerous ones. Since over 100 million people in the US drink chlorinated water and chlorination is widely used as a disinfectant in sewage treatment plants, the research raised serious questions about the safety of drinking water throughout the nation. It also served as impetus for the passage of the Safe Drinking Water Act, which was reluctantly signed into law by the President early in 1975.

Although Drs. Harris and Epstein were glad to see that bill passed and signed into law, they are critical of government agencies in charge of implementing and regulating water quality standards. "The Food and Drug Administration is clearly a captive of the industry," says Dr. Harris. "Thousands of chemicals released every year are never tested for their effect on human beings. Meanwhile the EPA says that they are delaying implementation of the Safe Drinking Water Act because they first have to determine a 'safe' level of carcinogens. The overwhelming conclusion of the scientific community is that there are *no* safe levels of carcinogens. These discharges must be completely eliminated, not just reduced."

EPA spokesmen say that on the basis of current knowledge, the benefits of chlorination far outweigh the potential harmful effects of compounds that may be created by the process, and there is not enough evidence at this time to require sweeping changes in current water treatment processes. They are however conducting a national study of the problem of carcinogens and other dangerous substances in drinking water. These results—to be drawn from the monitoring of 80 cities—should provide some of the evidence needed to begin making decisions on changing the treatment process.

Our water treatment methods, authorities agree, do need upgrading. What methods will be adopted is a matter of debate.

Some scientists are urging that we examine nature's oldest tools—biological tools—to see if they can't be used to solve the immense problems facing us today. Biological treatment—possibly the management of marshes planted with bulrushes and higher green plants—may prove to be the most effective, cheap and ecologically sound way to treat polluted waters in both industrialized and nonindustrialized nations.

The potential for biological treatment of water systems was the subject of a three-day conference sponsored by the Academy of Natural Sciences and the University of Pennsylvania in March of 1974. More than 100 scientists, city planners and environmental experts from a dozen countries came together to explore the best, most workable ways of biologically improving the quality and use of water, alone or in conjunction with conventional techniques. The three-day conference was called the International Conference on Biological Water Quality Improvement Alternatives.

"Interest in treatment systems using the natural cleansing ability of water, plants and animals is going to increase as costs of standard chemical and mechanical system continue to rise," says Edward W. Furia, Jr., a former regional administrator of EPA and conference chairman. "Substantial improvement of American drinking water supplies, municipal sewage and industrial pollution through conventional control is prohibitively expensive, plus it uses a great deal of energy since it relies on machines and pumps. These biological systems are no substitute for keeping pollutants out of the water in the first place, but they have tremendous potential for helping to undo the damage already done without further damage to the environment."

Currently many biological systems are at work in this country. More than 4000 municipalities already use some simple form of biological water purification in conjunction with other techniques, such as aeration lagoons where algae help to remove organic pollution. Dr. Harold R. Shipman, chairman of the United Nations Subcommittee on Water Resources and director of water supply and waste programs for the World Bank, estimates that there are more than 1000 biological water stabilization ponds in the United States alone, with uncounted numbers in the rest of the world. But scientists from here and abroad who have been at work on little publicized projects using higher green plants, namely bulrushes and reeds and a form of iris which is a granddaddy of our garden variety, brought fresh evidence to the conference of the ability of these plants to screen out, devour and bar toxic bacteria and chemicals. Others said that the microorganisms that cling to bulrushes, insects, fish, higher plants and even oysters may be the unsung heroes in any potential all-out war on water pollutants.

Projects using nature's tools in a managed way are being conducted, usually on an experimental basis, by small communities with available land or pond areas in Germany, Holland, Hungary, Poland, Yugoslavia, Finland, Israel, Italy and Japan. Pilot projects have been operating in the US since 1972 and a design system combining conventional engineering techniques with biological treatment of the effluent from the wettest mine in the Northern Hemisphere, the New Jersey Zinc Mine in Friedensville, Pennsylvania, is currently up before the state of Pennsylvania for approval. If approved this system will be the first to use bulrush filtration of nonorganic industrial wastes on such a large scale in this country.

Most of these designs have been inspired by the findings of Dr. Kaethe Seidel, a limnologist (specialist in the biology of fresh water bodies), who heads the Max Planck Institute in Germany. Dr. Seidel has discovered in working with bulrushes since 1957 that these hardy biblical plants prefer clear water so much that they actually *create* the clear water by a metabolic process that devours various organic and inorganic pollutants.

In Krefeld, Germany Dr. Seidel has successfully used artificial lagoons planted with bulrushes as part of a complex water treatment scheme that produces clear, potable water from the Rhine River. The Rhine is at least as dirty as the Mississippi, yet Dr. Seidel and her co-workers have discovered that Rhine water pumped through an artificially created bulrush marsh (the bulrushes are planted in gravel nets) emerges at the other end after a week or two of "travel" essentially free of nitrates, phosphates, sodium, potassium and calcium. Dr. Seidel reported to the conferees that bulrushes remove highly toxic organic substances like phenol; neutralize alkaline and acid waste waters; clean up waters polluted by food processing wastes; aerate water; provide a habitat for other living things like insects and fish, which also clean up pollution; reduce the amount of waste water; mechanically filter suspended solids with their root structures; absorb dissolved and suspended particles on roots; kill germs and produce no sludge.

Dr. Seidel also told of an installation of bulrushes in Urach that she has managed since 1964. There, waste water that includes unclarified sewage, domestic sewage, intermittent additions of extremely charged industrial wastes containing cyanides from a metal manufacturer and blood from a slaughter house runs first through sedimentation basins, then through stands of bulrushes, and comes out clean, drinkable and "delicious."

LENGTH: 2781 WORDS

Name Class Date

11 Dirty Water in the Bulrushes

SCORING: Reading time: _____ Rate from chart: _____ W.P.M.				
RETENTION	number right _____	× 4 equals _____	points
INFERENCES	number right _____	× 3 equals _____	points
COMPLETION	number right _____	× 3 equals _____	points
VOCABULARY	number right _____	× 3 equals _____	points
	(Total points: 100)	**Total** _____	points

RETENTION Based on the passage, which statements are True (T), False (F), or Not answerable (N)?

1. ____ Sudanese women use bulrushes to purify Nile water.
2. ____ Chlorine fights disease bacteria.
3. ____ Biological purifiers are really impractical for America.
4. ____ We release 500 new chemicals each year.
5. ____ Almost 100 million Americans drink chlorinated water.
6. ____ New Orleans has a much higher cancer rate than the national average.
7. ____ There are few, if any, bulrushes in the Mississippi river.
8. ____ Projects for biological purification are going on in Europe.
9. ____ The Rhine river is at least as dirty as the Mississippi.
10. ____ Bulrushes are effective against natural, not chemical, wastes.

INFERENCES

1. ____ Which of the following statements is most likely accurate?
   (a) Chlorinating our water may be more dangerous than we thought.
   (b) The Sudanese are much healthier than Americans or Europeans.
   (c) Fish and insects tend to pollute fresh water.
2. ____ Which of the following statements is most likely inaccurate?
   (a) Sophisticated water-purifying systems may be outmoded.
   (b) Microorganisms may be responsible for the bulrushes' effectiveness.
   (c) Our most serious problem now is with bacteria, not carcinogens.

COMPLETION Choose the best answer for each question:

1. ____ Bulrushes prefer clear water so much they: (a) die in salt water. (b) make clear water. (c) signal freshness. (d) create real mirages.
2. ____ Another plant that effectively purifies water is: (a) the red tulip. (b) the common water lily. (c) the Rhine-wort. (d) a variety of iris.
3. ____ The Environmental Protection Agency believes: (a) there is no water crisis yet. (b) people are going to get "spooked." (c) chlorination is an outmoded technique. (d) the Sudanese hold the secret to water purity.
4. ____ Dr. Seidel found that bulrushes filtered highly: (a) explosive (b) carcinogenic (c) toxic (d) repulsive substances from the water.
5. ____ Studies by environmental agencies found: (a) 5 (b) 66 (c) 500 (d) 6000 dangerous chemicals—carcinogens—in New Orleans's drinking water.
6. ____ The biological purifying systems are no substitute for: (a) chemical systems. (b) Sudanese systems. (c) prevention. (d) bulrushes.
7. ____ One authority fears chlorination may: (a) not work. (b) wear off. (c) fall out of favor in cities. (d) be dangerous in itself.
8. ____ As one scientist points out, life is a: (a) chancy thing. (b) matter of coping with new problems. (c) highly molecular machine. (d) serious risk factor.

VOCABULARY Choose the best definition for each vocabulary entry:

1. ____ elaborate: (a) big (b) significant (c) complex (d) lengthy (e) subtle
2. ____ incidence: (a) finding (b) occurrence (c) hitting (d) studying (e) causing
3. ____ abundant: (a) large (b) significant (c) slow (d) heavy (e) plentiful
4. ____ sophisticated: (a) ignorant (b) advanced (c) sly (d) weak (e) secondary
5. ____ insidious: (a) lost (b) difficult (c) evil (d) thorough (e) organized
6. ____ unsung: (a) tuneless (b) sorrowful (c) unharmed (d) precise (e) unknown
7. ____ monitor: (a) guide (b) subvert (c) watch (d) regarding water (e) make do
8. ____ toxic: (a) impure (b) insidious (c) alert (d) ruinous (e) poisonous
9. ____ hardy: (a) strong (b) bright (c) alert (d) sentimental (e) novelistic
10. ____ potable: (a) capable of being carried (b) suspicious (c) drinkable (d) transporting (e) wary of extremes

12

Stereotyping the Indians

Vine Deloria, Jr.

It is probably accurate to say that movies and television have given most Americans their only image of American Indians. The media has tended both to romanticize and to villify groups of people over the years, and for groups such as the Indians romanticization and villification have been equally harmful. Vine Deloria wonders if such stereotyping will ever end.

It was a rare war movie in the 1940s that actually showed a black or a Mexican as a bona fide fighting man. When they did appear it was in the role of cooks or orderlies serving whites. In most cases this was a fairly accurate statement of their situation, particularly with respect to the Navy.

World War II movies were entirely different for Indians. Each platoon of red-blooded white American boys was equipped with its own set of Indians. When the platoon got into trouble and was surrounded, its communications cut off except for one slender line to regimental headquarters, and that line tapped by myriads of Germans, Japanese, or Italians, the stage was set for the dramatic episode of the Indians.

John Wayne, Randolph Scott, Sonny Tufts, or Tyrone Power would smile broadly as he played his ace, which until this time had been hidden from view. From nowhere, a Navajo, Commanche, Cherokee, or Sioux would appear, take the telephone, and in some short and inscrutable phraseology communicate such a plentitude of knowledge to his fellow tribesman (fortunately situated at the general's right hand) that fighting units thousands of miles away would instantly perceive the situation and rescue the platoon. The Indian would disappear as mysteriously as he had come, only to reappear the next week in a different battle to perform his esoteric rites. Anyone watching war movies during the 40s would have been convinced that without Indian telephone operators the war would have been lost irretrievably, in spite of John Wayne.

Indians were America's secret weapon against the forces of evil. The typing spoke of a primitive gimmick, and it was the strangeness of Indians that made them visible, not their humanity. With the Korean War era and movies made during the middle 50s, other minority groups began to appear and Indians were pushed into the background. This era was the heyday of the "All-American Platoon." It was the ultimate conception of intergroup relations. The "All-American Platoon" was a "one each": one black, one Mexican, one Indian, one farm boy from Iowa, one Southerner who hated blacks, one boy from Brooklyn, one Polish boy from the urban slums of the Midwest, one Jewish intellectual, and one college boy. Every possible stereotype was included and it resulted in a portrayal of Indians as another species of human being for the first time in moving pictures.

The platoon was always commanded by a veteran of grizzled countenance who had been at every battle in which the United States had ever engaged. The whole story consisted in killing off the members of the platoon until only the veteran and the college boy were left. The Southerner and the black would die in each other's arms singing "Dixie." The Jewish intellectual and the Indian formed some kind of attachment and were curiously the last ones killed. When the smoke cleared, the college boy, with a prestige wound in the shoulder, returned to his girl, and the veteran reconciled with his wife and checked out another platoon in anticipation of taking the same hill in the next movie.

While other groups have managed to make great strides since those days, Indians have remained the primitive unknown quantity. Dialogue has reverted back to the monosyllabic grunt and even pictures that attempt to present the Indian side of the story depend upon unintelligible noises to present their message. The only exception to this rule is a line famed for its durability over the years. If you fall asleep during the Late Show and suddenly awaken to the words "go in peace my son," it is either an Indian chief bidding his son good-bye as the boy heads for college or a Roman Catholic priest forgiving Paul Newman or Steve McQueen for killing a hundred men in the preceding reel.

Anyone raising questions about the image of minority groups as portrayed in television and the movies is automatically suspect as an un-American and subversive influence on the minds of the young. The historical, linguistic, and cultural differences are neatly blocked out by the fad of portraying members of minority groups in roles which formerly were reserved for whites. Thus Burt Reynolds played a Mohawk detective busy solving the crime problem in New York City.

Diahann Carroll played a well-to-do black widow with small child in a television series that was obviously patterned after the unique single-headed white family.

In recent years the documentary has arisen to present the story of Indian people and a number of series on Black America have been produced. Indian documentaries are singularly the same. A reporter and television crew hasten to either the Navajo or Pine Ridge reservation, quickly shoot reels on poverty conditions, and return East blithely thinking that they have captured the essence of Indian life. In spite of the best intentions, the eternal yearning to present an exciting story of a strange people overcomes, and the endless cycle of poverty-oriented films continues.

This type of approach continually categorizes the Indian as an incompetent boob who can't seem to get along and who is hopelessly mired in a poverty of his own making. Hidden beneath these documentaries is the message that Indians really WANT to live this way. No one has yet filmed the incredible progress that is being made by the Makah tribe, the Quinaults, Red Lake Chippewas, Gila River Pima-Maricopas, and others. Documentaries project the feeling that reservations should be eliminated because the conditions are so bad. There is no effort to present the bright side of Indian life.

With the rise of ethnic studies programs and courses in minority-group history, the situation has become worse. People who support these programs assume that by communicating the best aspects of a group they have somehow solved the major problems of that group in its relations with the rest of society. By emphasizing that black is beautiful or that Indians have contributed the names of rivers to the road map, many people feel that they have done justice to the group concerned.

One theory of interpretation of Indian history that has arisen in the past several years is that all of the Indian war chiefs were patriots defending their lands. This is the "patriot chief" interpretation of history. Fundamentally it is a good theory in that it places a more equal balance to interpreting certain Indian wars as wars of resistance. It gets away from the tendency, seen earlier in this century, to classify all Indian warriors as renegades. But there is a tendency to overlook the obvious renegades, Indians who were treacherous and would have been renegades had there been no whites to fight. The patriot chiefs interpretation also conveniently overlooks the fact that every significant leader of the previous century was eventually done in by his own people in one way or another. Sitting Bull was killed by Indian police working for the government. Geronimo was captured by an army led by Apache scouts who sided with the United States.

If the weak points of each minority group's history are to be covered over by a sweetness-and-light interpretation based on what we would like to think happened rather than what did happen, we doom ourselves to decades of further racial strife. Most of the study programs today emphasize the goodness that is inherent in the different minority communities, instead of trying to present a balanced story. There are basically two schools of interpretation running through all of these efforts as the demand for black, red, and brown pride dominates the programs.

One theory derives from the "All-American Platoon" concept of a decade ago. Under this theory members of the respective racial minority groups had an important role in the great events of American history. Crispus Attucks, a black, almost single-handedly started the Revolutionary War, while Eli Parker, the Seneca Indian general, won the Civil War and would have concluded it sooner had not there been so many stupid whites abroad in those days. This is the "cameo" theory of history. It takes a basic "manifest destiny" white interpretation of history and lovingly plugs a few feathers, woolly heads, and sombreros into the famous events of American history. No one tries to explain what an Indian is who was helping the whites destroy his own people, since we are now all Americans and have these great events in common.

The absurdity of the cameo school of ethnic pride is self-apparent. Little Mexican children are taught that there were some good Mexicans at the Alamo. They can therefore be happy that Mexicans have been involved in the significant events of Texas history. Little is said about the Mexicans on the other side at the Alamo. The result is a denial of a substantial Mexican heritage by creating the feeling that "we all did it together." If this trend continues I would not be surprised to discover that Columbus had a Cherokee on board when he set sail from Spain in search of the Indies.

LENGTH: 1440 WORDS

Name Class Date

12 Stereotyping the Indians

SCORING: Reading time: _____ Rate from chart: _____ W.P.M.				
RETENTION	number right _____	× 4 equals _____	points	
INFERENCES	number right _____	× 3 equals _____	points	
COMPLETION	number right _____	× 3 equals _____	points	
VOCABULARY	number right _____	× 3 equals _____	points	
	(Total points: 100)	**Total** _____	points	

RETENTION Based on the passage, which statements are True (T), False (F), or Not answerable (N)?

1. _____ "The All-American Platoon" was a phenomenon of the 1950's.
2. _____ Indians, but not Blacks, were often fighting men in 1940's films.
3. _____ John Wayne helped "invent" the "All-American Platoon."
4. _____ Documentary films now play up the successes of the Indians.
5. _____ Indian poverty has not been a popular subject for movie makers.
6. _____ The current media approach to minorities is the "cameo" theory of history.
7. _____ The Mexicans were not really involved in the Alamo.
8. _____ Most minority study programs give a balanced approach, according to Deloria.
9. _____ Eli Parker was a Mohawk from the city.
10. _____ The portrayal of Blacks in 1940's war movies was totally inaccurate.

INFERENCES

1. _____ Which of the following statements is most likely accurate?
   (a) The media want to be totally fair to the minority groups.
   (b) Media distortions of minorities change with the fashion.
   (c) Indians were extraordinarily good fighters in World War II.
2. _____ Which of the following statements is most likely inaccurate?
   (a) Many platoons were racially and ethnically mixed in World War II.

(b) Current portrayals of minorities could contribute to more racial strife.

(c) Emphasizing the good points of minorities is our best hope now.

COMPLETION Choose the best answer for each question:

1. ____ The rise of ethnic studies and minority history programs has made the situation: (a) worse. (b) better. (c) more complicated. (d) ridiculous.

2. ____ 1940's movies portrayed a lot of Indian: (a) sign language. (b) John Waynes. (c) fighting men. (d) army telephone operators.

3. ____ It was the Indians': (a) curiosity, (b) strangeness, (c) silence, (d) brutishness, not their humanity, that made them visible.

4. ____ In the media, the Indians have remained: (a) poor. (b) stubborn, but amazing. (c) foolhardy, but brave. (d) a primitive, unknown quantity.

5. ____ The Makah tribe, the Quinaults, and the Red Lake Chippewas have: (a) been wiped out. (b) been stereotyped as drunks. (c) been legally adopted by John Wayne. (d) made incredible progress.

6. ____ Every significant Indian leader of the nineteenth century was done in: (a) sooner or later. (b) by the whites. (c) by his own people. (d) by stupidity.

7. ____ Group pride dominates the: (a) movies. (b) ethnic studies programs. (c) Pima-Maricopas. (d) motives for stereotyping.

8. ____ The "patriot chief" interpretation of history overlooks the Indians who were: (a) dead. (b) not chiefs. (c) obvious renegades. (d) not patriots.

VOCABULARY Choose the best definition for each vocabulary entry:

1. ____ incompetent: (a) able (b) slow (c) unskilled (d) disallowed (e) fallow

2. ____ ethnic: (a) pure (b) proud (c) minority (d) group (e) a circumstance

3. ____ essence: (a) odoriferous (b) right (c) clue (d) knowledge (e) basis

4. ____ blithely: (a) happily (b) willfully (c) slowly (d) stupidly (e) sorrowfully

5. ____ yearn: (a) spin (b) tell (c) know (d) desire (e) be mysterious

6. ____ durable: (a) good (b) worthwhile (c) lasting (d) first (e) ethnic

7. ____ species: (a) animal (b) kind (c) hardy (d) dangerous (e) particulars

8. ____ reconciled: (a) harmonized (b) afraid (c) beguiled (d) behaved (e) shorn

9. ____ unique: (a) special (b) dull (c) preserved (d) unusual (e) singular

10. ____ revert: (a) have (b) go back (c) turn off (d) insist (e) odd behavior

13

The Storyteller

Francis Steegmuller

In his book of sketches and reminiscences, the eminent writer and translator Francis Steegmuller describes some of his relatives and their experiences. One of the most interesting is his wife, Bea, a born storyteller who throughout her life has charmed grownups and children alike with her skills.

Not very surprisingly, perhaps, when Bea went to normal school, she specialized in storytelling. On her graduation, she was employed by welfare organizations to tell stories in settlement houses—chiefly to groups of children then known as court cases. These were neighborhood youngsters who had been, or whose parents had been, in difficulty with the law. Now and then, she was asked to tell stories in a hospital. Some of the childen's wards included defective children, in those days, and for that reason were kept locked. The nurse in charge would lock Bea in, and come back for her at the end of the session. Sometimes there were a few sick prostitutes locked in, too—"because," as a nurse once said, "they have to be locked in someplace."

Once, on an afternoon shortly before Christmas, when Bea arrived at one of the settlement houses to give a special program of Yule tales, she found her audience larger than usual, augmented by a number of uninvited teen-age youths whom she had never before seen. Quite a few of these, she noticed, were carrying knives. Before beginning her first story, she announced that all knives were to be

THE STORYTELLER From *Stories and True Stories* by Francis Steegmuller.

placed, for the duration of the program, on the table at which she sat. The adolescents courteously complied, and then listened to the tales with a demeanor no less rapt and respectful than that of the others. When the program was over, Bea induced them to stay on for one more story, "just for themselves." This, she felt, gave her regulars a fair chance of reaching home unscathed.

When I first knew Bea, she had already changed her profession, but occasionally I heard and saw her tell stories impromptu to youthful groups, usually composed of her nieces and nephews and their friends. The rapidity with which the children invariably fell under the spell of legend and folklore struck me as uncanny. The moment she began, there would be an instant, utter hush, and the sight of all the young faces staring intently at the storyteller always touched me—it was such a tribute to some eternal aspect of the telling of tales.

Some years ago, not having told stories except informally for a considerable time, Bea was invited to participate as a storyteller in a "preventive antidelinquency campaign" at a community center. The young supervisors in charge withdrew the invitation after two or three sessions, however. They were sorry, they said, but tody's New York children needed more sophisticated fare than "The Daughter Who Was Born a Frog" from West Africa or "The One Who Loved Him Most" from the American plains. These stories "lacked relevance and didn't release enough tension," they said. Bea regretted this decision, especially since the community center children, apparently unaware of the inadequacy of the tales, had been listening to them with the same absorption shown by the settlement house children a generation before.

It was strange how, even when Bea was no longer a professional storyteller, the stories she used to tell kept cropping up, bringing responses from all kinds of people. It usually happened quite unexpectedly. There was an impromptu storytelling session one Halloween, in our apartment; we lived in a great big place, with hundreds of other families, on the East Side, not far from where Bea was born. Our doorbell hadn't rung during dinner that evening, and we were beginning to think there would be no children's visits for "trick or treat"; if so, it would be the first Halloween without them in all our years in New York. Then, just as we were leaving the table, there was a peal. A group of four children was at the door. Despite their various disguises—bought costumes, they were, every one of them—I had no difficulty in recognizing the children as junior co-tenants whom I had often glimpsed in lobby and elevator. They trooped into our foyer, and we handed out the nickels that they certainly didn't need, and then apples. When the apples appeared, one diminutive female spook lamented, "My pockets are so full of apples already I'm afraid I haven't room for this one."

"Would you like a story instead?" Bea asked.

Instantly the spook put her apple down on a table, and she and the others arranged themselves on the parquet floor, their masked faces upturned. The well-known hush fell. My wife chose a very brief tale; she knew they had other calls to make. She told them "The Monkey and the Jellyfish." When she had finished, there was a pause. The pause grew longer. Then one of the other masked listeners—this one in buckskin and feathers—reached up and tentatively laid his apple, too, on the table. Bea then told "The Traveling Musicians." After that, two more apples were placed confidently on the table, and two more short tales were told. "I guess that's that," Bea said then. "Everybody will be wondering where you are." The visitors wordlessly got to their feet, and only when they had filed out through the front door, which I had opened for them, did they burst into shrill thank-yous. Their voices streamed behind them as they disappeared toward the elevator.

Once Bea and I went to a cocktail party where we met a handsome, black-haired young man, introduced by our host as being from Oklahoma. "Are you a Chippewa?" Bea asked him, sociably. He nodded. "Then you must know my favorite Indian forest story," she said. " 'The Man Who Married the Moon.' "

"Not by that title, but tell it to me, and I'll tell you if it's one of ours," he said.

It was. Bea faltered a few times in the telling, being rusty, but the young man put her right each time. It was a curiously primeval antiphony to listen to, up there, high above Park Avenue. They finished in triumphant unison: "Then he found the girl whose face he had watched so many nights in the moon, and *he never came back to earth.*" Quite a few of the other cocktail guests had gathered round to listen, and they seemed to find that ending entirely satisfactory.

At another party—a dinner, this time—there was a young woman who said proudly that her father had been a mighty teller of Irish tales. When Bea said that she, too, had told Irish stories, the young woman looked at her with mistrust. "Did you tell 'The Bee, the Harp, the Mouse, and the Bum-clock'?" she demanded.

"I did," Bea said.

"Well, when you got to the part about the pans and the pails, what did you do with your hands?"

"I did this with them," said Bea, making a crisscross gesture.

"Bless you!" said the young woman. "There are those who always do this"—she made a different gesture—"and that's dead wrong, as you well know."

And then, one morning, one of the handymen of our apartment house came to make some repairs, and told Bea apologetically that some of the things she wanted him to do were impossible. "Too bad you're not a Buddhist with an elephant," she said to him wistfully. "Everything is possible to a Buddhist if his elephant's the right one. Do you know the story called 'The Well-Trained Elephant'? It was white, and it could do all kinds of things, even when it was standing on one leg."

"I don't know the story, but I am a follower of yoga," the man replied with dignity. "I stand on my head every morning."

"I've never seen that done the yoga way," Bea said. "Would it be disrespectful if I asked you to show it to me?"

''Not at all,'' said the handyman, ''If you don't tell the superintendent.''

Bea asked his permission to call in the maid, who she knew would be interested, and, before the two ladies, the handyman placed his hands and forearms on the floor, unfolded upward gracefully and slowly, and was soon standing on his head, chatting amiably about the diet he followed and about what a shame it was that his wife was of too impatient a nature to learn the yoga positions that he found so beneficial.

''He stayed there on his head at least five minutes,'' Bea told me admiringly when I came home that night. ''He seemed utterly relaxed. He didn't even get red in the face. Then he did all kinds of things for me around the house. Extra things—things I'm sure he'd never have done if he hadn't first stood on his head. Not as many as if he'd had the Well-Trained Elephant to help him, naturally. He couldn't hope to—I told him this in consolation, when he looked unhappy at not being able to fix the faucet perfectly—because in the story, of course, the elephant turns out to be Buddha himself.''

LENGTH: 1332 WORDS

13 The Storyteller

SCORING: Reading time: ____ Rate from chart: ____ W.P.M.				
RETENTION	number right ______	× 4 equals ______	points
INFERENCES	number right ______	× 3 equals ______	points
COMPLETION	number right ______	× 3 equals ______	points
VOCABULARY	number right ______	× 3 equals ______	points
	(Total points: 100)	**Total** ______	points

RETENTION Based on the pasage, which statements are True (T), False (F), or Not answerable (N)?

1. ____ Bea was not a follower of yoga.
2. ____ The Steegmullers lived in New York.
3. ____ The community center authorities thought Bea's stories were old-fashioned.
4. ____ At the settlement house the uninvited guests were trick-or-treaters.
5. ____ One of Bea's stories was told at a cocktail party.
6. ____ Actually, Chippewa Indians do not tell stories.
7. ____ Bea used to be a professional storyteller.
8. ____ Some hospitals locked up defective children.
9. ____ Hand gestures are important features of some Irish stories.
10. ____ The handyman stood on his head for five minutes.

INFERENCES

1. ____ Which of the following statements is most likely accurate?
   (a) Storytellers can't make much of a living anymore.
   (b) Children respond best to stories with an ethnic flavor.
   (c) People have a strong positive response to storytelling.
2. ____ Which of the following statements is most likely inaccurate?
   (a) Juvenile delinquents do not seem responsive to storytelling.
   (b) Adults seem to like stories.
   (c) Stories are known to a relatively large community of people.

COMPLETION Choose the best answer for each question:

1. ____ The Well-Trained Elephant was: (a) the handyman. (b) Buddha. (c) yoga. (d) the storyteller with a memory.

2. ____ The stories were once described as: (a) telling, but sweet. (b) pans and pails. (c) legend and folklore. (d) triumphant.

3. ____ One story Bea told was: (a) an Indian forest story. (b) an African medley. (c) botched completely. (d) about a leaky faucet.

4. ____ The Halloween children traded: (a) apples for oranges. (b) fruit for candy. (c) something for nothing. (d) treats for stories.

5. ____ "The Daughter Who Was Born a Frog" was from: (a) France. (b) Northern Ireland. (c) West Africa. (d) the American plains.

6. ____ One of the Halloweeners was dressed in: (a) a frog costume. (b) buckskin and feathers. (c) a homemade spook costume. (d) various costumes.

7. ____ Bea told an extra story to the knifebearing children to give the rest of her audience a: (a) break. (b) chastening. (c) talking-to. (d) headstart.

8. ____ Sometimes Bea was locked in to the children's ward with: (a) prostitutes. (b) other storytellers. (c) real criminals. (d) the children's parents.

VOCABULARY Choose the best definition for each vocabulary entry

1. ____ uncanny: (a) worthless (b) unknown (c) amazing (d) dull (e) wobbly

2. ____ tentatively: (a) uncertainly (b) suddenly (c) ugly (d) latterly (e) homily

3. ____ impromptu: (a) sure (b) spontaneous (c) thoughtful (d) inconsiderate (e) now

4. ____ absorption: (a) loss (b) chemical (c) reasonable (d) concentration (e) feeling

5. ____ diminutive: (a) smart (b) alarmed (c) small (d) frightened (e) heavy

6. ____ sophisticated: (a) amazing (b) simple (c) complex (d) dull (e) unlettered

7. ____ consolation: (a) pride (b) joy (c) irritation (d) assurance (e) reassurance

8. ____ primeval: (a) modern (b) ancient (c) current (d) delinquent (e) thunder

9. ____ unison: (a) together (b) high (c) intense (d) unique (e) very special

10. ____ shrill: (a) soft (b) mellifluous (c) harmonic (d) loud (e) childlike

14

A Second Coal Age

David Sheridan

The first coal age ended sometime around 1950, when oil had all but replaced it as the national fuel. Now, with America's dependence on foreign oil supplies at such a peak, we have readdressed ourselves to coal, our most plentiful fossil fuel. And the problems which were not solved during the first coal age again demand solutions.

The first coal age began in wood-poor England and Scotland in the latter half of the 18th century and spread from there to the Continent and the United States, providing the fuel for the Industrial Revolution. By 1910 it was supplying 80 percent of our energy. That same year oil and gas surpassed wood as a fuel, and coal began to decline. Unable to compete, bulky, dirty coal petered out by midcentury, providing only 18 percent of our energy.

Now we are embarking on a second coal age, one that will surpass anything seen in the first in terms of tons produced. President Carter wants to double output by 1985, to well over a billion tons a year. Coal cannot solve our energy problems, despite the "Dig We Must" newspaper ads, but it certainly can help.

We paid dearly for the first coal age. In this century alone in the United States, more than 100,000 men lost their lives in coal mines. More than a million were permanently disabled in mine accidents. Even more—no one knows how many—contracted pneumoconiosis (black lung disease) and spent their last years gasping for breath. The federal government now pays black lung victims $1 billion a year in benefits which may rise to $8 billion by 1980.

The number of people who have died from breathing coal pollution is unknown. Epidemiological studies do show a direct correlation between air pollution, especially sulfur dioxide, and illness and premature death from respiratory ailments such as bronchitis, asthma, emphysema, and lung cancer. Coal-fired power plants emit about 50 percent of the sulfur dioxide in our air. And sulfur dioxide, it seems, paralyzes those tiny, hairlike structures called cilia found in the throat. Under normal conditions, the cilia beat with a motion that propels mucus and waste toward the mouth or stomach. They are the respiratory system's sentries. But when they are incapacitated, particles of dust and other material, possibly with toxic or carcinogenic chemicals adhering to them, pass relatively freely through the throat and nasal passage directly into contact with lung tissue.

Drainage from coal mines has polluted some 6,700 miles of streams in this country with a mixture of sulfuric acid, iron and aluminum salts—a compound sufficiently potent to kill aquatic life and poison wells and, in some cases, to corrode concrete. More than 90 percent of these streams are in Appalachia. Some 470,000 acres of land in the United States have been stripped for coal and never reclaimed—they are called "orphaned lands" in the coal business. Appalachia accounts for 81 percent of them.

These statistics come to life in a description of a strip-mined site by Kentuckian Harry Caudill: "All that is left of what was once a tree-covered, living ridge is a vast mesa where nothing moves except the clouds of dust on dry, windy days, or the sluicing autumn rains that carve new creekbeds across its dead surface. . . . Enormous gullies are cut into the slopes and sheets of soil are carried away from more nearly level surfaces. Streams that had run clear for thousands of years are now mud, 'too thin to plow and too thick to drink.' "

But despite the terrible costs of digging and burning it, coal does possess one redeeming characteristic—there is a lot of it. That is very important at a time when Americans are consuming natural gas and oil faster than they can find and produce it, and when technical as well as social problems continue to plague nuclear power. Beneath the wooded hills and hollows of Appalachia, the corn- and hayfields in the Midwest, the rolling grasslands of the Northern Great Plains and the arid plateaus and dry creeks of the Southwest lie vast beds of coal. This is an energy resource far richer than the much-heralded oil fields of Alaska or the North Sea. It is more extensive than the huge Persian Gulf oil deposits. Even if the United States were seriously to conserve energy—that is, substantially reduce its energy waste—increased coal production would be necessary. Coal represents 90 percent of the nation's remaining fossil fuel reserves.

How soon all this coal is developed depends largely on the federal government. Industry, and the bankers who will supply the money, are waiting to see what happens to the Clean Air Act now before Congress. If new laws require all coal-burning emissions to be "scrubbed," the low sulfur content of Western coal will no longer be the advantage it now seems. Industry also wants a resolution of the "checkerboard" pattern imposed on coal lands in the last century. The government granted large parcels to railroads along their rights-of-way, but kept alternating sections in federal hands. Mining companies say their equipment is designed for tracts larger than those now owned by railroads, and they cannot be developed unless the intervening federal parcels can be mined, too.

Some 16 billion tons of coal lie under federal land already leased to industry, but very little coal has been produced so far. Fifteen companies, only seven of them coal companies, control 70 percent of the leased land, but have produced coal from only 7 percent of it.

Most energy projections foresee these problems being resolved with the country increasing its reliance on coal energy—particularly for electric power production. President Carter's Energy Plan calls for an increase in coal production of heroic proportions—from 1976's 665 million tons to 1.2 billion in 1985, an unprecedented 535-million-ton increase in nine years. Coal's share of the nation's total energy consumption would rise to 29 percent under this plan.

Before attempting to discern some of the possible ramifications of the second coal age, let us first dispel some lingering misconceptions about coal.

American coal reserves are thought to be so vast that this is one resource which we need not worry about running out of. False. According to the General Accounting Office, if U.S. coal consumption keeps rising at the rate envisioned in the Carter plan, it will exhaust currently known reserves within 74 years. Of course, additional coal will be found in the interim, but the fact remains that coal is a finite resource.

It is often stated that most of the remaining coal reserves in the United States are west of the Mississippi. This is only true, however, if you are talking in terms of its tonnage. Using a more meaningful measure—energy content—we see that Western coal, while more plentiful, contains less energy. About 55 percent of the United States' coal energy, in the ground, lies east of the Mississippi in the old coal-bearing regions.

Another common misconception is that the nation's coal reserves are controlled by coal companies. But of the biggest holders of domestic coal reserves, few are independent coal companies—Westmoreland, Utah, North American. Several are oil companies—Continental Oil, Exxon, Occidental Petroleum, Kerr McGee, Gulf, Mobil, Sun, ARCO, Shell, Phillips, Standard. Two of the other biggest are railroads—the Burlington Northern and Union Pacific. The oil companies had sufficient capital and prescience to begin buying up coal properties in the mid-1960s, and they are now in a strong position to profit from the second coal age. The railroads had the good fortune to be given huge tracts of public lands by the government in the 19th century, and some of these turned out to contain extensive coal deposits.

Finally, consumers should not expect coal to be cheap in relation to other energy sources. Back before the world price of oil quadrupled, coal looked like a bargain at $8 a ton. But the price shot right up with oil to about $20 (spot prices actually rose as high as $45), and coal shows every indication of staying attached to the oil-price comet. Even if it does not, rising costs of capital, labor, pollution control, and land reclamation will keep coal and coal-generated electricity prices high.

In addition, states with coal reserves are beginning to grasp the real worth of their energy resources—much as the OPEC nations did with oil. Montana, for instance, now imposes a 20-to-30 percent tax on the dollar value of coal mined in the state. When State Senator Thomas Towe was asked whether this stiff tax would drive coal producers out of the state, he responded: "If this is the case, so be it. But we do not think that it is. The coal is here. You want it badly enough, however, you are going to have to get used to the idea that you must pay all the costs of your operations, direct and indirect. This is neither a punitive nor confiscatory tax. It is merely realistic. Montanans are through subsidizing the mining industry. Now you must pay your way or you cannot mine."

Producers seem to be paying, and there are signs that this tough new mood is spreading to other states such as Colorado, North Dakota and Wyoming. If an old coal state such as West Virginia ever follows Montana's lead, then the price impact could be truly profound. Currently, West Virginia imposes a 3.85 percent tax on the sale of coal mined in the state.

Indians own from 7 to 13 percent of the nation's coal reserves and they too are beginning to reevaluate the value of their holdings. This is particularly true in the case of the Northern Cheyenne, who have five billion tons under their southern Montana reservation. Other tribes with significant coal holdings include the Crow, the Navajo and the Hopi. Indeed, the Hopis were the first Americans to utilize coal—they used it as early as the 11th century to warm their homes and fire pottery. Indian lawyer George Crossland calls these tribes "the American Arabs."

The overriding impact of the second coal age will be to halt the United States' increasing dependence on oil imports. In 1976 foreign oil filled about 20 percent of our total energy demand—compared with 15 percent at the time of the Arab oil embargo of 1973–74. This situation is expected to get even worse—up to 24 percent or more by 1985. By pushing coal development, President Carter hopes to reduce oil imports to about 15 percent by 1985. But can coal be pushed without seriously endangering public health? The answer depends upon how well we learn to burn coal more cleanly.

Recall, for a moment, that as the last group of astronauts was returning from the moon, and when they were still several thousands miles out in space, they reported that the only evidence of Man on Earth they could see was a yellowish smudge emanating from the Four Corners electricity-generating plant at Farmington, New Mexico. Since then, pollution-control equipment has been installed in that plant and it removes about 90 percent of all the particulate matter from the smoke. Yet, the stacks still spew out more than 46 tons of particles per day. Moreover, the particles which escape tend to be the very small ones, and these pose the gravest threat to human health because they penetrate the body's respiratory filters and lodge in the small airways of the lungs where clearance is slower and less certain.

One of several promising options being pursued is something called fluidized-bed combustion. In this kind of boiler, air is forced through a grid at high speeds to support particles of limestone and ignited coal. The high velocity of air causes the solid particles to act as a fluid, thereby improving their heat transferability. Limestone helps to soak up the sulfur released from the burning coal. Georgetown University is installing a fluidized-bed boiler system to provide steam power to the campus. It will use high-sulfur coal, but will easily meet Environmental Protection Agency emission standards.

Sulfur dioxide in coal is just one health hazard. The soot that does escape into the atmosphere contains benzopyrene, already identified as a carcinogen in cigarette smoke. Fourteen heavy metals, all of them toxic, are found in American coal. Radioactive isotopes naturally present in the coal would add more radioactivity to the air than all the nuclear power plants currently in operation. And burning coal in the quantities envisaged in the Carter plan would add as much nitrogen oxides, a constituent of smog, to the air as do all the cars in the United States.

Coal-fired plants would also produce 600 million tons of carbon dioxide a year. The gas is not toxic, but there is a real concern over whether adding that much carbon dioxide to the atmosphere every year would raise the average temperature of the planet and change the climate in unknown ways.

Increased coal combustion will also hurt agriculture to a certain extent, especially in those areas where coal-fired power plants and gasification plants are concentrated. Coal pollution, especially sulfur dioxide, attacks plants directly—stunting growth and reducing seed output. Some species, such as alfalfa, are more sensitive than others. Coal pollution also has a secondary effect on all plants which may be even more serious: it weakens their ability to resist natural enemies such as insects, disease and drought. An environmental impact statement prepared for two proposed power plants at Colstrip, Montana, predicted crop and grass damage of up to 20 percent within a 500-mile radius.

Sulfur dioxide pollution also contributes to a phenomenon first detected in Sweden and then in Canada—acid rain. The acidity of rain in the United States has been steadily increasing over the last two decades, especially in the East and the Midwest. Acid rain can leach nutrients from the soil, stunt plant growth, including forests, and drastically reduce aquatic life in lakes and ponds. Biologists at Cornell University who have observed a precipitous decline in the tadpole population in ponds around Ithaca, New York, for example, think that acid rain may be the culprit.

Combustion by-products that do not make it up the stack can be a problem, too. A 1,000-megawatt plant burning low-sulfur coal operating for a year will produce 71,000 tons of ash in the boiler, 281,000 tons of fly ash collected in the stack and 212,000 tons of sulfur waste. (Some of the ash can be used in highways and other types of construction.) Put another way, the solid wastes from the coal-fired plants expected to be on line in 1980 will, during their 30-year lifetimes, cover 65,000 acres when piled 30 feet deep.

In the West, coal development creates another kind of water problem. For this is a region where, as historian Walter Prescott Webb noted, "there is a deficiency in the most essential climatic element—water." So when strip mining lowers the groundwater table 10 to 50 feet, as it has in the Decker, Montana, area, it is a serious matter, affecting not only wells but the entire land surface because water moves surfaceward through capillary action. Furthermore, areas receiving an average rainfall of less than 10 inches per year may not be reclaimable after strip mining, however diligent the miner's efforts. (The Ford Foundation found that rehabilitation in Western coal fields would cost anywhere from $925 to $2,750 an acre.)

Water Limits Coal Conversions

But it is the water demands of the new coal-fired power plants and coal gasification facilities which will cause the biggest headaches (SMITHSONIAN, February 1973). A National Academy of Sciences study concluded that "not enough water exists for large scale conversion of coal to other energy forms," and recommended that "alternate locations be considered for energy conversion facilities." There also may not be enough water for slurry pipelines proposed to transport coal from the West to the Southeast.

A case in point is the Kaiparowits Plateau in southern Utah. This arid area happens to contain one of the biggest deposits of low-sulfur coal in the nation. A coal-fired power plant larger than Four Corners was originally planned for the spot, but then was withdrawn after considerable environmental opposition developed. Now three utilities propose building a coal gasification plant there that would produce 300 million cubic feet of gas from 30,000 tons of coal per day. The plant would certainly cause a significant deterioration in the region's air quality and would strain its already overbooked water supplies. Of course, the plant would also create jobs.

New jobs may be one of the second coal age's most positive impacts, as Mrs. Arda Morrell of Loa, Utah, notes: "We are an economically depressed area and need jobs. Jobs will bring our young people home again, and our families will be complete." Identical sentiments are voiced in West Virginia, Kentucky and Pennsylvania as well. In its heydey, the coal-mining industry employed 700,000 people. As a result of automation, that level of employment will never be achieved again, but will rise noticeably from its low point in 1972 of 126,000. The coal work force should increase to 243,500 by 1985 and 390,600 by the year 2000. At present, unemployment in the coal regions of the country is more than 250,000. New coal-fired power and gasification plants and an expanded transportation system to move the coal will also create new jobs.

We are, indeed, on the threshold of some dramatic geographic shifts in populations. Between 1970 and 1975 the tide turned and the population increased by several hundred thousand. It is expected to go on growing at an accelerated rate in the next ten years.

In the West, the influx of coal miners and construction workers and their families has already hit towns like Gillette, Rock Springs and Green River, Wyoming; Forsyth, Montana; and Helper, Utah. They are or soon will be boom towns, and many others are on the way. Not since the homesteaders flooded the region at the turn of the century has there been anything like it.

The new jobs, new money, new shopping centers have been accompanied by some problems. Public facilities—schools, roads, sewage-treatment plants—can not keep up. Consider the case of Sweetwater County in southwestern Wyoming, a coal boom area (SMITHSONIAN, July 1974). In 1970 its population was 18,391. By 1975 it had climbed to 45,000 and was still growing. The county has one hospital (built in 1893) and six primary care doctors. It is in the throes of what clinical psychologist Elden V. Kohrs calls the "Gillette syndrome" after another coal boom town. The syndrome consists of about equal parts "alcoholism, accidents, absenteeism, depression, divorce, and delinquency." Sweetwater County has the third highest per capita suicide rate in the nation. Rock Springs, the county seat, has grown from 11,000 people in 1971 to 26,000 today—half of whom live in trailers. Wind in Rock Springs is often laden with dust from nearby strip-mining sites and the municipal water is frequently a dirty brown. More coal-related development is planned for Sweetwater County. The population is growing at a compound annual rate of 19 percent. Planners figure that sparsely populated counties like this one can absorb a growth rate of only 5 percent without serious socioeconomic troubles. There will be other Sweetwater Counties in the West before the coal is spent.

As the second coal age unfolds, logistical problems will arise. Railroads, mining equipment manufacturers and boiler producers will be hardpressed to deliver the goods and services demanded of them. Raising the necessary money could be a major hurdle. One study estimated that development of Western coal will require $16 billion in new capital, more than three times the industry's total capitalization right now. Temporary shortages could occur.

But these problems pale next to the ones facing our political institutions; the social stresses of the second coal age will be much greater than those of the first. During the first, concerns about coal miner safety, air and water pollution, and ravaged land were distinctly secondary to the business of producing and selling coal. Today this is no longer the case. Through laws passed by Congress and signed by Presidents, the nation has committed itself to the goals of safe mines, clean water, healthy air and reclaimed land. High growth in coal is also a national goal, however, and some conflicts are inevitable.

Coal development, as pointed out in a study made for the Office of Environmental Policy, must be a national program. Eastern strip mining provides large quantities of high-energy coal nationally at the cost of local land and water degradation. Water used in the West for power generation or coal gasification cannot be used for agriculture. Utilities need to know what they can burn and how much it will cost before they decide on the nature of future power plants. Coal companies must know how they can mine and to what level they must rehabilitate before they invest billions of dollars.

If it is any consolation, the second age of coal is unlikely to last longer than the first. It is clearly a transitional period. But a transition to what? That has yet to be determined. Perhaps to the first age of renewable energy—solar, organic, geothermal, wind and ocean-thermal gradients. Then, the Earth's remaining coal can be left to the makers of steel, aspirin, dyes, glue, cosmetics, fertilizer and margarine.

LENGTH: 3735 WORDS

14 A Second Coal Age

SCORING: Reading time: _____ Rate from chart: _____ W.P.M.				
RETENTION	number right _____	× 4 equals	_____	points
INFERENCES	number right _____	× 3 equals	_____	points
COMPLETION	number right _____	× 3 equals	_____	points
VOCABULARY	number right _____	× 3 equals	_____	points
		(Total points: 100)	**Total** _____	points

RETENTION Based on the passage, which statements are True (T), False (F), or Not answerable (N)?

1. ____ The population of Appalachia decreased after 1950.
2. ____ Coal is an ingredient in aspirin.
3. ____ The new coal age will mean more jobs than the first one offered.
4. ____ More than 100,000 men lost their lives in coal mines.
5. ____ The government has taken a "hands-off" policy regarding coal production.
6. ____ Coal companies were described as "the American Arabs."
7. ____ West Virginia levies a very high tax on its coal.
8. ____ Unlike with nuclear energy, there is no radioactive factor with coal.
9. ____ Heavy coal burning will not adversely affect plant growth.
10. ____ Much federal land contains huge coal supplies.

INFERENCES

1. ____ Which of the following statements is most likely accurate?
   (a) The second coal age will be worse than the first.
   (b) Coal will be much less expensive than oil.
   (c) Coal is not a long-term energy solution.
2. ____ Which of the following statements is most likely inaccurate?
   (a) Burning coal cleanly is not out of the question.
   (b) Economic depressions tend to break up families.
   (c) The coal age will have a serious impact on our economy.

COMPLETION Choose the best answer for each question:

1. ____ Five billion tons of coal are under land owned by: (a) the oil companies. (b) the Cheyenne. (c) Quaker State Mohawks. (d) federal agencies.
2. ____ By 1985 President Carter wants to: (a) clean up the environment. (b) start digging coal. (c) end oil dependency. (d) double coal output.
3. ____ The first coal age began in: (a) Pennsylvania. (b) England. (c) the coal-rich Saar Valley. (d) times of serious economic depression.
4. ____ Widespread coal production in the eighteenth century made possible the: (a) roads of Europe. (b) steam engine. (c) Industrial Revolution. (d) creation of ambitious social programs for Europe.
5. ____ The one redeeming virtue of coal is its: (a) color. (b) absolute solidity. (c) power-to-weight efficiency factor. (d) plentitude.
6. ____ The particles escaping from filtered plants are very dangerous because of their: (a) size. (b) metallic content. (c) quantity. (d) acid levels.
7. ____ Acid rain has a profound effect on: (a) coal miners. (b) statuary. (c) crops. (d) rainwear.
8. ____ The biggest headache for new coal-fired power plants will come from: (a) government agencies. (b) New Mexico. (c) water demands. (d) aspirin.

VOCABULARY Choose the best definition for each vocabulary entry:

1. ____ rehabilitate: (a) clothe (b) improve (c) reclaim (d) penalize (e) jail
2. ____ subsidize: (a) pay (b) cost-out (c) reclaim (d) penalize (e) jail
3. ____ impact: (a) affect (b) sound (c) improve (d) destroy (e) struggle
4. ____ profound: (a) heavy (b) serious (c) clever (d) deep (e) important
5. ____ extensive: (a) valuable (b) far-reaching (c) low (d) nervous (e) intense
6. ____ arid: (a) stuffy (b) wasted (c) dry (d) bitter (e) open; frank
7. ____ surpassed: (a) overtook (b) regarded (c) improved (d) outweighed (e) gave
8. ____ emit: (a) extrude (b) sluice (c) slight noise (d) give off (e) exit from
9. ____ toxic: (a) bad (b) prohibited (c) killing (d) diseaselike (e) metallic
10. ____ discern: (a) detect (b) have (c) reveal (d) high regard (e) feel for

15

The Garden of Allah

George Oppenheimer

Many people find the nostalgia of Hollywood to be irresistible. One of the most nostalgic Hollywood landmarks, a hotel on Sunset Strip called The Garden of Allah, no longer exists, but it lives on in legend. A haven for writers, actors, and screen buffs for twenty years, its eccentric ways and high-life parties are part of the lore of a Hollywood that is also gone.

Tallulah Bankhead called it "the most gruesomely named hotel in the western hemisphere." Others, perhaps thinking of its curious architecture or the monumental hangovers that accompanied its boozy high life, called it simply the most gruesome hotel. To most of its denizens, however—to the scores of stars, writers, directors, wits, and wags who would stay nowhere else when they went to Los Angeles to "make a movie"—it symbolized Hollywood itself.

It is gone today, replaced, fittingly perhaps, by a many-storied bank. But from the late 1920's until the years immediately after World War II, the Garden of Allah on Hollywood Sunset Strip was a hotel and an institution without peer. An uninitiated visitor might have passed it by without a glance. But rubbernecking tourists in buses that took them to see the homes of the stars were sure to have it pointed out to them. After gazing at the houses of the likes of Mary Pickford, John Gilbert, and Greta Garbo, they would roll past the restaurants and shops on the Strip, and then the guide with the megaphone would announce, "To your right, folks, the famous hotel, the Garden of Allah. Probably more luminaries liv-

THE GARDEN OF ALLAH Originally published as "Hollywood's Garden of Allah" in *American Heritage,* August 1977.

ing there right now than in all the rest of Hollywood put together.'' Through the window of the moving bus they got a fleeting glimpse of something sprawled out in a hollow below street level—red-tiled roofs smothered in tropical growth; a pink neon sign glaring in daylight among palm and pepper trees, sometimes with some of its letters failing to light up so that it announced THE DEN OF ALLAH.

''Garden'' and ''den'' were equally appropriate. Some awed guests recalled the Garden as an earthly paradise. But Lucius Beebe, raconteur and expert on luxuriously riotous living, announced shortly after moving into the hotel that he had seen nothing like it for ''concentrated alcoholism and general dementia'' since the old days of the Harvard-Yale boat races during Prohibition.

Generally, the hostelry lived up to its billing. The new arrival's neighbors often included stars such as Humphrey Bogart, Laurence Olivier, John Barrymore, Vivien Leigh, Gloria Swanson, Al Jolson, Clara Bow, W. C. Fields, and Errol Flynn, or perhaps such musicians as Igor Stravinsky, Leopold Stokowski, and Sergei Rachmaninoff, as well as swarms of celebrated writers, including William Faulkner, John Steinbeck, Ernest Hemingway, John O'Hara, F. Scott Fitzgerald, and Raymond Chandler.

The hotel began its life as a luxurious private home in 1920. Los Angeles County was then experiencing a mammoth real estate boom, and among the many speculators to profit from it was one W. H. Hay, who signalized his success by building himself a large house on Sunset Boulevard, surrounded by three and one half acres of formal gardens and framed by palms and other tropical trees. Under its tile roof were forty rooms, with floors of teak, and richly carved decorations in rosewood and pale mahogany. The mansion cost him some $200,000—considerably more than a million dollars in today's terms.

Hay enjoyed his munificent home for just four years, then leased it at $50,000 a year to Madame Alla Nazimova, a Crimea-born actress who was then one of the brightest stars of the silent screen. There was a blaze of publicity when she took possession of the place, and she spent a small fortune redecorating, adding new landscaping, and installing a free-form swimming pool whose shape, some claimed, had been inspired by the configuration of the Black Sea. When she was finished she modestly called the whole works the Garden of Alla.

Living there did not bring her much luck. Her picture career declined, she suffered personal as well as business troubles, and after two years of lavish entertaining, she had to turn over the lease to a corporation, which planned to convert the estate into a hotel. The house was remodeled to accommodate paying guests; many of the gardens were demolished; and single and duplex bungalows were built around the main building and the pool.

The grand opening of the new hotel on January 9, 1927, was in the gaudy tradition of the Hollywood première. Greeters in swallowtail coats and striped pants ushered thousands of unabashed gawkers through the rooms and bungalows, while a string quartet played in the lobby of the main building and a platoon of Japanese butlers served tea, punch, and sandwiches. When darkness fell, visitors gasped with wonder as colored lights lit up the grounds, and strolling troubadours in Spanish costumes sang and played beneath the night-blooming jasmine. The theatricality of the opening suggested the make-believe world of movies, and it was assumed by most visitors—and reported by the newspapers the next day—that the new establishment would appeal most to movie makers.

They came in droves, and by the end of the first week the management knew that the Garden of Alla was a hit. Within a few months, a common usage by the guests, and references by the Los Angeles newspapers, had permanently corrupted the spelling of the hotel's name; thereafter it became the Garden of Allah.

The Garden had opened at a turning point in Hollywood history; the Academy of Motion Picture Arts and Sciences had just been founded, and Al Jolson was at work on the Warner lot making the pioneer talking picture, *The Jazz Singer*. Jolson, an early Garden resident, typified the transplanted New Yorkers who first filled the hotel, setting an enduring tone that owed more to Broadway than to California and launching a home-away-from-home party that lasted more than twenty years. Once in a while during that time the hotel and cottages might have appeared somnolent; but the party smoldered on all the same.

"There were no rules," reminisced one early resident. "Nearly everybody drank, and drank hard. It was the thing to do, especially at the Garden. You would come back late at night and look around for a lighted window. That meant a party, where you'd be welcome." The informality took many forms. "If a stark naked lady of acting fame, her head crowned by a chattering monkey, chose to open the door to Western Union, no one was abashed, least of all the lady and the monkey," wrote Whitney Bolton, a New York drama critic who stayed at the Garden. But the informality was not for strangers and voyeurs. The hotel management posted a guard at the front gate and maintained a discreet patrol of the grounds after dark, one of the watchmen leading a formidable dog that residents fondly called the Hound of the Baskervilles. The private police were strictly for security; they had orders not to harass the guests or interfere with their personal foibles and pleasures.

Such guaranteed privacy soon produced a ceaseless stream of outrageous Hollywood stories. There was, for example, the tale of the Broadway playwright who was ensconced in a bungalow some distance from the main house. For weeks he had been trying to get into the office of an old acquaintance who was now the executive producer at a big studio. Day after day he had been turned away. Late one evening he heard a knock at his door and opened it. There stood the producer. "Hello, old boy," said the tycoon. "Come to my office tomorrow. I have a contract for you." The producer disappeared in the darkness, and next day the author signed his contract. Not till some time later did he learn that the producer had mistaken his bungalow for a similar one nearby in which he had recently installed a young lady.

Being on the Garden's guest list was a rough gauge of a film star's popularity. Clara Bow epitomized the flamboyance of the silent era at the Garden. Producers had advertised her to the world as the "It" Girl—"It" being sex appeal of overpowering voltage—and she was a popular figure at the poolside cocktail hour and at evening festivities as well. Occasionally diving off the high board in a dinner gown or pushing tuxedoed escorts into the pool, she made the evening-dress swimming party part of the Garden's early lore. But age overcame her and by 1937 her red Kissel roadster ceased to appear in its accustomed place in the parking lot, and her three chow dogs, whose coats matched their owner's hair, were no longer heard yapping at the bellboys. The "It" Girl was no longer a star.

By that time, Lucius Beebe had become one of the most active residents the place had ever seen. A columnist for the New York *Herald Tribune,* Beebe was an expert on railroading as well as good living, and had been engaged by director Cecil B. DeMille as technical adviser for the film *Union Pacific.* DeMille did not require Beebe's constant attendance at the studio, and so he had plenty of time to participate in—and lead—the life at the Garden. He would stand near the door of his bungalow as guests assembled and greet them with a cordial shout of "Welcome to Walden Pond." The Garden's room service especially impressed Beebe. The staff, he noted, could put a six-bartender private bar into operation on a minute's notice before lunch, so that those persons whom Beebe called "the maimed and dying from the previous night's party" could be given succor.

Not all the stories about the Garden were based on the Bacchanalia that went on there, though its reputation in that regard was so solidly recognized that H. B. Warner, who was about to play the role of Christ in a movie, was seriously warned by his director, C. B. DeMille, to remain in his bungalow and not get mixed up in the fleshpots of the hotel. Apart from the drinking, however, the resident wits gave the hostelry a general air of group merriment. Sheila Graham, from whose book *The Garden of Allah* many of these anecdotes come, termed it "the Algonquin Round Table gone West and childish." Musician Artie Shaw thought it "one of the few places so absurd that people could be themselves."

The Garden's easygoing management had a lot to do with the hotel's informal atmosphere. There was little pressure for prompt payment of bills, for example, even though some accounts carried charges for room service, gratuities to the staff, limousine hire, theater tickets, and cash advances in addition to rent. The owners had learned that in the long run they could depend on their tenants' high earning power.

One group of tenants, however, was denied credit. These were the Hallroom Boys, an assemblage of English actors who had flocked to Hollywood and who found occasional work as bit players in British Empire epics such as *The Lives of a Bengal Lancer.* These Englishmen, generally down-at-the-heels, inhabited the former servants' rooms in the hotel's main building. Their main occupation, it seemed, was to serve as stooges and jesters to the affluent residents of the bungalows. Wearing totally unwarranted Old Etonian ties, and blazers with the armorial emblems of Oxford and Cambridge colleges, with which they had no connection whatsoever, they amused their patrons with prattle about Sandhurst, the Guards, and tea on the vicarage lawn. According to John McClain, a New York drama critic and frequent Garden guest, the Hallroom Boys lived on tequila and nibblings from the cocktail buffet. One day, as McClain was settling his weekly account at the desk, a Hallroomer interceded disapprovingly: "You mustn't do this, old man. Embarrassing for the chaps. If you do it again, your name will be posted for payment of bill."

Perhaps the most loved and lovable of all the Garden's residents was humorist Robert Benchley, who came to Hollywood to star in a series of shorts and shared one of the larger bungalows with his friend, John McClain. The Garden of Allah suited Benchley perfectly, and he became the genial familiar spirit of the place in the period of its final glory, which began as the 1940's came on. It was here that he is supposed to have said after leaving the pool that he believed he would get out of his wet clothes and "into a dry martini," a witticism as often repeated at the time as the cable he is supposed to have sent to David Niven from Venice: "Streets full of water. Please advise."

Stories of Benchley's association with the Garden are legion. Once he tried to phone New York at night but was unable to rouse the hotel operator. He finally went to the main house, upended some furniture, and left a note on the switchboard, reading, "Let this be a lesson to you. I might have been having a baby." On another occasion, he held forth at the pool to British novelist P. G. Wodehouse on the Hollywood "nodders." They were lower, he explained to the British author, than the studio "yes men," for after the "yes men" yessed a producer, he said, the "nodders" nodded. There was also a memorable night when Benchley was lured against his will into playing The Game, which he loathed, and was given to act out the name of Ladislas Bus Fekete, a Hungarian screenwriter who was then working at one of the studios. Benchley immediately dropped to his hands and knees and began to crawl around the room. Then, as his bewildered teammates tried to guess what he was trying to convey, he crawled across the floor and out through some French doors, disappearing into the darkness—to be seen no more that night.

One of the best-remembered Benchley anecdotes concerned a new doorman at the Garden. As Benchley brushed past him, the doorman stretched out his hand for a tip and asked, "Aren't you going to remember me, sir?" "Why, of course," Benchley replied. "I'll write you every day." Nevertheless, everyone at the Garden liked to be near Benchley, to hear his booming laugh and bask in his warm generosity. Sometimes his kindness got him into trouble. One evening in a bar on Sunset Strip, he encountered an odd little man, wearing a derby and pince-nez, who told Benchley he was a song writer and was working on a number entitled "Stars Fell on Orchi Chornya." Benchley was so tickled by this that he invited the man to drop in on him at the Garden any time he felt like it. Accepting on the spot, the song writer accompanied Benchley to the hotel and established himself in the spare bedroom of Benchley's bungalow. The visit was a disappointment to his host, for the man said nothing worth remembering, although he ate and drank heartily. After several days of free-loading, he put on his derby and left, remarking as he departed, "I'm sorry to have to eat and run."

Like many guests, Benchley was an out-of-place New Yorker, somewhat uneasy with the close-to-nature California life. He got along well enough with the Garden's cats and dogs, but waged a celebrated war against the large number of birds that flew around the grounds. One rainy Sunday, Benchley was peering out the living room window when McClain heard him explode with laughter. "You know the bird who keeps me awake all night," Benchley asked, "the one who sits outside my window and keeps saying, *'Chicago, Chicago'*?" McClain said he knew of this bird, and Benchley went on, "Well, he just came in through the rain for a landing. The tile around the pool was so wet his feet went right out from under him and he slid three or four yards on his tail, coming up against the edge of the pool. Then he looked over and saw me watching him, and I swear he shrugged his wings and his expression was, 'All right, you know me and I know you and this time *you* have the laugh.' "

Former residents all recall the contrast between the tranquil Garden and the frightful rush of traffic just outside. Benchley took careful account of this peril whenever he wished to visit The Players, a restaurant on the other side of the Strip. Instead of risking passage across the street on foot, he is reported to have turned right, walked one block to Schwab's drugstore, and jumped into a cab, which then made a U-turn and deposited him in front of The Players.

The increasing traffic Benchley so deftly avoided actually reflected the growth of Los Angeles into a great city in which moving pictures had become one of many major industries. Gradually, the movie people began to feel the loss of their unique importance and, along with the Second World War, there came a chill in the atmosphere of the Garden. Though the hotel had a short period of postwar prosperity, it was due more to the housing shortage than to the old magic of the place. In time, Hollywood notables stopped coming, transients from New York began to find lively new places to stay, and the Garden began to get the reputation of a beloved, but shabby, has-been. The hotel went through a series of management and ownership changes, and continued to deteriorate. By the late 1940's, even the once-dazzling landscaping had grown drab, for heavy smog, a new and baleful element in Los Angeles, had settled over the area. The Garden stood in a natural funnel for the noxious fumes that rolled up the Strip in such concentration that they split the tiles, asphyxiated the big brown rats in the palm trees, and killed the radiant bougainvillea.

Some of the new guests seemed equally obnoxious. The harmless Hallroom Boys disappeared along with the rich movie people, and the bar was often occupied by smalltime chiselers and petty racketeers. Drunken fights broke out, and the management often had to call the police—something unheard of in happier times. In its last years the Garden seemed like a setting from a story of the Los Angeles underworld by Raymond Chandler, himself long since moved away. One could imagine his private eye, Philip Marlowe, leaving his coupé in the Garden parking lot and meeting some dubious character in the bar. Things grew still worse: one night armed thugs entered the lobby, looted the cash drawer, and shot the elderly night clerk dead.

The last owners gave up in April, 1959, announcing that they had sold the property to the Lytton Savings and Loan Association; the Garden would be razed to make way for a banking and commercial center. The furnishings were sold at auction: comedian Ben Blue bought the china and silver for his nightclub. On the night of August 22, 1959, an attempt was made to hold a gala grand closing to mark the official passing of a place that had actually died some years before. Many guests dressed as old-time picture stars and tried to evoke a mood of civilized nostalgia, but on the whole it was an unfortunate affair. Only one genuine silent star stopped by—Francis X. Bushman, still a handsome, dapper man at seventy-six. He stood for a moment looking at the empty bottles floating in the pool, then shook his head, walked back to his car, and drove home.

LENGTH: 2774 WORDS

15 The Garden of Allah

SCORING: Reading time: _____	Rate from chart: _____ W.P.M.		
RETENTION	number right _____	× 4 equals _____	points
INFERENCES	number right _____	× 3 equals _____	points
COMPLETION	number right _____	× 3 equals _____	points
VOCABULARY	number right _____	× 3 equals _____	points
	(Total points: 100)	**Total** _____	points

RETENTION Based on the passage, which statements are True (T), False (F), or Not answerable (N)?

1. ____ The Garden of Allah was torn down to make room for a bank building in the late 1940's.
2. ____ Robert Benchley was smart enough to buy into the hotel.
3. ____ Tallulah Bankhead approved of the hotel's name from the first.
4. ____ Al Jolson liked the place, but never stayed there.
5. ____ There was little or no smog in Los Angeles in the 20's and 30's.
6. ____ The hotel's early management protected its guests' way of life.
7. ____ Clara Bow did not care for dogs.
8. ____ Actually, the hotel only attracted one or two celebrities at a time.
9. ____ The Hallroom Boys were well-educated English stars.
10. ____ Philip Marlowe drove a coupé.

INFERENCES

1. ____ Which of the following statements is most likely accurate?
   (a) The publicity stemming from fleshy parties hurt the hotel.
   (b) The hotel fell victim to economic changes and social shifts.
   (c) Hollywood pulled together to try to save the hotel as a shrine.
2. ____ Which of the following statements is most likely inaccurate?
   (a) Hollywood stars loved privacy and tried to avoid each other.
   (b) Maintaining a legend for eccentricity was not altogether undesirable.
   (c) Having one's name associated with the "Den" might help a career.

COMPLETION Choose the best answer for each question:

1. ____ The next thing lower than a yes man is a: (a) sleeper. (b) snooper. (c) nodder. (d) no man.

2. ____ When the hotel was sold, Ben Blue bought the: (a) furnishings. (b) teak floor. (e) free-form pool. (d) dishes and silver.

3. ____ The smog actually: (a) drowned rats. (b) split tiles. (c) closed the hotel. (d) kept the New Yorkers away.

4. ____ Clara Bow was the: (a) original owner of the hotel. (b) "It" girl. (c) first casualty of the Talkies. (d) one great star who didn't drink.

5. ____ One of the most active residents the place had ever seen was: (a) Lucius Beebe. (b) John McClain. (c) Sherlock Holmes. (d) Philip Marlowe.

6. ____ Robert Benchley was described as: (a) a star. (b) being generally silly. (c) an unreliable friend. (d) totally caught up in movie-magic.

7. ____ The Garden of Allah was originally built as: (a) an investment. (b) a tax write-off for a star. (c) a private home. (d) studio barracks.

8. ____ The real decline of the hotel dates from: (a) the era of Prohibition. (b) the beginning of TV. (c) the end of the Blitz. (d) the end of the 40's.

VOCABULARY Choose the best definition for each vocabulary entry:

1. ____ uninitiated: (a) new (b) eccentric (c) alone (d) without hope (e) foolish
2. ____ raconteur: (a) drunk (b) star (c) storyteller (d) gangster (e) boss
3. ____ celebrated: (a) famous (b) liked (c) treated (d) applauded (e) lost
4. ____ succor: (a) fool (b) sharpster (c) friend (d) aid (e) prosperity
5. ____ noxious: (a) unlikely (b) gleaming (c) dangerous (d) fraud (e) salubrious
6. ____ affluent: (a) influential (b) solid (c) impecunious (d) overly larded (e) wealthy
7. ____ anecdotes: (a) jokes (b) cures (c) meanings (d) producers (e) breviaries
8. ____ tycoon: (a) actor (b) servant (c) royalty (d) producer (e) magnifier
9. ____ harass: (a) beguile (b) alarm (c) succeed (d) remove (e) annoy
10. ____ ensconced: (a) secured (b) lost (c) omitted (d) left behind (e) floored

SECTION 3

Vocabulary Preview

The following words come from the seven reading selections in Section 3. Study the list carefully, pronouncing the words aloud if possible. Conceal the definitions with a card or your hand and test your command of the meanings of the words.

abundance, *noun* plentiful supply
accelerate, *verb* to increase speed
adherent, *noun* member; one who believes
admonition, *noun* counsel or warning
allusions, *noun* indirect references; references to other works or events
anecdotes, *noun* brief, entertaining stories
antiquity, *noun* ancient times
aphorism, *noun* a saying
ascetic, *adj.* self-denying
attenuate, *verb* to weaken
bigotry, *noun* prejudice against those unlike oneself
candor, *noun* frankness
civilized, *adj.* raised from a primitive state; refined
communal, *adj.* shared by a community
conjecture, *verb* to guess
contingent, *adj.* dependent on something else
crevice, *noun* crack
criteria, *noun* standards for judgment
curriculum, *noun* a course of study
decadence, *noun* deterioration
denigrate, *verb* to speak damagingly about someone or something
derive, *verb* to receive or obtain from a source
deviate, *verb* to turn or veer from a set course
dialectical, *adj.* related to a logical process based on dialogue
diffusion, *noun* spreading throughout
distinction, *noun* a difference between things
durable, *adj.* lasting
eccentric, *adj.* deviating from accepted behavior
emancipate, *verb* to set free
empirical, *adj.* based on experience or observation

engender, *verb* to give birth to
enquiries, *noun* questions
epoch, *noun* a memorable period of history
ethical, *adj.* pertaining to values
fanaticism, *noun* intense enthusiasm
fervid, *adj.* enthusiastic
fidelity, *noun* loyalty
foliage, *noun* a mass of leaves
fortified, *adj.* well-protected
formidable, *adj.* frightening
fountainhead, *noun* principal source
habitat, *noun* the place where a plant or animal naturally grows or lives
hackneyed, *adj.* overused
humility, *noun* the quality of being humble
idolatrous, *adj.* making a god out of a physical object
illuminate, *verb* to make clear; to shed light upon
incapable, *adj.* unable to perform a certain task
indiscretion, *noun* an imprudent act; folly
inducement, *noun* motive; encouragement
inevitable, *adj.* sure to occur
intricate, *adj.* complicated
linear, *adj.* straight
metallurgy, *noun* the study of metals
obsolescence, *noun* condition of being no longer in use
orthodox, *adj.* conforming to an established doctrine
paradox, *noun* self-contradictory statement or situation
piety, *noun* devotion
preoccupation, *noun* excessive concern about something
prestige, *noun* importance
punitive, *adj.* involving punishment
ravine, *noun* a narrow steep-sided valley
realm, *noun* sphere; domain
redemptive, *adj.* saving
repudiate, *verb* to reject
resources, *noun* available supplies or funds
robust, *adj.* healthy
sanctify, *verb* to purify
terminology, *noun* special language used for a particular purpose
theological, *adj.* pertaining to the study of religion
transcendent, *adj.* going beyond ordinary limits
transmute, *verb* to alter or change in form
treatise, *noun* a written argument or study

ultimately, *adv.* finally
utilitarian, *adj.* serving a useful purpose
unique, *adj.* one-of-a-kind; unlike any other
vanity, *noun* conceit

Choose the word or phrase that best defines the vocabulary item:

1. ____ utilitarian: (a) harmful (b) enthusiastic (c) overused (d) useful (e) feeble
2. ____ fervid: (a) sickly (b) enthusiastic (c) strong (d) calm (e) excitable
3. ____ admonition: (a) time (b) getting in (c) course (d) warning (e) a fright
4. ____ incompetent: (a) unable (b) incomplete (c) useful (d) weakened (e) tough
5. ____ criteria: (a) importance (b) standards (c) purposes (d) time (e) food service
6. ____ obsolescence: (a) rejected (b) old (c) uselessness (d) out of fashion (e) being in a state of suspended animation.
7. ____ epoch: (a) bigness (b) period (c) site (d) explosion (e) place
8. ____ attenuate: (a) weaken (b) strike (c) alter (d) confound (e) berate
9. ____ paradoxical: (a) surprising (b) confusing (c) contradicting itself (d) in suspended judgment (e) twinlike in appearance
10. ____ anecdotes: (a) stories (b) verses (c) poison-reversers (d) tips (e) prose
11. ____ indiscretion: (a) folly (b) a "touch" (c) illness (d) peculiarity (e) crack
12. ____ repudiate: (a) suspect (b) reject (c) react (d) revile (e) despise
13. ____ conjecture: (a) question (b) examine (c) frame (d) entitle (e) guess
14. ____ foliage: (a) leaves (b) brush (c) hair (d) following (e) stumbling
15. ____ treatise: (a) help (b) delight (c) neatness (d) piece of writing (e) cause
16. ____ ethical: (a) slow (b) not relevant (c) moral (d) timely (e) refined
17. ____ robust: (a) shapely (b) energetic (c) healthy (d) opposing (e) alarming
18. ____ idolatrous: (a) loving (b) making idols (c) worshiping idols (d) being in church (e) with a sense of piety
19. ____ transmute: (a) change (b) evaluate (c) suffer (d) elongate (e) remark upon

20. ____ inevitable: (a) disguise (b) without merit (c) well-protected (d) certain (e) disputed

21. ____ emancipating: (a) striking (b) freeing (c) manly (d) virtue (e) completing

22. ____ sanctify: (a) belie (b) sanction (c) sustain (d) abet (e) purify

23. ____ contingent: (a) necessary (b) needful (c) dependent (d) state (e) continent

24. ____ redemptive: (a) slow (b) being rescued (c) accusing (d) cautious (e) fearful

25. ____ incapable: (a) unfilled (b) limited (c) bemused (d) not able (e) able

16

Arapesh and Mundugumor: Sex Roles in Culture

Margaret Mead

Margaret Mead, one of the world's most well-known anthropologists, describes her research into the ways of New Guinea tribespeople. She and her husband, Reo, were surprised, intrigued, and repulsed by the behavior of these Sepik river groups. They also discovered a great deal about themselves while learning about these completely unfamiliar cultural patterns.

They were a fierce group of cannibals who occupied the best high ground along the riverbank. They preyed on their miserable swamp-dwelling neighbors and carried off their women to swell the households of the leading men. In German times, the Mundugumor told us, the government had sent an occasional punitive expedition to burn down a village and kill anyone they found in the neighborhood. This neither distressed nor deterred them. The Australian administration, when it took over, devised a quite different method of stopping warfare. Instead of destroying villages, the village leaders were put in prison. So the two big men in Kenakatem, the village where we settled, had been imprisoned for a year, during which they sat wondering who had seduced each of their many wives.

When the leaders returned, they announced that warfare was over. This meant that all ceremonial life came to an abrupt end as well. Women had already been admitted to initiation, and so the central point of the ritual—the separation of men from women and children—was lost, and the ceremony would probably be abandoned. Furthermore, all the young men were to leave the village and go to work. This absolute acceptance of a break with the past, which is very characteristic of Sepik cultures, led to a kind of cultural paralysis.

We worked, of course. Reo decided that this time he would do the culture and that I could do the language, the children, and the technology. Since there was only one very good informant, we worked with him alternately. Reo collected endless accounts of battles about women; I worked out the details of the technology. The mosquitoes were frightful, and we found that the people themselves included in their anecdotes allusions to the mosquitoes and whether or not they were biting. It was extraordinarily hard and unrewarding work trying to record everything we could about a culture which the people themselves believed had ceased to exist.

In the middle of our stay I discovered that Reo, who had insisted that he alone would work on the kinship system, had missed a clue. The clue had come from the children's terminology, on which I was working. I felt that if he had not drawn so rigid a dividing line between his work and mine, we would have been able to put the material together much sooner. As it was, we might have missed the clue altogether, and this went against the grain. It was a flat contradiction of good scientific practice. I did not mind a division of labor based on what Reo wanted to do, in which I was left to do whatever he thought was least interesting, as long as the work got done. What worried me was the chance that it might not have got done.

In addition, I felt that I was getting no further in my exploration of sex styles. The Mundugumor contrasted with the Arapesh in every conceivable way. Fierce possessive men and women were the preferred type; warm and cherishing men and women were culturally disallowed. A woman who had the generosity to breastfeed another woman's infant simply did not find another husband when she was widowed. Both men and women were expected to be positively sexed and aggressive. In general, both rejected children and, where the children that were allowed to survive were concerned, adult men and women strongly favored children of the opposite sex. In Arapesh the women were kept away from the gardens for their own protection, because yams disliked anything to do with women. In Mundugumor people copulated in gardens belonging to someone else, just to spoil their yams. Here again, in Mundugumor, I found a very strong cultural styling of personality, but as in Arapesh, both men and women were expected to conform to a single type: the idea of behavioral styles that differentiated men and women was wholly alien. As far as my central problem was concerned, I felt completely stalemated. There would, of course, be plenty of new material, but not on the subject on which I had particularly wanted to work. On my two previous field trips I had had tremendously good luck working in cultures that had been as arbitrarily chosen as the Arapesh and the Mundugumor were. But it seemed that this time my luck was not holding.

Furthermore, I loathed the Mundugumor culture with its endless aggressive rivalries, exploitation, and rejection of children. The Mundugumor had developed a variation on the kinship systems of the area which was neither patrilineal nor matrilineal in its emphasis. People belonged to a "rope"—a woman belonged to her father's rope, to which his mother belonged, and a man belonged to his mother's rope, to which her father belonged. This meant that a man belonged to the same group as his mother's father, but he was not allied either with his father and his father's brothers or with his mother's brothers. And, of course, he belonged to a different "rope" from his sisters. With this system went ruthless intrasex competition and rivalry and merciless exploitation of the emotions of small children. Little boys of seven or eight were expected to stand up to their fathers who wanted to trade a daughter for an extra wife when, correctly, the boy's sister should have been kept to be given in exchange for the boy's wife. And little boys were sent as hostages to live for months among temporary allies; when they went they were told to learn the bush tracks carefully so that later they could guide a raiding party to the village. Lovemaking was accompanied by scratching and biting, and people committed suicide by getting into a temper tantrum and drifting down the river in a canoe to be captured and eaten by the next tribe.

Most difficult of all for me to bear was the Mundugumor attitude toward children. Women wanted sons and men wanted daughters, and babies of the wrong sex were tossed into the river, still alive, wrapped in a bark sheath. Someone might pull the bark container out of the water, inspect the sex of the baby, and cast it away again. I reacted so strongly against the set of the culture that it was here that I decided that I would have a child no matter how many miscarriages it meant. It seemed clear to me that a culture that so repudiated children could not be a good culture, and the relationship between the harsh culturally prescribed style and the acts of individuals was only too obvious.

Reo was both repelled and fascinated by the Mundugumor. They struck some note in him that was thoroughly alien to me, and working with them emphasized aspects of his personality with which I could not empathize. His way of treating illness in himself was to go out and climb a mountain, however raging his fever, in order to fight the sickness out of his system. When we were first married, he had taken care of me very gently during my first attack of malaria—which is frightening because one gets so cold that it is hard to believe one will ever be warm again and stop shaking. But later, as I became more of a wife—and so a part of him—he turned on me the same fierceness with which he treated his own fevers. When I had an infected finger that required a hot poultice, I was told to make it myself. And once in New York when I was ill, he refused to go out and get a thermometer; and when I called in a neighbor, I found that my temperature was 105°. So I had ceased to expect any sympathy. In Mundugumor I had a good deal of fever, and this, combined with Reo's unrelenting attitude toward illness, the mosquitoes, and the general sense of frustration over the people, made it a very unpleasant three months.

Just before Christmas we packed up our camp and went down to the mouth of the Yuat where it converged with the brown, swiftly flowing waters of the Sepik. The night we spent there, waiting for the government launch, was the worst in all our months with the Mundugumor. For the people had made a door to the latrine from a kind of palm frond that is edged with tiny thorns, and when I tried to open it, I ran hundreds of thorns into my hands.

Finally, in the morning, the patrol officer and the government launch arrived, and we began the long trip upstream to spend Christmas at Ambunti, the main government station on the river, some 250 winding miles above the river's mouth. This stretch of the Sepik is wide and deep with fens that stretch far back from both banks, and only here and there, on slightly rising land, tall trees make a dark green splash against the sky. We sailed past Tambunam, deep in shade, the most impressive village on the Sepik and one of the most beautiful villages in New Guinea with its great dwelling houses that have rattan faces woven into the gables and its great double-peaked men's house set in a green plaza planted with crotons. Again Reo and I responded with a pang of envy. This was a culture we would like to have studied.

LENGTH: 1560 WORDS

Name Class Date

16 Arapesh and Mundugumor: Sex Roles in Culture

SCORING: Reading time: _____ Rate from chart: _____ W.P.M.			
RETENTION	number right _____	× 2 equals _____	points
INFERENCES	number right _____	× 3 equals _____	points
COMPLETION	number right _____	× 3 equals _____	points
VOCABULARY	number right _____	× 2 equals _____	points
	(Total points: 100)	**Total** _____	points

RETENTION Based on the passage, which of the following statements are True (T), False (F), or Not answerable (N)?

1. _____ The Mundugumor are cannibals.
2. _____ Mundugumor are swampdwellers.
3. _____ At one time Germany controlled parts of New Guinea.
4. _____ Before the Meads arrived, the Arapesh and Mundugumors lived in peace.
5. _____ Yams are a principal crop of the Sepik peoples.
6. _____ Mosquitoes do not bite the local tribespeople.
7. _____ Margaret Mead was working on problems of Mundugumor technology.
8. _____ Arapesh men and women were expected to behave much alike.
9. _____ Reo missed a clue while he alone worked on the kinship system.
10. _____ The Mundugumor were particularly useful warriors for the Australians.
11. _____ The Meads did not always use good scientific methods.
12. _____ Boys and girls in the same families belonged to the same "rope."
13. _____ The Sepik culture repudiated children.
14. _____ Reo sometimes went mountain climbing.
15. _____ The Arapesh liked Reo's he-man lifestyle.
16. _____ The Meads left their village just before Christmas.
17. _____ The Meads chose their cultures for study in an arbitrary fashion.
18. _____ The Arapesh were actually excellent subjects for Margaret's interests.

19. ____ These cultures knew nothing of possessive people.

20. ____ Tambunam was the least impressive village on the Sepik.

INFERENCES

1. ____ Which of the following statements is most likely accurate?

   (a) The Meads had been married a long time before coming to New Guinea.

   (b) Their study helped the Meads learn about each other.

   (c) The Mundugumor convinced the Meads that they should have children.

2. ____ Which of the following statements is most likely inaccurate?

   (a) Cannibal tribes do not eat their own people.

   (b) Research into other cultures can offer numerous surprises.

   (c) The government was careful to protect the Meads from harm.

COMPLETION Choose the best answer for each question:

1. ____ Reo was repelled and (a) alarmed (b) bewildered (c) fascinated (d) amused by the Mundugumor.

2. ____ In New York, Reo once refused to get Margaret a: (a) research tool. (b) doctor. (c) thermometer. (d) different assignment.

3. ____ At the door of the latrine, Margaret was hurt by: (a) a Judas thornbush. (b) palm fronds. (c) native insults. (d) Reo's harsh comments.

4. ____ People drifted down the river in a canoe in order to: (a) meet new friends. (b) intimidate the tribes. (c) show off. (d) commit suicide.

5. ____ Babies were cast into the river wrapped in: (a) bark sheath. (b) swaddling clothes. (c) oilskin. (d) Sepik linens.

6. ____ Margaret Mead felt that often the children were: (a) exploited. (b) seen but not heard. (c) the real power in the village. (d) absent entirely.

7. ____ Disputes between tribespeople were often about: (a) yams. (b) fishing rights. (c) pole-cabins and their placement. (d) women.

8. ____ Sepik cultures can tolerate: (a) little or nothing. (b) extreme cold. (c) a great deal of examination by Europeans without becoming angry. (d) a break with the past.

VOCABULARY Choose the word or phrase from Column B that best defines the vocabulary item in Column A:

	Column A	*Column B*
1.	____ pang	a. stymie
2.	____ converged	b. deny
3.	____ poultice	c. hate
4.	____ punitive	d. agree with
5.	____ conceivable	e. met
6.	____ conform	f. remarkable
7.	____ loathe	g. feel for
8.	____ exploitation	h. bandage
9.	____ matrilineal	i. punishing
10.	____ tantrum	j. unfair use
11.	____ repudiate	k. pain
12.	____ empathize	l. imaginable
13.	____ terminology	m. on the mother's side
14.	____ possessive	n. fit
15.	____ deter	o. sympathetic
		p. language
		q. selfish
		r. insinuate

17

The Khyber Pass Local

Paul Theroux

The train through the Khyber Pass is one of the great feats of railroad engineering. It weaves, dips, dodges, and penetrates through the mountains separating Afghanistan and Pakistan, guarded by riflemen from one of the British Empire's great regiments. Its passengers comprise a remarkable cross-section of humanity, including railroad buffs, businesspeople, tribal people, and beggars.

The Khyber Pass on the Afghanistan side of the frontier is rockier, higher, and more dramatic than on the Pakistan side, but at Tor Kham—the border—it turns green, and for this foliage one feels enormous gratitude. It was the first continuous greenery I had seen since leaving Istanbul. It begins as lichen on the rock faces, and pale clumps of weed sprouting from crevices; then bushes and low trees the wind has twisted into a mass of elbows, and finally grassy slopes, turning leafy as one nears Peshawar. It is like a seasonal change in the space of a day, this movement from the sharp-featured heights and gorges outside Jalalabad to the cliffs of Landi Khana, bearded with windblown bouquets of wildflowers. The change is abrupt; there cannot be many countries so close geographically and yet so distinctly different. The landscape softens where the border line on the map begins, and the grizzled faces of Afghans, whose heads are sloppily swathed in white turbans, are replaced by the angular beakiness of Pakistanis, who wear narrow slippers and have the thin scornful mustaches of magicians and movie villains.

And there is the Khyber Railway, a further pleasure. Built fifty years ago at great cost, it is an engineering marvel. It has thirty-four tunnels, ninety-two bridges and culverts, and climbs to 3600 feet. The train is well guarded: on bluffs above the track, in little garrisons and pillboxes, the Khyber Rifles stand sentry duty, staring blankly at the plummeting blue black ravines on Afghanistan's inhospitable edge.

There is only one train a week on the Khyber Railway, and practically all the passengers are what the Pakistanis refer to as "tribal people," the Kuki, Malikdin, Kambar, and Zakka Khel, indistinguishable in their rags. They use the train for their weekly visit to the bazaar in Peshawar. It is an outing for them, this day in town, so the platform at Landi Kotal station in the Khyber Pass is mobbed with excited tribesmen tramping up and down in their bare feet, waiting for the train to start. I found a seat in the last car and watched a tribesman, who was almost certainly insane, quarreling on the platform with some beggars. A beggar would limp over to a waiting family and stick his hand out. The lunatic would then rush up to the beggar and scream at him. Some of the beggars ignored him; one hit back, rather lazily slapping him until a policeman intervened.

The lunatic was old. He had a long beard, an army surplus overcoat, and wore sandals cut from rubber tires. He squawked at the policeman and boarded the train, choosing a seat very near me. He began to sing. This amused the passengers. He sang louder. Beggars had been passing through the car—lepers, blind men led by little boys, men on crutches—the usual parade of rural unfortunates. They shuffled from one end of the car to the other, moaning. The passengers watched them with some interest, but no one gave them anything. The beggars carried tin cans of dry bread crusts. The lunatic mocked them: he made faces at a blind man; he screamed at a leper. The passengers laughed; the beggars passed on. A one-armed man boarded. He stood flourishing his good arm, presenting his stump, a four-inch bone at his shoulder.

"Allah is great! Look, my arm is missing! Give something to my wounded self!"

"Go away, you stupid man!" shouted the lunatic.

"Please give," said the one-armed man. He started down the car.

"Go away, stupid! We don't want you here!" The lunatic rose to torment the man, and as he did so the man pounced on him and gave him a terrific wallop on the side of his head, sending him reeling into his seat. When the one-armed man left, the lunatic resumed his singing. But now he had no listeners.

The translation of this dialogue was provided by two men sitting near me, Mr. Haq and Mr. Hassan. Mr. Haq, a man of about sixty-five, was a lawyer from Lahore. Mr. Hassan, from Peshawar, was his friend. They had just come from the border where, Mr. Haq said, "We were making certain enquiries."

"You will like Peshawar," said Mr. Hassan. "It is a nice little town."

"I would like to interrupt my learned friend to say that he does not know what he is talking,'' said Mr. Haq. ''I am an old man—I know what I am talking. Peshawar is *not* a nice town at all. It *was,* yes, but not now. The Afghanistan government and the Russians want to capture it. It was the Russians and Indians who took a piece of Pakistan away, what they are calling Bangladesh. Well. Peshawar was once great some time back. It is full of history, but I don't know what is going to happen to us.''

The train had started, the lunatic was now tormenting a small boy who appeared to be traveling alone, the tribesmen—all elbows—were at the windows. It was an odd trip: one moment the car would be filled with sunshine, and outside the head of the valley shifted to a view of a tumbling stone gorge; the next moment we would be in darkness. There are three miles of tunnels on the Khyber Railway, and as there were no lights on the train, we traveled those three miles in the dark.

''I would like very much to talk to you,'' said Mr. Haq. ''You have been to Kabul. You can tell me: is it safe there?''

I told him I had seen a lot of soldiers, but I supposed they were around because of the military coup. Afghanistan was ruled by decree.

''Well, I have a problem, and I am an old man, so I need some advice.''

The problem was this: a Pakistani boy, a distant relative of Mr. Haq's, had been arrested in Kabul. What with difficulties in obtaining foreign currency and the impossibility of traveling to India, the only place holiday-minded Pakistanis go to is Afghanistan. Mr. Haq thought the boy had been arrested for having hashish, and he had been asked whether he would go to Kabul to see if he could get the boy released. He wasn't sure he wanted to go.

''You tell me. You make the decision.''

I told him he should put the matter in the hands of the Pakistani embassy in Kabul.

''Officially we have diplomatic relations, but everyone knows we have no diplomatic relations. I cannot do.''

''Then you have to go.''

''What if they arrest me?''

''Why would they do that?''

''They might think I'm a spy,'' said Mr. Haq. ''We are almost at war with Afghanistan over the Pakhtoonistan issue.''

The Pakhtoonistan issue was a few villages of armed Pathan tribesmen, supported by Russia and Afghanistan, who were threatening to secede from Pakistan, declare a new state, and, deriving their income from dried fruit, become a sovereign power; the liberated warriors would then compete in the world market of raisins and prunes.

''My advice is don't go,'' I said.

''How can you say that! What about the boy? He is a relative—his family is very worried. I wish,'' said Mr. Haq, ''to ask you one further question. Do you know Kabul's jail?''

I said I didn't, but I had seen Kabul's insane asylum and did not find it encouraging.

"Kabul's jail. Listen, I will tell you. It was built in the year sixteen twenty-six by King Babar. Well, they call it a jail, but it is a number of holes in the ground, like deep wells. They put the prisoners in. At night they cover them up with lids. That is the truth. They do not give food. The boy might be dead. I don't know what I should do."

He fretted in Urdu with Mr. Hassan, while I snapped pictures of the ravines. We ducked into tunnels, emerging through spurs to reversing stations; above us were fortified towers and stone emplacements, bright in the midafternoon sun. It seems an impossible journey for a train. The 132-Down teeters on the cliff sides, breathing heavily, and when there is nothing ahead but air and a vertical rock face the train swerves into the mountain. Plunging through a cave, it dislodges bats from the ceiling, which the tribesmen at the windows swat with their sticks. Then into the sunlight again, past the fort at Ali Masjid, balancing on a high peak, and an hour later, after twenty sharp reverses, moves on a gentler slope in the neighborhood of Jamrud. Above Jamrud is its bulky fort, with walls ten feet thick and its hornworks facing Afghanistan.

Some tribesmen got out at Jamrud, moving Mr. Haq to the observation: "We do what we can with them, and they are coming right up."

He fell silent again and did not speak until we were traveling through the outskirts of Peshawar, beside a road of clopping *tongas* and beeping jalopies. Here, it was flat and green, the palms were high; it was probably hotter than Kabul had been, but so much green shade made it seem cool. Behind us the sun had dropped low, and the peaks of the Khyber Pass were mauve in a lilac haze so lovely it looked scented. Mr. Haq said he had business here—"I have to solve my great worry."

"But let us meet later," he said at Peshawar Cantonment Station. "I will not trouble you with my problems. We will have tea and talk about matters of world interest."

LENGTH: 1771 WORDS

17 Khyber Pass Local

SCORING: Reading time: _____ Rate from chart: _____ W.P.M.				
RETENTION	number right _____	× 2 equals _____	points
INFERENCES	number right _____	× 3 equals _____	points
COMPLETION	number right _____	× 3 equals _____	points
VOCABULARY	number right _____	× 2 equals _____	points
	(Total points: 100)	**Total** _____	points

RETENTION Based on the passage, which of the following statements are True (T), False (F), or Not answerable (N)?

1. _____ The Khyber Pass links Afghanistan with Pakistan.
2. _____ There is a bazaar every week in Peshawar.
3. _____ The author had a business appointment in Peshawar.
4. _____ There is no insane asylum in Kabul.
5. _____ There are only thirty-four tunnels on the Khyber Railway.
6. _____ The railway was built twenty-five years ago.
7. _____ Afghans wear white turbans; Pakistanis wear narrow slippers.
8. _____ The author sat in the last car of the train.
9. _____ There was a lunatic, but no beggars, on the train.
10. _____ The lunatic could yell, but not sing.
11. _____ Bone protruded from the one-armed man's stump.
12. _____ Pakistanis vacation in Afghanistan.
13. _____ Afghánistan has an elected government.
14. _____ Peshawar is a relatively new town.
15. _____ Kabul is in Afghanistan.
16. _____ Mr. Haq was worried about a boy, his son.
17. _____ The fort at Jamrud faces Pakistan.
18. _____ There are no official diplomatic relations between Pakistan and Afghanistan.

19. ____ Mr. Haq and Mr. Hassan had been in the Pakistani government.

20. ____ It was flat and green near Peshawar.

INFERENCES

1. ____ Which of the following statements is most likely accurate?
   (a) The Khyber Railway links politically tense nations.
   (b) In a war, the "tribal people" would be the first to fight.
   (c) The Khyber Railway has little or no military value.

2. ____ Which of the following statements is most likely inaccurate?
   (a) Mr. Haq and Mr. Hassan are "tribal people."
   (b) The future of Pakistan seems to be in some doubt.
   (c) There is some question of Mr. Haq's being a spy.

COMPLETION Choose the best answer for each question:

1. ____ The Khyber Railway is described as: (a) exciting, but unstable. (b) an engineering marvel. (c) a costly mistake. (d) a link in relations.

2. ____ The author's advice to Mr. Haq was: (a) gratefully accepted. (b) politely refused. (c) not helpful. (d) based on strong personal views.

3. ____ The cells in Kabul jail are: (a) plush. (b) primitive. (c) incomplete. (d) interesting.

4. ____ Urdu is probably: (a) a religion. (b) a town. (c) Mr. Haq's son. (d) a language.

5. ____ Pakistanis go to Afghanistan on: (a) Wednesdays. (b) vacation. (c) very urgent business only. (d) political expeditions.

6. ____ The Khyber Pass Railway runs: (a) every so often. (b) each week. (c) once every other week. (d) daily.

7. ____ Mr. Haq felt that the Russians and Indians: (a) could be quieter. (b) would go to war. (c) took part of Pakistan. (d) wanted world peace.

8. ____ When the train plunged into a cave: (a) everyone shouted. (b) no one dared speak. (c) Mr. Haq sobbed. (d) bats were dislodged from the ceiling.

VOCABULARY Choose the word or phrase from Column B that best defines the vocabulary entry in Column A:

Column A	*Column B*
1. ____ gorge	a. winding
2. ____ currency	b. independent
3. ____ secede	c. contemptuous
4. ____ sovereign	d. showy
5. ____ coup	e. sudden victory
6. ____ swathed	f. hopeful
7. ____ plummeting	g. wrapped
8. ____ indistinguishable	h. treating
9. ____ decree	i. perfumed
10. ____ bulky	j. ravine
11. ____ scented	k. rate
12. ____ dramatic	l. falling
13. ____ sinuous	m. money
14. ____ abrupt	n. large
15. ____ scornful	o. similar
	p. sudden
	q. edict
	r. drop out

18

The Semi-literate Shakespeare

Alvin Toffler

The transformation of the English language over the centuries has been so extensive that someone living in Shakespeare's time would know only slightly more than half the terms we use daily. Most of this change, however, has occurred over the last fifty years. And chances are that the changes will be even greater in the next half century.

If our images of reality are changing more rapidly, and the machinery of image-transmission is being speeded up, a parallel change is altering the very codes we use. For language, too, is convulsing. According to lexicographer Stuart Berg Flexner, senior editor of the *Random House Dictionary of the English Language,* "The words we use are changing faster today—and not merely on the slang level, but on every level. The rapidity with which words come and go is vastly accelerated. This seems to be true not only of English, but of French, Russian and Japanese as well."

Flexner illustrated this with the arresting suggestion that, of the estimated 450,000 "usable" words in the English language today, only perhaps 250,000 would be comprehensible to William Shakespeare. Were Shakespeare suddenly to materialize in London or New York today, he would be able to understand, on the average, only five out of every nine words in our vocabulary. The Bard would be a semi-literate.

This implies that if the language had the same number of words in Shakespeare's time as it does today, at least 200,000 words—perhaps several times that many—have dropped out and been replaced in the intervening four centuries. Moreover, Flexner conjectures that a full third of this turnover has occurred within the last fifty years alone. This, if correct, would mean that words are now dropping out of the language and being replaced at a rate at least three times faster than during the base period 1564 to 1914.

This high turnover rate reflects changes in things, processes, and qualities in the environment. Some new words come directly from the world of consumer products and technology. Thus, for example, words like "fast-back," "wash-and-wear" or "flashcube" were all propelled into the language by advertising in recent years. Other words come from the headlines. "Sit-in" and "swim-in" are recent products of the civil rights movement; "teach-in" a product of the campaign against the Vietnam war; "be-in" and "love-in" products of the hippie subculture. The LSD cult has brought with it a profusion of new words—"acid-head," "psychedelic," etc.

At the level of slang, the turnover rate is so rapid that it has forced dictionary makers to change their criteria for word inclusion. "In 1954," says Flexner, "when I started work on the *Dictionary of American Slang,* I would not consider a word for inclusion unless I could find three uses of the word over a five-year period. Today such a criterion would be impossible. Language, like art, is increasingly becoming a fad proposition. The slang terms 'fab' and 'gear,' for example, didn't last a single year. They entered the teen-age vocabulary in about 1966; by 1967 they were out. You cannot use a time criterion for slang any more."

One fact contributing to the rapid introduction and obsolescence of words is the incredible speed with which a new word can be injected into wide usage. In the late 1950's and early sixties one could actually trace the way in which certain scholarly jargon words such as "rubric" or "subsumed" were picked up from academic journals, used in small-circulation periodicals like *New York Review of Books* or *Commentary,* then adopted by *Esquire* with its then circulation of 800,000 to 1,000,000, and finally diffused through the larger society by *Time, Newsweek* and the larger mass magazines. Today the process has been telescoped. The editors of mass magazines no longer pick up vocabulary from the intermediate intellectual publications alone; they, too, lift directly from the scholarly press in their hurry to be "on top of things."

When Susan Sontag disinterred the word "camp" and used it as the basis of an essay in *Partisan Review* in the fall of 1964, *Time* waited only a few weeks before devoting an article to the word and its rejuvenator. Within a matter of a few additional weeks the term was cropping up in newspapers and other mass media. Today the word has virtually dropped out of usage. "Teenybopper" is another word that came and went with blinding speed.

A more significant example of language turnover can be seen in the sudden shift of meaning associated with the ethnic term "black." For years, dark-skinned Americans regarded the term as racist. Liberal whites dutifully taught their children to use the term "Negro" and to capitalize the "N." Shortly after Stokely Carmichael proclaimed the doctrine of Black Power in Greenwood, Mississippi in June, 1966, however, "black" became a term of pride among both blacks and whites in the movement for racial justice. Caught off guard, liberal whites went through a period of confusion, uncertain as to whether to use Negro or black. Black was quickly legitimated when the mass media adopted the new meaning. Within a few months, black was "in," Negro "out."

Even faster cases of diffusion are on record. "The Beatles," says lexicographer Flexner, "at the height of their fame could make up any word they like, slip it into a record, and within a month it would be part of the language. At one time perhaps no more than fifty people in NASA used the word 'A-OK.' But when an astronaut used it during a televised flight, the word became part of the language in a single day. The same has been true of other space terms, too—like 'sputnik' or 'all systems go.' "

As new words sweep in, old words vanish. A picture of a nude girl nowadays is no longer a "pin-up" or a "cheesecake shot," but a "playmate." "Hep" has given way to "hip"; "hipster" to "hippie." "Go-go" rushed eagerly into the language at breakneck speed, but it is already gone-gone among those who are truly "with it."

The turnover of language would even appear to involve non-verbal forms of communication as well. We have slang gestures, just as we have slang words—thumbs up or down, thumb to nose, the "shame on you" gesture used by children, the hand moving across the neck to suggest a throat-slitting. Professionals who watch the development of the gestural language suggest that it, too, may be changing more rapidly.

Some gestures that were regarded as semi-obscene have become somewhat more acceptable as sexual values have changed in the society. Others that were used only by a few have achieved wider usage. An example of diffusion, Flexner observes, is the wider use today of that gesture of contempt and defiance—the fist raised and screwed about. The invasion of Italian movies that hit the United States in the fifties and sixties probably contributed to this. Similarly, the upraised finger—the "up yours" gesture—appears to be gaining greater respectability and currency than it once had. At the same time, other gestures have virtually vanished or been endowed with radically changed meaning. The circle formed by the thumb and forefinger to suggest that all goes well appears to be fading out; Churchill's "V for Victory" sign is now used by protesters to signify something emphatically different: "peace" *not* "victory."

There was a time when a man learned the language of his society and made use of it, with little change, throughout his lifetime. His "relationship" with each learned word or gesture was durable. Today, to an astonishing degree, it is not.

LENGTH: 1320 WORDS

Name ____ Class ____ Date ____

18 The Semi-literate Shakespeare

SCORING: Reading time: _____ Rate from chart: _____ W.P.M.				
RETENTION	number right _____	× 2 equals	_____	points
INFERENCES	number right _____	× 3 equals	_____	points
COMPLETION	number right _____	× 3 equals	_____	points
VOCABULARY	number right _____	× 2 equals	_____	points
		(Total points: 100) **Total**	_____	points

RETENTION Based on the passage, which of the following statements are True (T), False (F), or Not answerable (N)?

1. ____ The civil rights movement contributed no new words to the language.
2. ____ Stuart Flexner is a lexicographer.
3. ____ Two-thirds of the changes in language occurred in the last fifty years.
4. ____ English is unusual in having so much language change.
5. ____ Russian lexicographers are hampered by party politics.
6. ____ "Turnover" is one of the new words added recently.
7. ____ Actually, the rate of language change has not altered much since 1564.
8. ____ The English language has about 450,000 usable words.
9. ____ Susan Sontag disinterred the word "camp."
10. ____ Scholarly jargon never enters into popular usage.
11. ____ *Newsweek* is a mass magazine, compared with *Commentary*.
12. ____ In 1945 "black" replaced "Negro" as a term of pride.
13. ____ "Psychedelic" was a term we got from a Beatles album.
14. ____ "Black" is an ethnic term.
15. ____ Slang gestures rarely, if ever, change.
16. ____ Italian movies have no influence on the English language.
17. ____ "V for Victory" was associated with Stokely Carmichael.
18. ____ There has not been a *Dictionary of American Slang*.

19. ____ Fads appear in art.

20. ____ Images of reality apparently can change.

INFERENCES

1. ____ Which of the following statements is most likely accurate?
   (a) No one can predict which words are going to change next.
   (b) There is money to be made from inserting new words in the language.
   (c) Slang words change even faster than the standard words in English.

2. ____ Which of the following statements seems most likely inaccurate?
   (a) Liberal whites were often caught off-guard in the 1960's.
   (b) Actually, it is difficult to inject a new word into wide usage.
   (c) People writing for large magazines often read scholarly journals.

COMPLETION Choose the best answer for each question:

1. ____ The term "A-OK" was used by: (a) Churchill. (b) Flexner, in 1954. (c) the LSD cults. (d) NASA people.

2. ____ One word picked up from the scholarly journals is: (a) "interface." (b) "subsumed." (c) "disinterred." (d) "legitimated."

3. ____ One space term is: (a) "Sputnik." (b) "Spacy." (c) "altitudinal." (d) "Highing into gear."

4. ____ "Diffusion" is a term for: (a) losing a word. (b) gaining a word. (c) more restricted use of a word. (d) greater use of a word.

5. ____ "Cheesecake" shots are now called: (a) "Go-go" shots. (b) "pin-ups." (c) "Foo-Dads." (d) "Playmates."

6. ____ Apparently, the development of gestures is watched closely by: (a) the cops. (b) parents. (c) professionals. (d) quick-witted photographers.

7. ____ Toffler assumes the number of English words in Shakespeare's time is: (a) the same as now. (b) larger than now. (c) about four-fifths of our current number. (d) impossible to determine.

8. ____ One important source for new words is: (a) the newspapers. (b) television. (c) advertisements. (d) dictionaries.

VOCABULARY Choose the word or phrase from Column B that best defines the vocabulary entry in Column A:

Column A	*Column B*
1. ____ endowed	a. answers
2. ____ durable	b. changing
3. ____ dutifully	c. given
4. ____ obsolescence	d. specialized language
5. ____ rejuvenation	e. scorn
6. ____ jargon	f. suggests
7. ____ turnover	g. sent
8. ____ contempt	h. long-lasting
9. ____ propelled	i. outdatedness
10. ____ profusion	j. good supply
11. ____ parallel	k. reluctantly
12. ____ altering	l. appear
13. ____ implies	m. big
14. ____ materialize	n. conscientiously
15. ____ comprehensible	o. regaining vigor
	p. change
	q. meaningful
	r. similar

19

Man's Selfhood

Reinhold Niebuhr

Reinhold Niebuhr, a religious thinker, observes that the individual, or self, is nurtured in a community. It gives and is given to. And, as religions have long taught, the more one gives the more one receives. Niebuhr shows that the theories of modern psychology parallel this religious view of human experience. The concept of self is both scientific and spiritual.

Man's self-seeking and self-giving are intricately related in the human self. Human freedom makes for a unique and dialectical relation of the individual to the community. On the one hand, it transmutes nature's instinct for survival into a variety of forms of self-realization, including vanity, the will-to-power and the desire for a full selfhood, which must include always relations to neighbors and communities. On the other hand, the freedom of the self gives man an infinite variety of relationships with his community, from social dependence to social creativity. Thus man's selfhood is involved in an intricate relation of self-seeking and self-giving. The paradoxical observation of Jesus about this relation is accurate. He said, "He who finds his life will lose it, and he who loses his life for my sake will find it." This aphorism might be interpreted as follows: consistent self-seeking is bound to be self-defeating; on the other hand, self-giving is bound to contribute ultimately to self-realization.

The social substance of human existence makes this paradoxical relation inevitable. The community, chiefly the family in the infancy of the self, is the primary source of the self's security which enables the self to love and relate its life to others. The psychoanalytic study of the child has shown how the security of the self is derived from the love it experienced in childhood from "the mothering one." On the other hand, the family and a whole complex of communities are the arena in which the self, freed of undue self-concern, is able to relate itself to others, first in parental affection and responsibility to the children and to the mate in the family, which continues to be the most primary, as it is the most primordial, of all human communities.

Thus the gift of security given by parents to children is transmuted naturally into the ability of even those parents, who are otherwise self-seeking, to be "self-giving" in their relations to their family. Thus modern psychiatry has validated and given new emphasis to what was defined in orthodox religious thought as "common grace." This element of "grace" may be defined as the "gift" of security, without which the self is incapable of becoming free of preoccupation with its own security so that it might relate itself to others and achieve true fulfillment of the self.*

Naturally, in civilized communities, the family is not the only community through which the self is made secure and in turn is offered the opportunity of self-fulfillment through self-giving. These other communities include not only the various civic communities, from tribe to city-state, to empire and nation. They also include all communities of culture which engage creatively the reason and imagination of the self, thus leading to self-realization by the fulfillment of all its talents.

All this does not change the basic fact that self-seeking, practiced too consistently without regard to the social substance of self-fulfillment, must be self-defeating. Nor do all the achievements of civilized life alter the other part of the paradox, namely that the capacity of the self to relate itself to others cannot be achieved by a robust moral will. It is a gift of the original security of the self; that is, it is a matter of "grace."

Erich Fromm in his *Man for Himself,* as also others, defines the capacity to love as a "phenomenon of abundance," but mistakenly he assumes that the abundance of security which enables the self to love is derived from its previous self-seeking. It is more correct to regard the abundance of security as furnished by the love and devotion which others give the self, as Erik Erikson, for example, illustrates with his concept of "basic trust." Thus we have a complete circle of the paradox: consistent self-seeking is self-defeating; but self-giving is impossible to the self without resources furnished by the community, in the first instance, the family.

*The word "grace" is a translation of the Greek *charis* and the Latin *gratias*. Its original meaning is therefore a free gift, not a reward for merit. The theological usage of the word frequently obscures the original meaning, but it is reflected in such general usage of the meaning of gift, in the words "gracious" or "graceful" in which the freedom of the gift is emphasized. "Grateful" is obviously meant to designate the response to a free gift.

Thus modern empirical studies support the paradox of Jesus. But there are two aspects of the intricate relation between self-seeking and self-giving which have been confused, rather than illuminated, by orthodox doctrine, both Catholic and Reformation. The first is the confusion pertaining to the theological distinction between "common grace" and "saving grace." This distinction is valid only insofar as the community of faith or the religious tradition is able to supply an additional resource for freeing the self from idolatrous forms of communal loyalties. By definition and tradition, "saving grace" is induced by a religious experience in which the conscience of the individual self transfers devotion from a contingent community, such as family, race or nation, to an ultimate loyalty to God, the fountainhead of the whole realm of value.

Actually the force of "saving grace" has a different course in history than the one marked out for it according to the theory. It has emphasized the loyalty of individuals to the immediate community, rather than emancipating them from idolatrous worship of common loyalties. Thus loyalty to religious faith and to its ethical traditions has affected the standards of fidelity in marriage, as are shown even in the statistics of the Kinsey report. But the religious commitment in itself does not necessarily make the family, the community of loyal individuals, for example, responsible for the well-being of other families. The family as family cannot detach itself from its own self-interest to seek actively the well-being of other families.

In the community of faith—the church or the denomination—this domestication of love is shown not only passively in lack of concern but also positively in the sins of religious fanaticism and bigotry.

Ideally the church is a community of "saved" individuals, who know themselves to be "forgiven sinners." This ideal should make for humility; but the long history of religious self-righteousness reveals that religious experience is more effective in inducing repentance for deviation from common standards than in inducing repentance for the hatred, bigotry, and prejudice involved in the common standards of race and nation, or church. The adherent of religion must come to terms with the historic facts, that in all collective behavior religious piety is likely to sanctify historical and contingent viewpoints. Historically speaking, religious piety is more apt to be found claiming the divine for an ally of its own partial viewpoints—"It has seemed good to the Holy Spirit and to us"—rather than showing a humble awareness of the relative aspects of all historical loyalties or as bringing forth the fruits of repentance for shortcomings as judged by the transcendent God.

All this is a human rather than a peculiarly or uniquely religious phenomenon. Both the French and the Russian revolution showed it was easy to do this without benefit of clergy. Thus it was the curious quirks of the collective self which prompted all men to claim ultimate validity for contingent collective values. In both Jacobin and communist fanaticism, "truth" or "reason" or "Marxist-

Leninist science'' was worshipped as an asbsolute. Perhaps human self-hood in its collective form constitutionally is unable to imagine any higher value than the common value of its devotion. Hence, the redemptive value of dissident individuals, the prophet, the critic, even the rebel, in a free community.

Orthodox religious doctrine in a second way has confused this basic paradox of self-giving, self-striving and self-fulfilling. It has assumed that it is possible to suppress self-regard and to make the self unselfish and disinterested. This perfectionist hope is expressed in Catholicism particularly in its ascetic tradition and theology. In Protestantism it is found both in the Lutheran doctrine of the ''heavenly realm'' and in various perfectionist Protestant sects as also more generally in Protestant moralism.

This belief in perfectability has given the religious community too often the aura of self-righteousness. Religious people were ostensibly more ''unselfish'' than other mortals, although common experience refuted this pretension. Another consequence of this belief in perfectability was that all forms of self-regard and self-realization were denigrated and regarded as ''sinful.'' Thus the truth in Jesus' original paradox was obscured. He had observed merely that a consistent desire for self-fulfillment was self-defeating. This is true because the self needs other selves in order to be itself. This is the nature of the self, and also is its destiny.

LENGTH: 1250 WORDS

Name Class Date

19 Man's Selfhood

SCORING: Reading time: _____	Rate from chart: _____ W.P.M.		
RETENTION	number right _____	× 2 equals _____	points
INFERENCES	number right _____	× 3 equals _____	points
COMPLETION	number right _____	× 3 equals _____	points
VOCABULARY	number right _____	× 2 equals _____	points
	(Total points: 100)	**Total** _____	points

RETENTION Based on the passage, which of the following statements are True (T), False (F), or Not answerable (N)?

1. _____ The self needs other selves in order to be itself.
2. _____ The self 's first community is the family.
3. _____ One's culture is not a community.
4. _____ The Lutherans did not develop a perfectionist view.
5. _____ Niebuhr cites Jesus' observation about the self as paradoxical.
6. _____ One paradox is why Jesus discusses the self at all.
7. _____ Catholicism has an ascetic tradition as well as a theology.
8. _____ Adherents of religion need not come to terms with historic facts.
9. _____ Ideally the church is a community.
10. _____ Religious faith has no effect on marriage.
11. _____ Religious commitment does not necessarily make the family responsible for the well-being of other families.
12. _____ Self-righteousness has been associated with the religious community.
13. _____ "Grace" may be defined as the gift of security.
14. _____ Self-seeking can confound self-fulfillment.
15. _____ Children give the gift of security to parents.
16. _____ Modern psychiatry cannot help us interpret grace.
17. _____ Self-giving contributes to self-realization.
18. _____ Niebuhr says nature has an instinct for survival.

19. ____ There is no mention made of human freedom.

20. ____ The tribe is a civic community.

INFERENCES

1. ____ Which of the following statements is most likely accurate?
   (a) Religion is beginning to make a comeback.
   (b) Religion may have relevance for modern life.
   (c) Religion is solving its problems through psychiatry.

2. ____ Which of the following statements is most likely inaccurate?
   (a) The development of self depends on a community or family.
   (b) The family has ceased to be the most primary human community.
   (c) The lack of a mother figure could cause psychiatric problems.

COMPLETION Choose the best answer for each question:

1. ____ Niebuhr's program for self-giving is: (a) not mentioned. (b) concerned with daily worship. (c) natural to the community. (d) psychiatrically sound.

2. ____ Even without religion, the Russian revolution produced: (a) martyrs. (b) idolatrous worship. (c) a genuine clergy. (d) the Kinsey report.

3. ____ The dissident individual has: (a) no chance. (b) more problems than others. (c) something to teach us. (d) a redemptive value.

4. ____ Communists are said to have worshipped: (a) the devil. (b) non-creeds. (c) at the altar of Jacobinism. (d) truth or reason.

5. ____ "Grace" can be translated as: (a) charity. (b) a free gift. (c) a religious paradox. (d) self-fulfillment.

6. ____ One religious ideal is: (a) humility. (b) righteousness come what may. (c) fidelity to the cause. (d) community in the imperial sense.

7. ____ The "mothering one" is: (a) any woman. (b) central to the tribe. (c) the Holy Spirit. (d) in the family.

8. ____ Erich Fromm mistakenly feels that the security which enables one to love comes from: (a) parents. (b) previous self-seeking. (c) the social environment. (d) contact with the brotherhood of religious adherents.

VOCABULARY Choose the word or phrase from Column B that best defines the vocabulary entry in Column A:

Column A	*Column B*
1. ____ adherent	a. dependent upon
2. ____ quirk	b. impression; feelings
3. ____ contingent	c. endless
4. ____ pertaining to	d. reduced
5. ____ inducing	e. hearty
6. ____ aura	f. steady
7. ____ robust	g. odd quality
8. ____ aphorism	h. veering from
9. ____ infinite	i. necessary to
10. ____ consistent	j. member; believer
11. ____ ultimately	k. relevant
12. ____ inevitable	l. causing
13. ____ deviation	m. hidden
14. ____ prompt	n. cause
15. ____ obscured	o. saying
	p. at last
	q. sudden; unexpected
	r. certain

20

The Charmed Life

Katherine Anne Porter

Katherine Anne Porter, a distinguished American writer, lived in Mexico for many years. In this narrative, she describes a man whose life was devoted to Mexico and theories about its history. He gave up home and family to follow his dreams of archaeology, to dig up lost Indian cities.

In 1921, he was nearly eighty years old, and he had lived in Mexico for about forty years. Every day of those years he had devoted exclusively to his one interest in life: discovering and digging up buried Indian cities all over the country. He had come there, an American, a stranger, with this one idea. I had heard of him as a fabulous, ancient eccentric completely wrapped up in his theory of the origins of the Mexican Indian. "He will talk your arm off," I was told.

His shop was on the top floor of a ramshackle old building on a side street in Mexico City, reached by an outside flight of steps, and it had the weathered, open look of a shed rather than a room. The rain came in, and the dust, and the sunlight. A few battered showcases and long rough tables were piled up carelessly with "artifacts," as the Old Man was careful to call them. There were skulls and whole skeletons, bushels of jade beads and obsidian knives and bronze bells and black clay whistles in the shape of birds.

I was immensely attracted by the air of authenticity, hard to define, but easy to breathe. He was tough and lean, and his face was burned to a good wrinkled leather. He greeted me with an air of imperfect recollection as if he must have known me somewhere. We struck up an easy acquaintance at once, and he talked with the fluency of true conviction.

Sure enough, within a quarter of an hour I had his whole theory of the origin of the ancient Mexicans. It was not new or original; it was one of the early theories since rejected by later scientists, but plainly the Old Man believed he had discovered it by himself, and perhaps he had. It was religion with him, a poetic, mystical, romantic concept. About the lost continent, and how the original Mexican tribes all came from China or Mongolia in little skiffs, dodging between hundreds of islands now sunk in the sea. He loved believing it and would listen to nothing that threatened to shake his faith.

At once he invited me to go with him on a Sunday to dig in his latest buried city, outside the capital. He explained his system to me. He had unearthed nearly a half-hundred ancient cities in all parts of Mexico. One by one, in his vague phrase, he "turned them over to the government." The government thanked him kindly and sent in a staff of expert scientists to take over, and the Old Man moved on, looking for something new.

Finally by way of reward, they had given him this small and not very important city for his own, to settle down with. He sold in his shop the objects he found in the city, and with the profits he supported the digging operations on Sunday.

He showed me photographs of himself in the early days, always surrounded by Indian guides and pack-mules against landscapes of cactus or jungle, a fine figure of a man with virile black whiskers and a level, fanatic eye. There were rifles strapped to the bales on the pack-mules, and the guards bristled with firearms. "I never carried a gun," he told me. "I never needed to. I trusted my guides, and they trusted me."

I enjoyed the company of the Old Man, his impassioned singleness of purpose, his fervid opinions on his one topic of conversation, and the curiously appealing unhumanness of his existence. He was the only person I ever saw who really seemed as independent and carefree as a bird on a bough.

He ate carelessly at odd hours, fried beans and tortillas from a basket left for him by the wife of his head digger, or he would broil a scrawny chicken on a stick, offer me half, and walk about directing his men, waving the other half. He had an outdoors sort of cleanliness and freshness; his clothes were clean, but very old and mended. Who washed and mended them I never knew. My own life was full of foolish and unnecessary complications, and I envied him his wholeness. I enjoyed my own sentimental notion of him as a dear, harmless, sweet old man of an appealing sociability, riding his hobby-horse in triumph to the grave, houseless but at home, completely free of family ties and not missing them, a happy, devoted man who had known his own mind, had got what he wanted in life, and was satisfied with it. Besides he was in perfect health and never bored.

Crowds of visitors came and bought things, and he dropped the money in a cigar-box behind a showcase. He invited almost everybody to come out and watch him dig on Sundays, and a great many came, week after week, always a new set. He received a good many letters, most of them with foreign postmarks, and after a few rapid glances he dropped them into the drawer of a long table. "I know a lot of people," he said, shuffling among the heap one day. "I ought to answer these. Big bugs, too, some of them."

One day, among a pile of slant-eyed clay faces, I found a dusty, dog-eared photograph of a young girl, which appeared to have been taken about fifty years before. She was elegant, fashionable, and so astonishingly beautiful I thought such perfection could belong only to a world-famous beauty. The Old Man noticed it in my hand. "My wife," he said in his impersonal, brisk tone. "Just before we were married. She was about eighteen then."

"She is unbelievably beautiful," I said.

"She was the most beautiful woman I ever saw," he said, matter-of-factly. "She is beautiful still." He dropped the photograph in the drawer with the letters and came back talking about something else.

After that, at odd moments, while he was polishing jade beads or brushing the dust off a clay bird, he dropped little phrases about his wife and children. "She was remarkable," he said. "She had five boys in eight years. She was just too proud to have anything but boys, I used to tell her."

Again, later: "She was a perfect wife, perfect. But she wouldn't come to Mexico with me. She said it was no place to bring up children."

One day, counting his money and laying it out in small heaps, one for each workman, he remarked absently: "She's well off, you know—she has means." He poured the heaps into a small sack and left the rest in the cigar-box. "I never wanted more money than I needed from one week to the next," he said. "I don't fool with banks. People say I'll be knocked in the head and robbed some night, but I haven't been, and I won't."

One day we were talking about a plot to overthrow the Government which had just been frustrated with a good deal of uproar. "I knew about that months ago," said the Old Man. "One of my politician friends wrote me. . . ." He motioned toward the table drawer containing the letters. "You're interested in those things," he said. "Would you like to read some of those letters? They aren't private."

Would I? I spent a long summer afternoon reading the Old Man's letters from his international big bugs, and I learned then and there that hair *can* rise and blood *can* run cold. There was enough political dynamite in those casually written letters to have blown sky-high any number of important diplomatic and financial negotiations then pending between several powerful governments. The writers were of all sorts, from the high-minded and religious to the hearty, horse-trading type to the worldly, the shrewd, the professional adventurer, down to the natural moral imbecile, but they were all written in simple language with almost boyish candor and an indiscretion so complete it seemed a kind of madness.

I asked him if he had ever shown them to anyone else. "Why, no," he said, surprised at my excitement.

I tried to tell him that if these letters fell into certain hands his life would be in danger. "Nonsense," he said vigorously. "Everybody knows what I think of that stuff. I've seen 'em come and go, making history. Bah!"

"Burn these letters," I told him. "Get rid of them. Don't even be caught dead with them."

"I need them," he said. "There's a lot about ancient Mexican culture in them you didn't notice." I gave up. Perhaps the brink of destruction was his natural habitat.

A few days later, I went up the dusty stairs and, there, in a broad square of sunlight, the Old Man was sitting on a cowhide chair with a towel around his neck, and a woman was trimming his moustache with a pair of nail scissors. She was as tall as he, attenuated, with white hair, and the beauty of an aged goddess. There was an extraordinary pinched, starved kind of sweetness in her face, and she had perfect simplicity of manner. She removed the towel, and the Old Man leaped up as if she had loosed a spring. Their son, a man in middle age, a masculine reincarnation of his mother, came in from the next room, and we talked a little, and the wife asked me with gentle pride if I did not find the shop improved.

It was indeed in order, clean, bare, with the show-windows and cases set out properly, and tall vases of flowers set about. They were all as polite and agreeable to one another as if they were well-disposed strangers, but I thought the Old Man looked a little hunched and wary, and his wife and son gazed at him almost constantly as if they were absorbed in some fixed thought. They were all very beautiful people, and I liked them, but they filled the room and were not thinking about what they were saying, and I went away very soon.

The Old Man told me later they had stayed only a few days; they dropped in every four or five years to see how he was getting on. He never mentioned them again.

Afterward when I remembered him it was always most clearly in that moment when the tall woman and her tall son searched the face of their mysterious Wild Man with baffled, resigned eyes, trying still to understand him years after words wouldn't work any more, years after everything had been said and done, years after love had worn itself thin with anxieties, without in the least explaining what he was, why he had done what he did. But they had forgiven him, that was clear, and they loved him.

I understood then why the Old Man never carried a gun, never locked up his money, sat on political dynamite and human volcanoes, and never bothered to answer his slanderers. He bore a charmed life. Nothing would ever happen to him.

LENGTH: 2054 WORDS

20 The Charmed Life

SCORING: Reading time: _____ Rate from chart: _____ W.P.M.				
RETENTION	number right _____	× 2 equals _____	points
INFERENCES	number right _____	× 3 equals _____	points
COMPLETION	number right _____	× 3 equals _____	points
VOCABULARY	number right _____	× 2 equals _____	points
	(Total points: 100)	**Total** _____	points

RETENTION Based on the passage, which of the following statements are True (T), False (F), or Not answerable (N)?

1. ____ The Old Man had a shop in Mexico City.
2. ____ In 1921, the man was almost 80 years old.
3. ____ The Old Man's theory was that the Mexican tribes came from China.
4. ____ Even in tough times, the Old Man never carried a gun.
5. ____ The government did not take official notice of the man.
6. ____ Funeral sculptures were the fastest sellers in his shop.
7. ____ The Old Man never had diggings on Sunday.
8. ____ The Old Man's family visited him every five or six months.
9. ____ Some of the Old Man's letters contained political dynamite.
10. ____ At one time the Old Man had black whiskers.
11. ____ His clothes were both old and mended.
12. ____ The Old Man was from England.
13. ____ The Old Man kept his money in goldbacks.
14. ____ The author convinced the Old Man to burn his letters.
15. ____ Actually, the author had never heard of the Old Man.
16. ____ The government gave the Old Man one of the cities he discovered.
17. ____ The Old Man had found cities only on the Eastern coast.
18. ____ The Old Man's wife did not think Mexico a good place to raise children.

19. ____ The man and his wife had at least five sons.

20. ____ The man's wife married him when she was about eighteen.

INFERENCES

1. ____ Which of the following statements is most likely accurate?
   (a) The Old Man seemed more interested in the past than the present.
   (b) People such as the Old Man usually wind up in plenty of trouble.
   (c) Were it not for such people, historical discoveries would not be made.

2. ____ Which of the following statements is most likely inaccurate?
   (a) The origin of Mexican tribes is obscure.
   (b) Selling Mexican artifacts is not unusual.
   (c) Porter thought the man happy and well-balanced.

COMPLETION Choose the best answer for each question:

1. ____ One thing the author liked about the Old Man was his: (a) wry sense of humor. (b) beard. (c) outdoors sort of cleanness. (d) capacity to theorize.

2. ____ Katherine Anne Porter also felt that the: (a) feelingfulness (b) eccentricity (c) belligerence (d) unhumanness of his existence was curiously appealing.

3. ____ When she saw a picture of the man's wife, Porter thought she must have been: (a) a child-bride. (b) an angel. (c) a famous beauty. (d) dead.

4. ____ After making a sale, the Old Man dropped the money in: (a) his pocket. (b) a cigar-box. (c) the greasy till. (d) a government envelope.

5. ____ Porter describes the man as in perfect health and never: (a) sickly. (b) bored. (c) cantankerous. (d) a rapscallion.

6. ____ Despite everything, Porter felt the man's family: (a) hoped he would come home. (b) despised him. (c) didn't understand him. (d) forgave him.

7. ____ Porter lamented that her own life was: (a) wasted. (b) full of unnecessary complications. (c) futile by comparison. (d) not charmed in any way.

8. ____ Among the artifacts mentioned were: (a) bronze bells. (b) singing birds. (c) sinks and funnels. (d) clay tablets with runic accounts.

VOCABULARY Choose the word or phrase from Column B that best defines the vocabulary item in Column A.

Column A	*Column B*
1. ____ resigned	a. incomplete; uncertain
2. ____ fabulous	b. weakened; thin
3. ____ fluency	c. out of the ordinary
4. ____ fervid	d. edge
5. ____ impassioned	e. talkative
6. ____ virile	f. easiness; fullness
7. ____ pending	g. splendid
8. ____ brink	h. amazing; remarkable
9. ____ attenuated	i. having submitted
10. ____ wary	j. imbecilic
11. ____ elegant	k. thoughtful; canny
12. ____ eccentric	l. where one lives
13. ____ shrewd	m. enthusiastic
14. ____ habitat	n. suspicious
15. ____ candor	o. one's passion
	p. masculine
	q. emotional
	r. honesty

21

Our Advertising Was Honest

Robert Thomas Allen

The early days of advertising were anything but glamorous. Copywriters for department stores had no illusions about their work stirring up hot copy about socks and knee pads. The author admits that it was hard work and not too inspiring. But he stresses that in his day advertising struggled to be honest. He is not so sure this is the way things are today.

I'm not sure that my generation was any more honest than the present young generation. We probably weren't. But we believed in honesty. Perhaps this is what the young mean by hypocrisy, and they may be right. But we were at least clearheaded about it. We knew when we were being crooked, which must be a minor virtue. Today, young people must be utterly confused on the subject, when lying over world hook-ups is an accepted technique of international diplomacy, and when respected guests on TV panel shows tell so many lies that they now always say "This is the truth," before they tell another one, and everyone, including the M.C. sits there pretending to believe it. When this kind of thing happens, something fundamental has slipped.

I'll say one thing for the kind of retail department-store advertising I started writing, there was a real effort made to be honest, as a store policy. We had what was called a comparison department, staffed by suspicious, thin-lipped men who checked out the claims of the buyers, the advertising department, and the manufacturer. They would go to the men's wear department and get an actual pair of

---

socks which had been claimed to be 100 percent wool, and put them through a shredder or something to make sure they were, and they laid down rules governing the use of English to defraud. We could never say a thing—say, a tube of toothpaste—was free unless a customer could walk in, say "Give me a tube of toothpaste, please," and walk out again without spending a cent.

This kind of advertising still had some historic connection with the ancient marketplace. It dealt with real things, like chairs and saucepans. It was relatively realistic and unpretentious. If a writer got delusions of grandeur about his talents as a crafty composer of compelling literature, he heard about it from some furious, red-faced buyer of men's socks who yelled over the phone: "I don't want any of that crap about these socks giving you happy feet, I want you to tell what they're *made of!*" In those days you had to take your own ad down to the department manager the day after the merchandise was on sale and find out how many pairs of socks he sold from *your* ad, and mark the quantity on the ad with a black grease pencil. It was entered in a book that was photostated and bound for posterity. If the geniuses of today's TV commercials had to show the client how much of his product their commercials sold, about 98 percent of them would lose their jobs.

Nobody kidded himself—advertising was a rather ghastly way to make a living. But there was a merry kind of prison life going on there all the same, and we made the time pass more pleasantly by tossing dimes and putting fifty-cent bets on the horses with a bookie who was the brother of one of the proofreaders. We sat in little cubicles at old typewriters, trying to think up things to say about curtains and cedar chests and men's socks. The socks would lie there beside your typewriter. Often your mind would rebel at having to do anything so ridiculous. You couldn't think of a single intelligent thing to write. The way you overcame this was just to start writing anything. "I am looking at a pair of men's socks," you'd write. "The men's wear manager is a brassbound bastard. I hate making a living writing ads about men's socks, especially socks like this, which are a kind of nauseous green—" Eventually, by sheer accident, you'd put down a phrase about socks that made sense, and you'd begin to get the glimmer of a coherent paragraph.

This principle is well known to all writers who, hot or cold, have to produce. I knew a tall, buck-toothed, talkative man who made his living writing magazine short stories, back in the days when this was an active market. He used to employ a method something similar to this to get started when his muse was asleep. He used to fascinate me by telling me how he wrote a story last night, starting with no idea other than the desire for a check. "I sat down at my typewriter and said to myself, 'What's a good name for a girl? Daphne. I haven't used Daphne for a long time. Okay,' I typed 'Daphne.' I asked myself 'What was Daphne doing?' 'Daphne sat up in bed.' I typed 'Daphne sat up in bed.' 'Why did Daphne sit up in bed?' " (You have to remember that this man was writing in the pre-pornography days of art and literature.) " 'Daphne heard a sound,' I told myself. I typed 'Daphne heard a sound.' 'What did Daphne hear?' "

This guy would hang over me, jiggling and laughing and licking his buck teeth and dropping cigarette ashes over me with the sheer fun of the game of starting the creative juices. All this might strike some people as rather horrible evidence of why the magazine short story disappeared. But I've never seen any relation between the quality of a piece of writing and the motives or methods of getting up momentum to get it written. Writers will write what they are capable of writing, no more, no less, whether they write to save humanity or to save their equity in a house.

I disliked advertising almost from the moment I got into it, but one of the things I really enjoyed about the advertising department where I worked was that almost everybody was interested in something other than advertising—art, writing, producing plays, playing clarinets. It was full of people who were really knowledgeable in art and music. An artist would be sitting there with his thoughts on, perhaps, a concert he was going to that night. His head would appear above his partition: "What's that symphony that goes 'da-dum da-dum?' " he'd ask, apparently to an empty room. "That's the middle of the second movement in Beethoven's Fifth," a voice would say. The artist's head would sink below the partition again, like a seal submerging, as he went back to drawing a pressure cooker.

There was a kind of innocence about financial matters among artists that guaranteed that they'd never have much money. They'd come back from lunch hours with purchases they'd made in the junk stores downtown, proudly displaying things like a secondhand set of gram weights, eighteenth-century sabers and kettle drums. "I got this for a dollar," someone would say, holding up a starboard lamp from a schooner, convinced, somehow, that he had beaten the system. We visited art galleries during our lunch hours and sketched and played pianos in rooms that were rented by the hour as practice and teaching studios by a big music company across the street. When a new employee came along who was really keen on advertising we were all suspicious of him. I know men I don't trust to this day because they came into the advertising office and began to show an interest in advertising.

We had entered the era of the first manipulation of words on a national scale. I remember when Ipana toothpaste began to scare people about bleeding gums, which Ipana was supposed to do something about, and warned them of "pink toothbrush." I went into a drugstore with a friend of mine who wanted to buy some toothpaste, and if he had something that was good for pink toothbrush. I waited for the clerk to recommend washing the toothbrush, and was even more horrified to hear the clerk say without change of expression, "Ipana is very good for pink toothbrush." Both my friend and the clerk had been brainwashed.

But in retail advertising, certainly in the store where I worked, we still had the idea that language should be used for communication. Public relations men and information officers had hardly been heard of, or the profession, which many of them were to develop, of skillfully removing all meaning from words. These men have almost created a counterprofession of trying to get information out of them. A while ago I spent ten minutes trying to get a tall, distinguished-looking public relations head of a brewery to describe the flavor of his beer, which he had said was different from other beers. "Why don't you just say that our beer is palatable, Mr. Allen," he told me with a courtly manner, while I tried to explain that I could say the same thing of potatoes, and that I still wanted to know how his beer tasted. (The brewmaster, who was short and undistinguished-looking but who hadn't forgotten how to talk, told me. "It's bitter," he said.)

Some of the people I worked with had no feeling for words, but they were completely free from intention to mislead.

One girl who, I'll never know how, became a copywriter, could create the most intriguing effects with words just by using the right words in a peculiar order. She used to write ads for hardware, and the manager of the hardware department would explain to her that some household paint or varnish was non-toxic and was harmless if a kid chewed on something painted with it. This girl would study her notes and come up with one of her inimitable sentences, running everything together: "This paint will not harm linoleum, toilet seats, or babies." One time the department was selling foam rubber that women could use for kneeling pads. (These were days when many women still got down on their knees and scrubbed floors by hand.) It could also be used for machinery mounts, to absorb vibration. She wrote: "Ideal for mounting machinery or busy housewives." This girl could innocently have started wars with her use of language, but she was a pleasant woman who was doing no harm and who at least tried to communicate.

LENGTH: 1740 WORDS

Name Class Date

21 Our Advertising Was Honest

SCORING: Reading time: _____ Rate from chart: _____ W.P.M.			
RETENTION	number right _____	× 2 equals _____	points
INFERENCES	number right _____	× 3 equals _____	points
COMPLETION	number right _____	× 3 equals _____	points
VOCABULARY	number right _____	× 2 equals _____	points
	(Total points: 100)	**Total** _____	points

RETENTION Based on the passage, which of the following statements are True (T), False (F), or Not answerable (N)?

1. ____ The buck-toothed writer wrote advertising, not fiction.
2. ____ Pink toothbrush was part of an advertising campaign.
3. ____ Daphne was identified as a copywriter.
4. ____ The bookie was the brother of a proofreader.
5. ____ A copywriter was held responsible for sales from his ad.
6. ____ The author met a short story writer who used a technique like his own.
7. ____ People in advertising seem to have been narrow-minded.
8. ____ The author feels that writers will write what they are capable of, no more, no less.
9. ____ Robert Thomas Allen loved advertising almost from the moment he got in it.
10. ____ The magazine short story seems to have an active market today.
11. ____ One public-relations head of a brewery could not describe his beer.
12. ____ Ipana is a grooming aid.
13. ____ Allen was suspicious of those who didn't like advertising.
14. ____ The writer who mixed up her words amused Allen.
15. ____ Allen does not mention his buying something from the junk stores.
16. ____ None of Allen's advertising friends was knowledgeable about music.
17. ____ Apparently, Beethoven wrote at least five symphonies.

18. ____ Dishonesty is an accepted technique of modern diplomacy.

19. ____ Allen feels his generation was more honest than the present generation.

20. ____ When Allen advertised a "free" product it did not have to be absolutely free.

INFERENCES

1. ____ Which of the following statements is most likely accurate?
   (a) Allen implies that the world has changed.
   (b) Advertising's level of sophistication is unchanged.
   (c) Gambling and honesty do not mix.

2. ____ Which of the following statements is most likely inaccurate?
   (a) TV advertising is different from department store advertising.
   (b) Allen envies the TV advertising budgets.
   (c) Allen wrote ads because he was inspired, not because he needed money.

COMPLETION Choose the best answer for each question:

1. ____ Allen compliments his generation on knowing: (a) the score. (b) when it was being dishonest. (c) how to lie well. (d) a real bargain.

2. ____ The Comparison Department checked out the ad writer's: (a) background. (b) grammar. (c) bookie-charts. (d) claims.

3. ____ Sometimes Allen wrote copy: (a) asleep. (b) late into the night. (c) with the product next to him. (d) in a mad rush so as to get an early start.

4. ____ Allen felt honest advertising had a connection with: (a) the ancient marketplace. (b) good government. (c) hypocrisy. (d) department stores.

5. ____ The magazine writer began a story with nothing more than a desire for: (a) fame. (b) his main character. (c) peace and quiet. (d) a check.

6. ____ Artists, Allen says, have a kind of: (a) silliness (b) innocence (c) happy-go-luckiness (d) basic shrewdness about financial affairs.

7. ____ The kneeling-pads were good for knees and: (a) machines. (b) ankles. (c) tired bankers. (d) altar boys.

8. ___ The idea in Allen's department store was that language should be used: (a) again and again. (b) carefully. (c) early. (d) for communication.

VOCABULARY Choose the word or phrase from Column B that best defines the vocabulary item in column A:

Column A	*Column B*
1. ___ palatable	a. age
2. ___ intriguing	b. sickening
3. ___ era	c. tiny room
4. ___ non-toxic	d. resist
5. ___ momentum	e. interesting
6. ___ cubicle	f. poisonous
7. ___ ghastly	g. cheat
8. ___ nauseous	h. harmless
9. ___ rebel	i. misapprehensions
10. ___ defraud	j. tasty
11. ___ diplomacy	k. buildup of speed
12. ___ hypocrisy	l. frightening
13. ___ unpretentious	m. unique
14. ___ delusions	n. simple
15. ___ inimitable	o. deceit
	p. modest
	q. tactful dealings
	r. unavailable

22

Birches

Robert Frost

Robert Frost was a poet of the New England countryside. The birches he describes here are a familiar New England sight. To Frost they suggest the adventures of his childhood. They also take on a greater significance to him as an adult. Reflecting on the birches, he considers the character of his entire life.

When I see birches bend to left and right
Across the lines of straighter darker trees,
I like to think some boy's been swinging them.
But swinging doesn't bend them down to stay
As ice-storms do. Often you must have seen them
Loaded with ice a sunny winter morning
After a rain. They click upon themselves
As the breeze rises, and turn many-colored
As the stir cracks and crazes their enamel.
Soon the sun's warmth makes them shed crystal shells
Shattering and avalanching on the snow-crust—
Such heaps of broken glass to sweep away
You'd think the inner dome of heaven had fallen.
They are dragged to the withered bracken by the load,
And they seem not to break; though once they are bowed
So low for long, they never right themselves:

You may see their trunks arching in the woods
Years afterwards, trailing their leaves on the ground
Like girls on hands and knees that throw their hair
Before them over their heads to dry in the sun.
But I was going to say when Truth broke in
With all her matter-of-fact about the ice-storm
I should prefer to have some boy bend them
As he went out and in to fetch the cows—
Some boy too far from town to learn baseball,
Whose only play was what he found himself,
Summer or winter, and could play alone.
One by one he subdued his father's trees
By riding them down over and over again
Until he took the stiffness out of them,
And not one but hung limp, not one was left
For him to conquer. He learned all there was
To learn about not launching out too soon
And so not carrying the tree away
Clear to the ground. He always kept his poise
To the top branches, climbing carefully
With the same pains you use to fill a cup
Up to the brim, and even above the brim.
Then he flung outward, feet first, with a swish,
Kicking his way down through the air to the ground.
So was I once myself a swinger of birches.
And so I dream of going back to be.
It's when I'm weary of considerations,
And life is too much like a pathless wood
Where your face burns and tickles with the cobwebs
Broken across it, and one eye is weeping
From a twig's having lashed across it open.
I'd like to get away from earth awhile
And then come back to it and begin over.
May no fate willfully misunderstand me
And half grant what I wish and snatch me away
Not to return. Earth's the right place for love:
I don't know where it's likely to go better.
I'd like to go by climbing a birch tree,
And climb black branches up a snow-white trunk
Toward heaven, till the tree could bear no more,
But dipped its top and set me down again.
That would be good both going and coming back.
One could do worse than be a swinger of birches.

Name *Class* *Date*

22 Birches

SCORING: Reading time: _____	Rate from chart: _____ W.P.M.			
RETENTION	number right _____	× 2 equals _____	points
INFERENCES	number right _____	× 3 equals _____	points
COMPLETION	number right _____	× 3 equals _____	points
VOCABULARY	number right _____	× 2 equals _____	points
	(Total points: 100)	**Total** _____	points

RETENTION Based on the passage, which of the following statements are True (T), False (F), or Not answerable (N)?

1. ____ The straight trees are darker than the birches.
2. ____ Swinging on the birches takes the stiffness out of them.
3. ____ Boys learned baseball in town, not out in the country.
4. ____ Ice storms only bend the birches temporarily.
5. ____ The worst ice storms come in spring.
6. ____ Ice storms are said to enamel the trees.
7. ____ Frost mentions boys, but not girls.
8. ____ Actually, Frost doesn't like to think of boys swinging birches.
9. ____ Earth's the right place for love.
10. ____ Frost imagined himself climbing a tree toward heaven.
11. ____ Birches grow in clumps, not singly.
12. ____ Twigs can hurt eyes.
13. ____ Sometimes life can be like a wood.
14. ____ Frost describes the nighttime look of the icy trees.
15. ____ The inner dome of heaven is said to be made of glass.
16. ____ Truth can be very matter-of-fact.
17. ____ The boy Frost describes played alone often.
18. ____ Fate does not enter into this poem.

19. ____ The boy Frost describes swings on a neighbor's trees.

20. ____ There are no cobwebs in the wood.

INFERENCES

1. ____ Which of the following statements is most likely accurate?
   (a) Frost is glad to see an end to the cold weather and ice storms.
   (b) It is better for boys to bend birches than for ice to bend them.
   (c) Birches get bent no matter what happens, so one must be optimistic.

2. ____ Which of the following statements is most likely inaccurate?
   (a) Deep down, the poem is about boyhood.
   (b) Actually, the poem is basically about ecology.
   (c) One of the poem's deepest meanings is religious.

COMPLETION Choose the best answer for each question:

1. ____ Frost says one could do: (a) a lot better (b) less (c) worse (d) nothing more fun than be a swinger of birches.

2. ____ Frost says that he himself: (a) grew birches. (b) liked ice storms. (c) once played baseball. (d) was a swinger of birches.

3. ____ The boy Frost describes landed: (a) in the bracken. (b) feet first. (c) dangerously, but all right. (d) in a matter-of-fact fashion.

4. ____ Frost says that climbing the birches for him would be like: (a) heaven. (b) a storm in itself. (c) getting away from earth. (d) a brief vacation.

5. ____ The boy climbed to the top of the tree as carefully as: (a) filling a cup. (b) a bear. (c) his enthusiasm let him. (d) he possibly could.

6. ____ When the boy finished climbing the birches there was: (a) just time for dinner. (b) no ice left on the trees at all. (c) no tree left to conquer. (d) nothing Frost could think to say to him.

7. ____ In winter the trees would be loaded with ice: (a) after a rain. (b) even in the towns. (c) unless they were stark upright. (d) all the time.

8. ____ One of Frost's wishes is: (a) to begin over. (b) to have birches of his own. (c) connected with his boyhood. (d) linked to having a son.

VOCABULARY Choose the word or phrase from Column B that best defines the vocabulary item in Column A:

Column A	*Column B*
1. ____ dipped	a. clear
2. ____ considerations	b. shriveled
3. ____ craze	c. bending
4. ____ crystal	d. lifeless
5. ____ withered	e. on purpose
6. ____ arching	f. concerns
7. ____ fetch	g. grace
8. ____ subdued	h. partially bestow
9. ____ limp	i. not lively; conquered
10. ____ poise	j. crack
11. ____ pains	k. bent
12. ____ flung	l. proudfully; soaring
13. ____ willfully	m. cares
14. ____ half grant	n. retrieve
15. ____ weary	o. captively; unsupported
	p. like a chandelier
	q. tired
	r. thrown

SECTION 4

Vocabulary Preview

The following words come from the six reading selections in Section 4. Study the list carefully, pronouncing the words aloud if possible. Conceal the definitions with a card or your hand and test your command of the meanings of the words.

abyss, *noun* bottomless pit
adamant, *adj.* unyielding; inflexible
advent, *noun* beginning
austere, *adj.* having a severe or stern manner; forbidding
benign, *adj.* mild; kind
blithe, *adj.* of a cheerful disposition; carefree
brocade, *noun* a rich silk fabric with raised designs of gold or silver
buttes, *noun* steep-sided hills
catastrophe, *noun* a momentous and terrible event
causative, *adj.* producing an effect; causing
chasm, *noun* a steep-walled valley
cordon, *verb* encircle or shut off
coercion, *noun* exercise of force to persuade
derisive, *adj.* making fun of
diminution, *noun* lessening; reduction
dubious, *adj.* doubtful
engender, *verb* to bring into being; produce
exiguous, *adj.* scanty; meager
Geiger counter, *noun* instrument for detecting and counting ionized particles
glean, *verb* to gather information or other material bit by bit
grandiose, *adj.* grand in an impressive way; pompous
horde, *noun* crowd
illusory, *adj.* deceptive; unreal
impervious, *adj.* unaffected; not allowing entrance or passage
incarcerated, *adj.* confined; imprisoned
insidious, *adj.* harmful but attractive; treacherous
intimation, *noun* an indirect suggestion; hint
irradiate, *verb* to make clear; enlighten
isotope, *noun* any of two or more forms of an element having the same, or very closely related, chemical properties

juncture, *noun* a joining or being joined; a point of time
malevolent, *adj.* wishing evil or harm to others
malicious, *adj.* spiteful; intentionally mischievous or harmful
manifest, *verb* make clear or evident
mesa, *noun* a flat-topped hill with steep sides
misanthrope, *noun* person who hates mankind
oligarchy, *noun* government by the few
ominous, *adj.* having the character of an evil omen; sinister
oppressive, *adj.* tyrannical; weighing heavily on the spirit or senses
ostensibly, *adv.* apparently; seemingly
otiose, *adj.* idle; useless
paean, *noun* a song of joy, triumph, or praise
panorama, *noun* a view in all directions
paradigm, *noun* example or model
parapet, *noun* a low wall or railing
plashy, *adj.* full of puddles; marshy
postulate, *verb* to assume to be true without proof; to claim
prehensile, *adj.* adapted for seizing or grasping, as a monkey's tail
promontory, *noun* a peak of high land that juts out into a body of water
protégé, *noun* a person guided and helped by another influential person
reconcile, *verb* to make friendly again; settle disputes
reconnaissance, *noun* an exploratory survey or examination as in seeking out wanted information
recourse, *noun* a turning or seeking for aid, safety
replete, *adj.* plentifully supplied
scant, *adj.* few
schist, *noun* mica stone
sediment, *noun* the material which settles to the bottom of a liquid
sovereign, *adj.* above or superior to all others; supreme
stigmata, *noun* identifying marks or characteristics
subsistence, *noun* existence; minimum needed to maintain life
symptomatic, *adj.* characteristic; indicative
tangible, *adj.* concrete; able to be touched
totalitarian, *adj.* completely authoritarian or dictatorial
validate, *verb* to verify; confirm
vestigial, *adj.* remaining trace of something vanished
virulent, *adj.* extremely poisonous or injurious; deadly
vista, *noun* a distant view

Choose the word or phrase that best defines the vocabulary item:

1. ____ oligarchy: (a) divinity (b) rule by the few (c) tyranny (d) a senate (e) faultiness of judgment
2. ____ abyss: (a) chasm (b) depression (c) loss (d) wrong (e) nun
3. ____ vestigial: (a) formal (b) uniformly (c) store-bought (d) trace (e) tight
4. ____ ostensibly: (a) few (b) slowly (c) apparently (d) mild (e) correctly
5. ____ dubious: (a) doubtful (b) doubling (c) debilitate (d) disparate (e) regal
6. ____ ominous: (a) crown (b) all knowing (c) threatening (d) trying (e) totality
7. ____ adamant: (a) fun (b) loving (c) alarmed (d) firm (e) in front of
8. ____ scant: (a) few (b) forgiving (c) slight (d) weighty (e) look for
9. ____ derisive: (a) happily (b) making fun of (c) people-hater (d) gripping (e) elusive
10. ____ panorama: (a) wide view (b) put-down (c) movie (d) stunning (e) awing sight
11. ____ coercion: (a) shut off (b) noise (c) force (d) toughness (e) singing
12. ____ subsistence: (a) feeling state (b) existing (c) ebbing (d) being under the weather (e) reclining
13. ____ diminution: (a) decreasing (b) reviling (c) growing less visible (d) in a state of grace (e) distinction
14. ____ insidious: (a) crafty (b) sullen (c) partial (d) free (e) enlightened
15. ____ validate: (a) devalue (b) stifle (c) require (d) authorize (e) decide
16. ____ grandiose: (a) fat (b) regal (c) slough (d) impressive (e) fleshy
17. ____ illusory: (a) visual (b) supple (c) deceptive (d) frightful (e) uncertain
18. ____ replete: (a) faulty (b) full (c) apparently (d) produced (e) touchy
19. ____ sovereign: (a) supreme (b) governmental (c) hardly (d) soothing (e) clean

20. ____ benign: (a) sort (b) free (c) sustained (d) kind (e) perverse

21. ____ malevolent: (a) secret (b) maladjusted (c) evil (d) working (e) faulty

22. ____ tangible: (a) valid (b) touch (c) poured (d) terrible (e) concrete

23. ____ engender: (a) heavy thinking (b) produce (c) beginning (d) evidence (e) in the first place

24. ____ manifest: (a) clarify (b) handhold (c) party (d) serious (e) destiny

25. ____ impervious: (a) filled (b) slight (c) mean (d) unpassable (e) defrauded

23

The Nuclear Disaster They Didn't Want to Tell You About

Andrew Cockburn

Ever since the harnessing of nuclear energy became a reality, people have been concerned with the dangers of nuclear weapons, including a nuclear holocaust started "by mistake." But are we sufficiently aware of other dangers? Andrew Cockburn investigates an explosion of nuclear waste in Kyshtym, Russia. Both the disaster itself and its cover up by government officials in several countries may have terrible implications for us all.

For the first forty-eight hours after the accident, the authorities were unsure how dangerous it was going to be for the surrounding area. Officially, radioactive-waste dumps were not supposed to explode into the atmosphere, and therefore there had been no studies on how to handle it. It took at least two days to order a general evacuation of the area over which the radioactive cloud was drifting. By that time many of the inhabitants were already showing signs of radiation sickness.

The victims soon filled up all the hospitals in the cities to the north and south of the plant, so that old people's rest homes, clinics, and even some hotels had to be commandeered as emergency treatment centers. Eventually some of the casualties had to be sent to clinics two hundred miles away. All the fresh food from the farms of the area was seized and destroyed, and new supplies were trucked in.

THE NUCLEAR DISASTER THEY DIDN'T WANT TO TELL YOU ABOUT Originally appeared in *Esquire*, April 25, 1978. Reprinted with permission.

For reasons of security, no official announcement of what had happened could be made, and the population over a wide region grew hysterical with fear. Hundreds, perhaps thousands, of people died because they lived in the region over which strong winter winds blew the radioactive cloud. Today, twenty years later, some are still dying. All fishing in the many lakes in the area was, of course, forbidden, and all food not immediately destroyed had to be constantly checked for radiation with Geiger counters. These were only available to leading citizens; the rest of the public had to have their food checked at the entrances of markets.

The main north-south highway, which ran through the heart of the danger zone, had to be closed for nine months. When it reopened, drivers were warned by huge signs to move at top speed for the next thirty miles, with all windows closed. Stopping for any reason was expressly forbidden.

The central disaster zone was otherwise cordoned off, and where nearby spots had been irradiated, the topsoil was scraped off by bulldozers and buried in dumps known locally as "graveyards of the earth." Ten years after the accident it was thought necessary to advise pregnant women who had to live nearby to abort, because of the lingering danger of the radiation. Only after the accident were procedures for handling nuclear waste and all radioactive materials tightened up. Under conditions of the strictest security, scientists were allowed to study the environmental effects of the disaster and, much later, to publish their results in suitably censored form. Otherwise, the world's first great nuclear accident has officially never happened, and the country in which it occurred is pressing on with all speed toward a fully nuclear economy.

The demonology of nuclear power is replete with near disasters that only by the slightest chance avoided producing the consequences described here. A reactor fire that occurred on what is known as the day "we nearly lost Detroit," the Brown's Ferry incident in Alabama, the Windscale fire of 1957 in England, and numerous others might all have led to evacuation, panic, death. Which makes it all the more curious that so little attention has been paid to the Kyshtym disaster of 1957, which was, indeed, the world's first great nuclear accident, where all the postulations came true. When I asked the United States Department of Energy for its view of the scattered accounts that have been appearing over the past year, its spokesman replied, "This is all pure speculation, on which we cannot be expected to comment."

Kyshtym is a town in central Russia, on the eastern side of the southern Ural Mountains at the edge of the Siberian plain. Halfway between the great cities of Sverdlovsk and Chelyabinsk, it is part of one of the most highly industrialized and densely populated regions of the Soviet Union. From the time of Peter the Great, that part of the country had been a center of the arms industry, Kyshtym itself being owned and exploited by the Stroganov family. In World War II, when the Germans overran European Russia, a large part of the country's industrial plant was relocated around there, and when, at the end of the war, Stalin gave top priority to the development of nuclear weapons, the logical place to build the necessary plants was again there in the southern Urals.

In 1948, people began arriving in Chelyabinsk, the city to the south of Kyshtym. They had been told to leave their hometown because a military plant was being constructed there, and entry to the town was thereafter restricted. Those remaining in Kyshtym were given special privileges in terms of food and consumer goods, which they were sometimes able to pass out to less fortunate friends and relatives living outside. Many of the scientists and technicians at the plant were recruited from the Sverdlovsk Institute of Technology.

When the explosion came, probably in December, 1957, the people not directly affected could only get news of what had happened by rumor because, officially, disasters—earthquakes, plane crashes, and nuclear accidents—do not happen in the Soviet Union. Thus, precise knowledge of the facts remained a highly classified Soviet secret, and when news of this catastrophe reached Western intelligence services and the Atomic Energy Commission shortly afterward, they kept it classified, too.

It was not until November, 1976, that the Western public was given any inkling that nuclear accidents were not just a matter of remote probability. Even then the news came out by the merest accident.

Dr. Zhores Medvedev had been forced into exile from the Soviet Union in 1973. Though not an outright anti-socialist like his friends Solzhenitsyn and Sakharov, he had been a continual nuisance to the Russian authorities because of his criticism of the political control of Soviet science and the censorship of scientific correspondence. In 1970, the KGB had had him picked up and incarcerated in a mental institution. His identical twin brother, Roy, a historian, had rushed out to see the director of the institution. Eventually Roy rounded up enough support among the scientific elite, and Zhores was released. But harassment continued, and he found it increasingly difficult to carry on his scientific work as a biochemist. In January, 1973, he therefore accepted an invitation to do research for a year at the National Institute for Medical Research in London. His citizenship was revoked six months after he left the Soviet Union, and thus he, his wife, and one of his sons became unwilling British residents.

November, 1976, happened to be the twentieth anniversary of a lively British science magazine called *New Scientist*. For part of a retrospective issue the editors asked Medvedev to write about twenty years of scientific dissidence in the U.S.S.R. To illustrate a point in his article Medvedev detailed what had happened in the southern Urals twenty years before and the terrible consequences, assuming that anyone interested in nuclear science would already be aware that the disaster had happened. He was thus surprised when the first denials of his story appeared. They came not from Moscow but from London.

Sir John Hill, chairman of the United Kingdom Atomic Energy Authority, chairman of British Nuclear Fuels Ltd., chairman of The Radiochemical Center

Ltd., is a straightforward man. He sincerely believes that nuclear energy is the best, cheapest and safest available source of power. He is fond of pointing out that "they kill more people in the mines than we do." In the winter of 1976, he and the British energy bureaucracy were facing an unexpected problem. He had completed negotiations with the Japanese to reprocess the wastes of their nuclear industry at a new plant to be built at Windscale on the northwest English coast, the Japanese being unwilling to carry out the task on their own soil. The unexpected problem was the widespread disquiet among the British public at the proposal that Britain should become the world's nuclear dustbin. Every stage of the nuclear process has questions of safety associated with it, but nuclear waste, which remains dangerous for hundreds, thousands, of years, poses the most frightening questions of all. No one, confident predictions notwithstanding, has the slightest idea what to do with it.

To Sir John, therefore, the announcement that the contents of a radioactive-waste dump had been scattered over the homes of thousands of unfortunate Russians twenty years before carried implications that could make the British public even more restive than it already was. This was why he told the Press Association news agency that the story was "rubbish" and a "figment of the imagination."

If such dismissive remarks had been left to Tass, all might have remained quiet, but Hill's denial was a bad mistake, for it naturally enough spurred Medvedev to prove his story. Medvedev is a quiet and humorous man, but after battling with the Russian authorities for years he was quite ready for a fight with the British nuclear industry. He was especially angry, though he himself will only admit to "surprise," at the fact that no nuclear official, from Britain or anywhere else, contacted him to ask if he had any evidence to back up his story. "I was very disappointed," he told me later, "because I felt that responsible officials in the nuclear industry or scientists who work in this field would be very interested to find out all the details, because from the substance of my article it was quite clear that I mentioned the matter casually, without any details, and that I could tell a great deal more about what really happened. But nobody approached me with any questions or inquiries."

Medvedev did indeed know a great deal about the accident, because he had been asked to work on the research program that studied its environmental effects. In the spring of 1958, his professor at the Moscow Agricultural Academy, Vsevolod Klechkovsky, asked him if he wanted to join the team being assembled for work on the waste disaster area. He turned it down because he knew that the work would be highly classified, and that therefore he would in all probability never be allowed to leave the country again. But Klechkovsky's invitation was not the first intimation Medvedev had had of the accident. In January, 1958, a friend of his had visited Sverdlovsk, where the signs of a recent catastrophe were all too evident: there were food restrictions and it was difficult to find a hospital room because the hospitals were full of people from the south who were sick and dying of radiation sickness.

In fact, this alarming intelligence did not make quite the impact on Medvedev and his friends that might have been expected. He explains: "It was still the time when the tests of nuclear weapons in the atmosphere were permitted, so in the press you would often read that the Americans had carried out a big test and that the Russians were going to explode their own large weapons, so that when the papers talked about this sort of thing all the time you didn't consider that an accident of this kind was something really peculiar or unexpected." In other words, accidents will happen. Because of this attitude, Medvedev never thought to cross-question his informants, including the scientists who did accept Klechkovsky's invitation, about the precise origins of the explosion: "I just knew that waste was the cause. I was told that it was a nuclear waste explosion. The people who had gone to work on the experimental station used to visit our laboratory and discuss scientific problems with us. And it was clear from the discussions we had that it was waste and nobody had any doubt that it was waste."

While the British press generally confined its comments on Medvedev to quoting the derisive reaction of nuclear officials and scientists, two American newspapers printed follow-up articles that were curious in light of the official sensitivity about waste. Within two weeks of Medvedev's article, the *Los Angeles Times* and *The Washington Post* quoted "nuclear intelligence sources" as giving authoritative explanations of what had happened, which were mutually contradictory and which suggested that nuclear waste, in itself, was not the cause. The *L.A. Times* came out for a reactor "meltdown"—nasty in itself, but a mishap that has been often postulated and that present-day reactors are designed to avoid. *The Washington Post,* equally confident of its sources, asserted that a storage tank had been cracked open by an earthquake, one of two that occurred at about that time north of Lake Baikal, over two thousand miles away. The *Post* explained that quake forces could have moved laterally underground and could have caused other tanks to break open. I do not know if the *Post* consulted a seismologist, as I did later. But the man I talked to said the quakes were far too distant to have caused such damage.

But the following month, December, 1976, Medvedev got confirmation of a more authoritative kind. Another exiled Russian scientist, Professor Lev Tumerman, who now lives in Israel, wrote to *The Jerusalem Post* confirming the fact of the accident and additionally confirming that the cause was waste. Now, Tumerman is a firm believer in nuclear power. He wrote to *The Jerusalem Post* because anti-nuclear lobbyists in Israel had taken up the accident story to show that Israel should not develop nuclear reactors. They had received a garbled version of the story that left out any mention of waste. Anxious to show that reactors were blameless in this instance, Tumerman described how he had driven through the dead area in June, 1960: "Only chimneys remained of towns that once were there. As far as the eye could see, there were no villages, no towns, no people, no cattle herds." When he asked scientist friends working at a nearby civilian power plant the reason for this sinister landscape, he was told that it was the result of the great Kyshtym waste accident of a few years before.

No one could accuse Tumerman, as they had Medvedev, of concocting the story to help denigrate the Western nuclear power program. In fact, when I interviewed him he could hardly be deflected from paeans of praise for the future benefits and necessity of nuclear power. Nevertheless, back in Britain, Sir John Hill had no reason to appreciate subtlety. Commenting on Tumerman's account, he made it clear that it was not reports of a nuclear accident as such that he objected to but rather the question of waste. Even now he remains adamant that "there may have been an accident, but at a time when the public are concerned about the problems of nuclear waste I feel it is my duty to make it absolutely clear that in my view the burial of nuclear waste could not lead to the type of accident described."

In the meantime, Medvedev had hit on a way of obtaining independent, documentary evidence of the story. Recalling the names of colleagues who had gone to work in the disaster area, he searched the Russian scientific journals to see if they had published any of their results. Nothing had appeared until 1965, in itself a curious silence for such an eminent group of biologists. When they did begin to publish, their findings were ostensibly the results of controlled experiments—the deliberate irradiation of small areas for experimental purposes. But the very high levels of radioactivity mentioned made it clear that they must have been talking about an accidental release. Furthermore, the very size of the areas of these "experiments" was far greater than any researcher would dream of deluging with radioactivity. From the types of plants and animals mentioned, Medvedev could also pinpoint the scene of the research as the southern Urals of the U.S.S.R., a deduction that turned out to be otiose, as in one 1974 paper the censor slipped up, allowing the place-name "Chelyabinsk" to appear.

Put together, these papers not only pointed to the fact of a huge and uncontrolled release of radioactivity in the southern Urals province in 1957 but also indicated something else. The only radioactive isotopes referred to were long-lived isotopes, cesium-137 and strontium-90. This was crucial to the waste theory.

When waste leaves a reactor, military or civilian, the isotopes start to decay. Some die off in seconds, some in hours, or days, weeks, or months. The shorter-lived an isotope, the more virulent it is likely to be. Strontium-90 and cesium-137 are long-lived, remaining hot in waste after all the others have decayed. In the Russian papers there is not only no mention of any other isotopes but no evidence of their having been present to cause damage to the environment. If they had been there initially, all the pine trees in the affected area would have been dead. But they were not dead. This means—could only mean—that whatever was in the cloud that drifted east of Kyshtym had to have already been out of the reactor for a long time—waste. Medvedev concluded this formidable piece of detective work with the tart observation that "the nuclear authorities in Britain and the U.S. probably put more trust in the expensive information they receive from monitoring global fallout or from space satellite surveillance. They certainly do not read such Soviet journals as *Voprosy Ichtiologii, Genetika,* or *Zoologicheskii Zhurnal.*"

Although they may not have paid proper attention to their subscription copy of *Zoologicheskii Zhurnal,* the nuclear authorities did have more intelligence about what happened than Medvedev supposed, or at least the CIA did. In the late Fifties, despite enormous effort and great expense, the agency's information from inside Russia was exiguous, gleaned mostly from defectors, stray gossip by Russians at international conferences, returning German POWs, and, most importantly, U-2 reconnaissance flights.

At that time the head of the Office of Scientific Intelligence at the CIA was Herbert Scoville. A protégé of Allen Dulles, he was edged out in 1963, after John McCone took over the CIA. Now retired to his elegant house not far from Fort Langley, CIA headquarters, he confirmed to me that the agency did have some scattered reports at the time that there had been a nuclear accident, the origin of which was still a mystery by the time he left the agency. But he emphasized that this was before the advent of the surveillance satellites, which came along in the Sixties. Lyndon Johnson once remarked that the entire multibillion-dollar cost of the space program, moon shots and all, was justified by the intelligence benefits of these spy satellites.

Throughout the Sixties the technology steadily improved as satellites developed the ability not only to pick up small details, such as abandoned villages, but also to detect radiation in the atmosphere and, indeed, the specific type of radiation involved. Such post-accident satellite information would, Scoville points out, have certainly been circulated to responsible authorities such as the Atomic Energy Commission. Some of the early CIA intelligence reports have now become available, in heavily sanitized form. They were first obtained through a Freedom of Information Act request by a Ralph Nader group, the Critical Mass Energy Project, and subsequently recirculated with much fanfare.

The most vivid of these reports describes how "in the winter of 1957 an unspecified accident occurred at the Kasli atomic plant [near Kyshtym]. All stores in Kamensk Uralskiy (about sixty miles away) which sold milk, meat, and other foodstuffs were closed as a precaution against radiation exposure and new supplies were brought in two days later by train and truck. The food was sold directly from the vehicles, and the resulting queues were reminiscent of the worst shortages of World War II. The people in Kamensk Uralskiy grew hysterical with fear, with an incidence of unknown 'mysterious' diseases breaking out. A few leading citizens aroused the public anger by wearing small radiation counters which were not available to everyone."

Despite this chilling intelligence, available to anyone with the price of a postage stamp and the address of the CIA, Dr. Carl Walske, president of the Atomic Industrial Forum, the powerful industry pressure group, informed me blithely that their researches into the story consisted of probing Medvedev's own political beliefs, "and that was about as far as we could track it."

Perhaps he should have gone to Israel. Following Tumerman's revelations I looked there to see if any other Russian immigrants had had direct experience of the disaster. According to the Jewish Agency in Vienna, only a few dozen families from the Sverdlovsk area have ever been allowed to emigrate. But among these I found two persons who have remarkable reminiscences of what a nuclear accident can mean to those living over sixty miles away, even many years after the event. They now live in southern Israel.

When Gary Powers was shot down in May, 1960, just outside Sverdlovsk, his descent was observed by a young man then studying at the Sverdlovsk Institute of Technology. His parents lived on the edge of Chelyabinsk, and for several years he had been taking the bus home on weekends, down the highway past Kyshtym. In December, 1957, the road was suddenly closed without explanation, and he did not see his parents until late the next summer. In the meantime he visited a Sverdlovsk hospital to have a wart removed from his finger and was told by a doctor there that the whole building, and all the other hospitals in the city, and all the hospitals in Chelyabinsk, were full of the victims of the Kyshtym disaster. "I was told that there were thousands, and that most of them died." When he last drove through the area, in 1971, it was still empty and dead.

In 1967, ten years after the accident, a young woman from the Ukraine married a Soviet officer and moved to a rebuilt Kyshtym. The next year she became pregnant and was instructed by the doctor to have an abortion—"He said there was danger from the radiation." Because of her husband's rank she was given a personal radiometer to use when buying fresh food and when picking berries or mushrooms in the countryside. Occasionally on these rural walks she and her husband would come across the "graveyards of the earth," places where the heavily irradiated topsoil was buried and enclosed behind barbed wire and warning signs. Through the wire they could see that "giant mushrooms" were growing inside. None of the people in the town had lived there for longer than eight years, so no one ever told her what it all meant.

Thus it is that despite the cynicism of atomic energy officials in the West there is overwhelming evidence of this major disaster in Kyshtym, established by personal recollection of scientists, verifiable biological data from scientific literature, and memories of people living there at the time and since. There is, furthermore, evidence that the cause of the disaster lay with waste, a fact with startling implications—given the worldwide sensitivity about the waste issue—for the debate over nuclear energy.

It is a strange attribute of "catastrophist" news coverage that an impending disaster is more appealing, in terms of coverage and speculation, than one that has already occurred. But a major nuclear accident *has* occurred, with very little coverage or public analysis in the worlds of science, politics, or journalism. Official U.S. and British agencies have been as keen to tamp down speculation about the disaster as the Soviets.

Although the Soviet press is usually eager to give heavy coverage to riots and other demonstrations symptomatic of the decline of the West, there have been some curious omissions in the past year. No mention has been made in any Russian paper or TV broadcast of the huge anti-nuclear demonstrations in France, Germany, Japan, Australia, or in the U.S. Perhaps they are merely repaying the compliment paid by Western nuclear establishments in ignoring the Kyshtym disaster. We live in a nuclear world.

LENGTH: 4833 WORDS

24

Science and Liberty

Aldous Huxley

English novelist and critic Aldous Huxley was profoundly concerned with the nature of Western society and its future direction. Signs of totalitarianism frightened him enough to write the new classic Brave New World, *a novel intended to warn the world. Whether we have listened to his warning is still unclear. In this piece, Huxley describes the far-reaching effects science has had on our modern technological economy. It, too, contains a warning.*

By supplying the ruling oligarchy with more effective instruments of coercion and persuasion, applied science has contributed directly to the centralization of power in the hands of the few. But it has also made important indirect contributions to the same end. It has done this in two ways; first, by introducing over ever larger areas of the industrial and agricultural economy the methods of large-scale mass production and mass distribution; second, by creating, through its very progressiveness, an economic and social insecurity which drives all those concerned, owners and managers no less than workers, to seek the assistance of the national state. Let us now consider these two power-centralizing factors in greater detail.

a) In applying the results of disinterested scientific research, inventors and technicians have paid more attention to the problem of equipping large concerns with the expensive machinery of mass production and mass distribution than to that of providing individuals or co-operating groups with cheap and simple, but effective, means of production for their own subsistence and for the needs of a local market.

The reason for this is that there has been more money in working for the mass producers and mass distributors; and the mass producers and mass distributors have had more money because financiers have seen that there was more profit for them, and more power, in a centralized than in a decentralized system of production.

Here, in parenthesis, let us note that concentration of financial power preceded the scientific revolution of the eighteenth and nineteenth centuries and was largely responsible for making our industrial civilization the hateful thing it was and, for the most part, still is. Throughout Europe land and natural resources were not owned outright by the people, represented by a multitude of small holders; nor were they the property of a sovereign, leasing to small tenants and spending the rent (which is the monetary expression of the social value of land) for social purposes. The best part of the land and its natural resources was the monopoly of a small class of landlords, who appropriated the social values of what should, quite obviously, have been everybody's property, to their own private use. Hence the early centralization of financial power—a power that was used to exploit the new technological discoveries for the benefit, not of individual small producers or co-operating groups, but for that of the class, which alone possessed accumulations of money. Centralized finance begot centralized industry, and in due course the profits of centralized industry increased the power of centralized finance, so that it was able to proceed ever further in the direction of completely centralized production and distribution.

The centralizing of industrial capacity in big mass-producing factories has resulted in the centralization of a large part of the population in cities and in the reduction of ever-increasing numbers of individuals to complete dependence upon a few private capitalists and their managers, or upon the one public capitalist, the state, represented by politicians and working through civil servants. So far as liberty is concerned, there is little to choose between the two types of boss. Up to the present, state-controlled enterprises have been closely modeled upon those of capitalist big business. Nationalization has not stopped short at land and natural resources, nor have the land and natural resources been nationalized with the purpose of giving individuals or co-operating groups free access to the means of small-scale production, personal liberty and self-government. On the contrary, the objects nationalized include, besides land and natural resources, the tools of production, and that nationalization has been undertaken with a view to strengthening the state (that is to say, the politicians momentarily in power) against its subjects and not at all with the purpose of liberating individual men and women from economic dependence upon bosses. But economic dependence upon bosses is always bad, because, quite obviously, it is not easily reconcilable with local and professional self-government or with civil and personal liberty. Democratic institutions are likely to work best at times and in places where at least a good part of the citizens have access to enough land and possess sufficient tools and professional skill to be able to provide for their subsistence without recourse to financially potent private capitalists or to the government. Where, as in the contemporary Western world, great numbers of the citizens own nothing (not even, in many cases, a skill, since the operation of semi-automatic machines does not require a skill), personal liberty and political and civil rights are to a more or less considerable extent dependent upon the grace of the capitalistic or national owners and managers of the means of production and distribution, and upon their willingness to abide by the rules of the democratic game. To forward their interests and to protect themselves against oppression, propertyless workers combine in trade unions. These have done much to bridle the ambition and covetousness of capitalists and to improve the conditions of labor. But trade unions are as subject to gigantism and centralization as are the industries to which they are related. Consequently it happens all too frequently that the masses of unionized workers find themselves dependent upon, and subordinated to, two governing oligarchies—that of the bosses and that of the union leaders. Over the first they have no control at all, except by strike and the threat of strike; over the second their control is at best remote and rather shadowy. Self government, which is the very essence of democratic freedom, is more or less completely absent from their professional lives. This is ultimately due, as we have seen, to propertylessness and consequent dependence upon the private or public owners and managers of the means of mass production and mass distribution; and propertylessness is due in its turn to (among other things) the progress of applied science—a progress which, under the auspices of centralized finance, has hitherto favored mass production at the expense of production on a small scale for personal or cooperative use, or to supply a local market.

In the most highly industrialized countries, applied science and its ally, and master, centralized finance, have profoundly changed the traditional pattern of agricultural life. Thus, in the United States, the percentage of the population making its living from the land has been reduced in recent years to only a fifth of the total. Meanwhile the size of individual holdings of land has tended to increase, as powerful corporations add field to field in the effort to exploit mechanized farming to its economic limit. Small-scale farmers, who used to be primarily concerned with subsistence, secondarily with a cash crop, have been largely replaced by men whose primary concern is with cash crops and who use the cash so earned to buy "nationally advertised," processed and denatured foods at the grocers.

In Russia the process of centralizing and consolidating the control of land and of industrializing agricultural production has been carried out by government decree and by means of the liquidation of a whole class of society. It would appear, however, that a measure of small-scale private ownership, or quasi-ownership, has had to be reintroduced in order to increase agricultural efficiency by improving the morale of the workers.

b) Among the ordinary results of the rapid progress of applied science are technological unemployment and the sudden and unexpected necessity of changing long-established habits of agricultural and industrial production. When too rapid, changes of position or state are very disturbing to living organisms, sometimes even fatal. That is why, when we get out of a plane in mid-air, we use a parachute, why, when we take a Turkish bath, we do not plunge immediately into the hottest chamber. Analogously, social, economic and political changes can take place too rapidly and too frequently for human well-being. A highly progressive technology entails incessant and often very rapid and startling changes of economic, political and ethical state; and such changes tend to keep the societies subjected to them in a chronically uncomfortable and unstable condition. Some day, perhaps, social scientists will be able to tell us what is the optimum rate of change, and what the optimum amount of it at any one time. For the present, Western societies remain at the mercy of their progressive technologies, to the intense discomfort of everybody concerned. Man as a moral, social and political being is sacrificed to *homo faber,* or man the smith, the inventor and forger of new gadgets.

And meanwhile, of course, technological unemployment is always with us; for every labor-saving device, every substitution of a new and more efficient technique for an older and less efficient one, results in a local and temporary diminution of the labor force. In the long run the persons displaced, as the result of technological advance, may find themselves reabsorbed by other industries or even (since increased efficiency results in lowered prices, greater demand and an expansion of production sufficient, in some cases, to offset the original technological unemployment) by the industry from which they were discharged. But what may happen in the long run is of little interest to propertyless persons who are compelled by hunger and the elements to do their living exclusively in the short run. For such persons the chief consequence of progressive science is a chronic social and economic insecurity.

Here, as in an earlier paragraph, it is necessary to stress the fact that the progress of applied science is not the only causative factor involved. Mass unemployment and periodical slumps have a variety of interlocking causes—meteorological, financial and psychological causes as well as those connected with science and technology. Concerning the relative importance of these factors the experts are not yet agreed. Many theories of slumps and unemployment have been formulated, each of which emphasizes one of the known causative factors at the expense of all the rest. None of these theories is universally accepted; but all of them—and this, for our present purpose, is the important point—are agreed that technological unemployment is a reality and that the progress of applied science does in fact play an important part in creating that economic and social insecurity, which is the plague of modern industrial societies.

LENGTH: 1700 WORDS

Name Class Date

24 Science and Liberty

SCORING: Reading time: ____	Rate from chart: ____ W.P.M.	
RETENTION	number right ____ × 2 equals ____ points	
MAIN POINT	number right ____ × 4 equals ____ points	
AUTHOR'S ATTITUDE	number right ____ × 2 equals ____ points	
COMPLETION	number right ____ × 4 equals ____ points	
VOCABULARY	number right ____ × 2 equals ____ points	
	(Total points: 100) **Total** ____ points	

RETENTION Based on the passage, which of the following statements is True (T), False (F), or Not answerable (N)?

1. ____ Landlords comprise a class.
2. ____ Huxley mentions disinterested scientific research.
3. ____ The oligarchies created science as their weapon.
4. ____ There is less profit in mass production than in a decentralized system.
5. ____ Science has given oligarchies more effective means of persuasion.
6. ____ Centralized industry was begotten by centralized finance.
7. ____ State-controlled industry has been modeled on capitalist industry.
8. ____ There is little reciprocal action between industry and finance.
9. ____ Rent is not a monetary expression of land values.
10. ____ Nationalization often includes the tools of production.
11. ____ The people can be dispossessed of skills as well as land.
12. ____ Applied science is not related to technological unemployment.
13. ____ A small amount of private ownership boosts morale in nationalized states.
14. ____ Democracy works best when many people have access to land and tools.
15. ____ Technological unemployment does not exist in states like Russia.
16. ____ Trade unions can become centralized.

17. ____ People adjust quickly to rapid economic and social changes.

18. ____ *Homo faber* is man the inventor.

19. ____ For some people the progress of science means economic insecurity.

20. ____ Civil rights can depend upon owners and managers.

MAIN POINT Which of the following statements best represents the main point of the passage? ____

1. Modern economies and modern nations are pretty much alike.
2. Scientists would not have wanted their skills abused as they are.
3. No one could have foreseen the development of the modern state.
4. Insecurity, social and economic, can be traced to modern science.
5. Industry and finance have schemed to get control of the state.

AUTHOR'S ATTITUDE Which of the following statements best describe the author's attitude? ____; ____; and ____

1. People ought to share equally in ownership of land.
2. Degrees in science ought to go to poor people only.
3. The state, captialist or communist, is the people's boss.
4. Progress does not necessarily involve constant change.
5. Technological unemployment is the realistic cost of modernity.
6. Science has not freed us as much as it seems to.

COMPLETION Choose the best answer for each question:

1. ____ Laborsaving devices: (a) help people. (b) create unemployment. (c) are strictly modern inventions. (d) defer technological employment.

2. ____ The moral, social, and political man is sacrificed to: (a) man the inventor. (b) centralized industry. (c) science. (d) the politicians of the state.

3. ____ In the Western world great numbers of citizens: (a) work. (b) are in science. (c) have given up entirely. (d) own nothing.

4. ____ Huxley stresses that science is: (a) not the (b) the (c) only one (d) widely recognized as the cause of economic insecurity.

5. ____ Economic and social insecurity have a disastrous effect on our: (a) future. (b) liberty. (c) efforts in science. (d) decisions regarding centralization.

VOCABULARY Choose the word or phrase from Column B that best defines the vocabulary entry in Column A:

Column A	*Column B*
1. ____ chronic	a. killing off
2. ____ incessant	b. ethics; good behavior
3. ____ analogously	c. come before
4. ____ access	d. total control
5. ____ potent	e. permanent
6. ____ liquidation	f. similarly
7. ____ morale	g. took; seized
8. ____ precede	h. approach; ability to approach
9. ____ monopoly	i. powerful
10. ____ oligarchy	j. ceaseless
11. ____ coercion	k. not personally involved
12. ____ disinterested	l. too much
13. ____ subsistence	m. spirit
14. ____ appropriated	n. force
15. ____ accumulations	o. living
	p. masses
	q. go on; continue
	r. ruling group

25

The Missing Link

Loren Eiseley

Archaeologists work with evidence from the distant past. But every so often, and when one least expects it, the past transforms itself into the present. Such a moment is described here. In an alien environment, and in a moment of repose, Loren Eiseley is surprised to find himself looking at evidence of the missing link, the connection between man's deep past and man's distant future.

"The greatest prize of all," once confessed the British plant explorer F. Kingdon Ward, "is the skull of primitive man." Ward forgot one thing: there are other clues to primitive men than those confined to skulls. The bones of fossil men are few because the earth tolerated them in scant numbers. We call them missing links on the road to ourselves. A little less tooth here, a little more brain there, and you can see them changing toward ourselves in that long historyless time when the great continental ice sheets ebbed and flowed across the northern continents. Like all the students of that age, I wanted to find a missing link in human history. That is what this record is about, for I stumbled on the track of one.

Some men would maintain that a vague thing called atmosphere accounts for such an episode as I am about to relate, that there are houses that demand a murder and wait patiently until the murderer and his victim arrive, that there are great cliffs that draw the potential suicide from afar or mountains of so austere a nature that they write their message on the face of a man who looks up at them.

This all may be. I do not deny it. But when I encountered the footprint in the mud of that remote place I think the thing that terrified me most was the fact that I knew to whom it belonged and yet I did not want to know him. He was a stranger to me and remains so to this day. Because of a certain knowledge I had, however, he succeeded in impressing himself upon me in a most insidious manner. I have never been the same since the event took place, and often at night I start up sweating and think uncannily that the creature is there with me in the dark. If the sense of his presence grows, I switch on the light, but I never look into the mirror. This is a matter of old habit with me.

First off, though, we must get straight what we mean by a missing link.

A missing link is a day in the life of a species that is changing its form and habits, just as, on a smaller scale, one's appearance and behavior at the age of five are a link in one's development to an adult man or woman. The individual person may have changed and grown, but still the boy or girl of many years ago is linked to the present by a long series of steps. And if one is really alive and not already a living fossil, one will go on changing till the end of one's life and perhaps be the better for it. The term "missing link" was coined because some of the physical links in the history of man as a species are lost, and those people who, like myself, are curious about the past look for them.

My album is the earth, and the pictures in it are faded and badly torn and have to be pieced together by detective work. If one thinks of oneself at five years of age, one may get a thin wisp of disconnected memory pictures. By contrast, the past of a living species is without memory except as that past has written its physical record in vestigial organs like the appendix or a certain pattern on our molar teeth. To eke out what those physical stigmata tell us, we have to go grubbing about in caves and gravel for the bones of very ancient men. If one can conceive of the trouble an archaeologist might have in locating one's remains a half-million years from now, supposing they still existed, one will get an idea of the difficulties involved in finding traces of man before his bones were crowded together in cities and cemeteries.

I was wandering inland along a sunken shore when the thing happened—the thing I had dreamed of so long. In other words, I got a clue to man. The beaches on that coast I had come to visit are treacherous and sandy and the tides are always shifting things about among the mangrove roots. It is not a place to which I would willingly return and you will get no bearings from me. Anyway, what it was I found there could be discovered on any man's coast if he looked sharp for it. I had come to that place with other things in mind, and a notion of being alone. I was tired. I wanted to lie in the sun or clamber about like an animal in the swamps and the forest. To secure such rest from the turmoil of a modern city is the most difficult thing in the world to accomplish and I have only achieved it twice: once in one of the most absolute deserts in the world and again in this tropical marsh.

By day and night strange forms of life scuttled and gurgled underfoot or oozed wetly along outthrust branches; luminous tropical insects blundered by in the dark like the lamps of hesitant burglars. Overhead, on higher ground, another life shrieked distantly or was expectantly still in the treetops. Somehow, alone as I was, I got to listening as if all that world were listening, waiting for something to happen. The trees drooped a little lower listening, the tide lurked and hesitated on the beach, and even a tree snake dropped a loop and hung with his face behind a spider web, immobile in the still air.

A world like that is not really natural, or (the thought strikes one later) perhaps it really is, only more so. Parts of it are neither land nor sea and so everything is moving from one element to another, wearing uneasily the queer transitional bodies that life adopts in such places. Fish, some of them, come out and breathe air and sit about watching you. Plants take to eating insects, mammals go back to the water and grow elongate like fish, crabs climb trees. Nothing stays put where it began because everything is constantly climbing in, or climbing out, of its unstable environment.

Along drowned coasts of this variety you only see, in a sort of speeded-up way, what is true of the whole world and everything upon it: the Darwinian world of passage, of missing links, of beetles with soldered, flightless wings, of snakes with vestigial feet dragging slowly through the underbrush. Everything is marred and maimed and slightly out of focus—everything in the world. As for man, he is no different from the rest. His back aches, he ruptures easily, his women have difficulties in childbirth—all because he has struggled up upon his hind legs without having achieved a perfect adjustment to his new posture.

On this particular afternoon, I came upon a swamp full of huge waterlilies where I had once before ventured. The wind had begun to rise and rain was falling at intervals. As far as I could see, giant green leaves velvetly impervious to water were rolling and twisting in the wind. It was a species of lily in which part of the leaves projected on stalks for a short distance above the water, and as they rolled and tossed the whole swamp flashed and quivered from the innumerable water drops that were rolling around and around like quicksilver in the great cupped leaves. Everything seemed flickering and changing as if in some gigantic illusion, but so soft was the green light and so delicate the brushing of the leaves against each other that the whole effect was quite restful, as though one could be assured that nothing was actually tangible or real and no one in his senses would want it to be, as long as he could sway and nod and roll reflecting water drops about over the surface of his brain.

Just as I finally turned away to climb a little ridge I found the first footprint. It was in a patch of damp, exposed mud and was pointed away from the water as though the creature had emerged directly out of the swamp and was heading up the shore toward the interior. I had thought I was alone, and in that place it was wise to know one's neighbors. Worst of all, as I stood studying the footprint, and then another, still heading up the little rise, it struck me that though undoubtedly human the prints were different in some indefinable way. I will tell you once more that this happened on the coast of another country in a place where form itself is an illusion and no shape of man or beast is totally impossible. I crouched anxiously in the mud while all about the great leaves continued to rotate on their stems and to flash their endlessly rolling jewels.

But there were these footprints. They did not disappear. As I fixed the lowermost footprint with every iota of scientific attention I could muster, it became increasingly apparent that I was dealing with some transitional form of man. The arch, as revealed in the soft mud, was low and flat and implied to the skilled eye an inadequate adjustment to the upright posture. This, in its turn, suggested certain things about the spine and the nature of the skull. It was only then, I think, that the full import of my discovery came to me.

Good Lord, I thought consciously for the first time, the thing is alive. I had spent so many years analyzing the bones of past ages or brooding over lizard tracks turned to stone in remote epochs that I had never contemplated this possibility before. The thing was alive and it was human. I looked uneasily about before settling down into the mud once more. One could make out that the prints were big but what drew my fascinated eye from the first was the nature of the second toe. It was longer than the big toe, and as I crawled excitedly back and forth between the two wet prints in the open mud, I saw that there was a remaining hint of prehensile flexibility about them.

Most decidedly, as a means of ground locomotion this foot was transitional and imperfect. Its loose, splayed aspect suggested inadequate protection against sprains. That second toe was unnecessarily long for life on the ground, although the little toe was already approximating the rudimentary condition so characteristic of modern man. Could it be that I was dealing with an unreported living fossil, an archaic ancestral survival? What else could be walking the mangrove jungle with a foot that betrayed clearly the marks of ancient intimacy with the arboreal attic, an intimacy so long continued that now, after hundreds of thousands of years of ground life, the creature had squiggled his unnecessarily long toes about in the mud as though an opportunity to clutch at something had delighted his secret soul.

I crouched by the footprint and thought. I remembered that comparisons with the living fauna, whenever available, are good scientific procedure and a great aid to precise taxonomy. I sat down and took off my shoes.

I had never had much occasion to look critically at my own feet before. In modern man they are generally encased in shoes—something that still suggests a slight imperfection in our adaptations. After all, we don't normally find it necessary to go about with our hands constantly enclosed in gloves. As I sat contemplating and comparing my feet with the footprints, a faintly disturbing memory floated hazily across my mind. It had involved a swimming party many years before at the home of one of the most distinguished comparative anatomists in the world. As we had sat on the bench alongside his pool, I had glanced up suddenly and caught him staring with what had seemed unnecessary fascination at my feet. I remembered now that he had blushed a deep pink under his white hair and had diverted my inquiring glance deftly to the scenery about us.

Why I should have remembered the incident at all was unclear to me. I thought of the possibility of getting plaster casts of a footprint, and I also debated whether I should attempt to trail the creature farther up the slope toward which he appeared to have been headed. It was no moment for hesitation. Still, I did hesitate. The uneasy memory grew stronger, and a thought finally struck me. A little sheepishly and with a glance around to see that I was not observed, I lowered my own muddy foot into the footprint. It fitted.

I stood there contemplatively clutching, but this time consciously, the mud in my naked toes. I was the dark being on that island shore whose body carried the marks of its strange passage. I was my own dogging Man Friday, the beast from the past who had come with weapons through the marsh. The wind had died and the great green leaves with their rolling jewels were still. The mistake I had made was the mistake of all of us.

The story of man was not all there behind us in the caves of remote epochs. Even our physical bodies gave evidence that the change was not completed. As for our minds, they were still odd compounds of beast and saint. But it was not by turning back toward the marsh out of which we had come that the truly human kingdom was to be possessed and entered—that kingdom dreamed of in many religions and spoken of in many barbarous tongues. A philosopher once said in my presence, "The universe is a series of leaping sparks—everything else is interpretation." But what, I hesitated, was man's interpretation to be?

I drew a foot out of the little steaming swamp that sucked at it. The air hung heavily about me. I listened as the first beast might have listened who came from the water up the shore and did not return again to his old element. Everything about me listened in turn and seemed to be waiting for some decision on my part. I swayed a moment on my unstable footing.

Then, warily, I stepped higher up the shore and let the water and the silt fill in that footprint to make it, a hundred million years away, a fossil sign of an unknown creature slipping from the shadows of a marsh toward something else that awaited him. I had found the missing link. He walked on misshapen feet. The stones hurt him and his belly sagged. There were dreams like Christmas ornaments in his head, intermingled with an ancient malevolent viciousness. I knew because I was the missing link, but for the first time I sensed where I was going.

I have said I never look into the mirror. It is a matter of old habit now. If that other presence grows too oppressive I light the light and read.

LENGTH: 2563 WORDS

Name Class Date

25 The Missing Link

SCORING: Reading time: _____ Rate from chart: _____ W.P.M.			
RETENTION	number right ____	× 2 equals ____	points
MAIN POINT	number right ____	× 4 equals ____	points
AUTHOR'S ATTITUDE	number right ____	× 2 equals ____	points
COMPLETION	number right ____	× 4 equals ____	points
VOCABULARY	number right ____	× 3 equals ____	points
	(Total points: 100)	**Total** ____	points

RETENTION Based on the passage, which of the following statements is True (T), False (F), or Not answerable (N)?

1. ____ Eiseley tells us exactly where the footprint was.
2. ____ The footprint belongs to a friend, Mr. Friday.
3. ____ The story of man is not all there behind us in caves.
4. ____ Eiseley never looks into the mirror.
5. ____ In mangrove swamps life moves from one element to another.
6. ____ Tree snakes eat spiders.
7. ____ His footprint reveals incomplete adaptation to life on land.
8. ____ Some tropical insects are luminous.
9. ____ From the first, Eiseley knew he was not alone.
10. ____ The second toe of the footprint was longer than the first.
11. ____ F. Kingdon Ward felt the greatest prize of all was the human femur.
12. ____ A missing link represents a change in the life of a species.
13. ____ There may be such things as living fossils.
14. ____ Caves are a source of evidence for early man's existence.
15. ____ Apparently, Eiseley was on the coast when this event occurred.
16. ____ The swamp was strangely devoid of flowers or lilies.
17. ____ Some fish come out and breathe air.
18. ____ Man is said to be very different from the rest of creation.

19. ____ Beetles have their missing links, too, but not in swamps.

20. ____ Some plants eat insects.

MAIN POINT Which of the following statements best represents the main point of the passage? ____

1. Mangrove swamps are among the important research areas for man.
2. You never can tell exactly where archaeological evidence will show up.
3. Looking in the mirror makes one aware of our connections with the past.
4. Processes of change in human life are still going on in ourselves.
5. No one can truly say where the missing link will be discovered.

AUTHOR'S ATTITUDE Which of the following statements best describe the author's attitude? ____; ____; and ____

1. Humankind developed from visitors from outer space.
2. Evidence for man's prehistory is around us if we can interpret it.
3. Looking in the mirror can harm our sense of what to expect from life.
4. Humankind shows signs of imperfect adjustment to a new way of life.
5. Signs of change indicate the continuing development of life on earth.
6. Very little is to be achieved by individual "finds" such as this.

COMPLETION Choose the best answer for each question:

1. ____ The mind of man is said to be a mixture of saint and: (a) sinner. (b) priest. (c) mangrove. (d) beast.

2. ____ Eiseley says that because of its constant motion and constant change, the world of the mangrove swamp is not really: (a) essential. (b) natural. (c) helpful to archaeologists. (d) comfortable for him.

3. ____ The missing link, Eiseley realized, was: (a) not worth worrying about. (b) afraid of his shadow. (c) himself. (d) upright, courageous, and alert.

4. ____ Good scientific procedure is to: (a) compare (b) analyze (c) make a deal (d) do away with the living fauna.

5. ____ Apparently, Eiseley's feet are: (a) quite the same as (b) somewhat different from (c) longer than (d) unrelated to most people's feet.

VOCABULARY Choose the word or phrase from Column B that best defines the vocabulary entry in Column A:

Column A	*Column B*
1. ____ tangible	a. related to trees
2. ____ marred	b. find bit by bit
3. ____ diverted	c. damaged
4. ____ arboreal	d. era
5. ____ austere	e. with skill
6. ____ vestigial	f. upset; activity
7. ____ impervious	g. insecure
8. ____ deftly	h. distracted
9. ____ eke out	i. adroit
10. ____ turmoil	j. economical
11. ____ malevolent	k. solid; real
12. ____ unstable	l. weighty
13. ____ epoch	m. not likely to be disturbed
14. ____ intermingled	n. threatening; evil
15. ____ oppressive	o. disorder
	p. impairing
	q. mixed
	r. left over

26

The Image of Wholeness

Alvin Kernan

In this article, a distinguished Princeton professor considers the question of people's loyalty to today's universities. He reviews the useful functions which universities no longer fill. Yet, the public continues to loyally support them. In this review of the character and the function of the American university, Kernan uncovers new reasons for the continued support and the affection it receives from our society.

We often say these days that the university is no longer trusted and supported by society. But in a surprising, paradoxical way the whole society still seems to be increasingly fascinated by, even in love with, institutions of higher learning that go out of their way to reject the practical wisdom and the immediate daily concerns of society.

The educational systems of most societies have been strictly vocational and have been valued to the extent that they effectively taught what were agreed to be the most useful social skills—rhetoric or dance steps, Latin or magic. But our universities do not function in the obviously practical way that societies have usually demanded of education and other such crucial institutions as the law, government, or medicine. These institutions may not always work well, but there is never much doubt about what they are actually supposed to do. With the university, it is the function that is not clear at present, and therefore the loyalty that the institution engenders is surprising.

There are, of course, many hostile views of this situation. The lack of immediate connections between our most pressing social needs and our universities is sometimes said to show the decadence of our society, the weakness of one of our most fundamental institutions, and the operation of a caste system in a society affluent enough to be able to afford to teach its richer children those things that it is useless to know. Or it is sometimes said that the university is the most conservative of all institutions and that its organization and its curriculum are simply the lingerings-on of the dead past in a changed world.

I do not myself accept these hostile views of the university—although there are obvious traces of truth in such charges—but I have never been sure that the best defense is the usual one of trying to show that if we only understood and explained the universities' workings properly, it would be evident how really functional they are and how the skills they teach are necessary to government, business, and technology. It may be true that someone trained in the liberal arts will eventually make a better businessman—though I doubt it—or that the discoveries made in the physics laboratory today provide the technology of tomorrow, but such explanations seem to argue the weakest case. Utilitarian explanations can never fully justify the modern university, nor explain why it commands such powerful loyalties in a society that is ordinarily quite hard-headed about the necessity of its institutions' working in very direct, efficient ways.

We might come closer to explaining the value of the university not by defending the potential social usefulness of any of its subjects but rather by speaking of the entire curriculum and the image that the university creates as a whole. The arts-and-sciences center, the school of philosophy as it were, provides the central definition of the university, and it does so, I believe, not because of the usefulness of any one of its single subjects but because of the shapeliness, coherence, and inclusiveness of its entire structure. Society identifies so strongly with the university not because the economics department teaches us to understand the marketplace, or because physics teaches the ways of the energy that drives the cosmos, or because history provides a way of understanding and thereby living in linear time—although the practical worth of knowing these things is obvious—but because these and the many other subjects the university teaches gather together to form a deeply needed and powerfully reassuring image of the world.

What kind of an image? Well, an image that divides the world into a theoretically limitless number of specific categories or departments, each tended by specialists who understand the fine detail of their particular aspects of reality. But all the individual subjects fit in turn into four great comprehensive categories: the physical sciences, which deal in an objective manner with the nature and workings of the universe of matter; the life sciences, which explore the vital functioning of living organisms and the organization of creatures; the social sciences, which deal with the workings of human beings and the kind of social structures and institutions they construct to achieve desired human ends; and the humanities, which explore what is thought of as being distinctive about man, not the scientific laws governing his nature but the special needs and powers that are believed to mark him off from the rest of being.

There are many who consider the humanities' conception of man as outdated, and particularly fierce intellectual wars are fought along the borders of the humanities and the social sciences, where it is never clear whether history is an objective social science or a humanistic art of mythmaking; whether anthropology does not provide a better, a "thicker" (to use Clifford Geertz's term) description of human culture than art and literature; and whether psychology and the sociology of knowledge have not replaced philosophy. As along the edges of the continental plates, so along the borders of all of the academic divisions, there is constant restless shifting and frequent grating of sharp claims and counterclaims. Economics constantly threatens to become a "hard" or "exact" science, while psychology shifts back and forth between the life sciences and the social sciences. As biologists become more interested in such matters as ecological systems and the relationships of the structure of organisms to those of communities, they begin to interact with the social sciences; while at the same time biochemistry and the many forms of biophysics take the study of life in the direction of the physical sciences.

It is at these junctures of the academic divisions that the university curriculum is under most stress, as any administrator can tell you, and it is here that the volcanoes and earthquakes rumble and stir as they do at those places where the earth's continental plates meet and move against one another. The academic event can be ominous, and even frightening at times, like the geological one, but it is also reassuring because it shows that the university is alive and continuing to move, to grow and adapt, and because it tells us that the university is still a whole, that its parts meet and interact with one another, always seeking meaningful adjustment, seeking wholeness and symmetry.

It is in seeking and in manifesting this quality of wholeness that the university has its most powerful effect on modern society. The modern research university is an institutionalized form of a myth, or, to use Thomas S. Kuhn's term from *The Structure of Scientific Revolutions,* a "paradigm" of wholeness that manifests a belief that the world, for all its manifold parts and its bewildering complexity, does finally hang together, does make sense, is comprehensible to and therefore can potentially be controlled by the human mind. My argument is not that it does not matter which subjects are taught or whether or not they are taught well—quite the contrary. Any university that successfully projects an image of wholeness does so only by including in its curriculum all those subjects—physics, anthropology, literature, biology, and numerous other crucial disciplines—that are at the present time thought of as major aspects of reality, and by doing research in and teaching these subjects with real power and seriousness.

The image of wholeness is further enhanced by the distinction of the faculty, the quality of the architecture, the coherence of the campus and the community, the success of graduates and athletic teams, all of which help to authenticate the institutional statement of the coherence of the universe and to demonstrate that it really works. But the university's statement to the world will finally and most powerfully be made not in the form of the content of any of its courses or the arrangement of its physical plant but as an expression by the entire university of the possibility that the world is coherent.

Different universities exploit different possibilities to create their particular versions of the image of wholeness, and those that have succeeded in embodying that myth with real power and effectiveness command an enormous social loyalty, even from people who may know little or nothing of the vast range of particulars taught there. None of us, of course, knows more than a small fraction of that totality, but all of us seem to have an absolute need to sense that, for all its multiplicity, the world is ultimately a whole, that it is a structured totality. The increasing importance of the universities in the society may well come from the fact that other institutions that once provided an image of wholeness—the church, the family, the law, and the state—no longer (perhaps because their systems are tighter and more absolute) seem to be able to organize our vast and conflicting range of knowledge, our surplus of facts, to provide effectively the assurance of an ordered psychological, social, and physical cosmos. But the university, in the very looseness of its structure, is able to pull together and hold the range of knowledge in at least a livable tension of restless opposites.

It may well be that the tolerance of the university for pluralism and multiplicity of values is what suits it best for the modern world. Whatever the reasons, it is in satisfying the almost metaphysical need for cosmic orientation, by providing reassurance that although old certainties have been battered almost into oblivion, we still have, or at least somebody might conceivably have, a grasp of the outlines of reality and a method for getting on with the work of understanding ourselves and the world, that a university best serves its graduates and the society at large. It is also, I think, the confidence that such knowledge gives that finally marks and strengthens those graduates who have really deeply absorbed what the university has to say about a cautious confidence that the world is ultimately understandable; that, as Einstein put it, "God is subtle but He is not malicious."

LENGTH: 1680 WORDS

Name Class Date

26 The Image of Wholeness

SCORING: Reading time: _____ Rate from chart: _____ W.P.M.			
RETENTION	number right ____	× 2 equals ____	points
MAIN POINT	number right ____	× 4 equals ____	points
AUTHOR'S ATTITUDE	number right ____	× 2 equals ____	points
COMPLETION	number right ____	× 4 equals ____	points
VOCABULARY	number right ____	× 2 equals ____	points
	(Total points: 100)	**Total** ____	points

RETENTION Based on the passage, which of the following statements is True (T), False (F), or Not answerable (N)?

1. ____ The function of the university is not clear at the present.
2. ____ On the whole, American universities are highly vocational.
3. ____ The central definition of the university is supplied by the Arts College.
4. ____ Clifford Geertz is a "mythmaker."
5. ____ Mythmaking is a humanistic art.
6. ____ An image of the world is deeply needed.
7. ____ At least Economics never threatens to be a "hard" science.
8. ____ Many people consider the humanities to be outdated.
9. ____ The modern research university is an institutionalized form of a myth.
10. ____ Anthropology is a crucial discipline in the university.
11. ____ Athletic teams have nothing to do with authenticating the university.
12. ____ Kernan was himself a football player at Princeton.
13. ____ Different universities offer different images of the world.
14. ____ The distinction of the faculty helps the image the university creates.
15. ____ Kernan is not arguing about how well subjects are taught.
16. ____ The university is tolerant of pluralism.
17. ____ The church, the family, the law, and the state share no common ground.

18. ____ The tightness of university structure is critical to its function.

19. ____ A university serves its graduates, but not society at large.

20. ____ The university curriculum includes disciplines thought of as aspects of reality.

MAIN POINT Which of the following statements best represents the main point of the passage? ____

1. Universities have a tremendous responsibility to the public.
2. People will always believe what they want to about universities.
3. The university creates a sense of coherence that clarifies reality.
4. The university has substituted for church and state in our time.
5. We will be depending more and more on universities in the future.

AUTHOR'S ATTITUDE Which of the following statements best describe the author's attitude? ____; ____; and ____

1. Rejecting "practical wisdom" may not be unwise for universities.
2. Vocational colleges offer the most sensible education for today.
3. University survival will depend on effective curricula and teaching.
4. The university serves to create the myth we accept as reality.
5. All universities are pretty much the same five years after graduation.
6. People have a basic need to integrate diverse ideas and facts.

COMPLETION Choose the best answer for each question:

1. ____ One widespread idea is that universities: (a) will always be with us. (b) are no longer trusted. (c) are phony. (d) have tragic flaws.

2. ____ The old certainties, Kernan tells us, have been: (a) rediscovered. (b) the province of the church. (c) subtle, but not malicious. (d) battered.

3. ____ The educational systems of most societies have been strictly: (a) controlled. (b) confidential. (c) reserved for the rich. (d) vocational in character.

4. ____ The humanities offer a description of: (a) nothing. (b) useless stuff. (c) human culture. (d) progress and decline in predictable rhythms.

5. ____ The greatest turmoil in the academy occurs at the: (a) center (b) lowest point (c) juncture (d) interstices of academic disciplines.

VOCABULARY Choose the word or phrase from Column B that best defines the vocabulary item in Column A:

Column A	*Column B*
1. ____ manifesting	a. class
2. ____ ominous	b. related to employment
3. ____ vital	c. wealthy
4. ____ exploit	d. extremely important
5. ____ paradoxical	e. living
6. ____ utilitarian	f. traditional
7. ____ caste	g. training
8. ____ vocational	h. exhibiting
9. ____ image	i. make use of
10. ____ crucial	j. titling
11. ____ affluent	k. useful
12. ____ conservative	l. threatening
13. ____ engender	m. sex; sexual
14. ____ decadence	n. apparently contradictory
15. ____ curriculm	o. concept; idea
	p. deterioration
	q. beget
	r. program of studies

27

Where Solitude Is Easy to Find

Joseph Wood Krutch

The Grand Canyon is an awesome place. As the famed naturalist Joseph Wood Krutch tells us, it is one of the few remaining places where solitude can easily be found. Its walls harbor a panorama of life as it might have been had mankind never existed. It is truly one of the wonders of the world.

Twenty years ago I was one of the tourist thousands who saw Grand Canyon for the first time. In those days, travelers approaching from the south by car or bus had no warning until they stood actually upon the brink. Usually they descended at the front door of Bright Angel Lodge, passed through the lobby, and wandered across the terrace at the other side, wondering as they went where the Canyon was. Then, suddenly, they were at the brink with only a low parapet between them and a vast abyss.

First there is the sheer drop of several thousand feet, then the wide Tonto Plateau, then another sheer drop to an invisible bottom whose depth the visitor can only guess. Apparently this was the way Cárdenas, the first white man to see the Canyon, came upon it in 1540. Since then thousands of men and women have shared his wonder and delight. Though I have made many visits since my first, I still get a real if diminished shock.

Today a new road, built only a few years ago, gives automobilists a glimpse into the chasm as they approach. That spoils a bit of the drama; but perhaps it is just as well. On my first visit a fellow traveler took one look and then ran back to throw his arms around a tree. When I saw him last, he was desperately resisting the efforts of two women companions to pry him loose.

At first glance the spectacle seems too strange to be real. Because one has never seen anything like it, because one has nothing to compare it with, it stuns the eye but cannot really hold the attention. For one thing, the scale is too large to be credited. The Canyon is ten miles across from rim to rim at the point where one usually sees it first and almost exactly a mile deep. But we are so accustomed to thinking of skyscrapers as high and of St. Peter's or the Pentagon as massive that we can hardly help misinterpreting what the eye sees; we cannot realize that the tremendous mesas and curiously shaped buttes which rise all around us are the grandiose objects they are. For a time it is too much like a scale model or an optical illusion. One admires the peep show and that is all. Because we cannot relate ourselves to it, we remain outside, very much as we remain outside the frame of a picture. And though we may come back to a picture again and again, we cannot look at it continuously for any considerable period of time. To pass on to another picture is the almost inevitable impulse. And this is the reaction of a majority of visitors to the Canyon.

To get into the picture one must relate one's self to it somehow and that is not easy to do in a short time. A few of the more hardy take the daylong journey on muleback to the bottom and return. A few of the more foolhardy brush warnings aside and plunge gaily downward on foot only to discover—unless they are seasoned hikers—that they have to be rescued in a state of exhaustion from an illusory panorama through which, as in a dream, they seem unable to make any progress. They have related themselves, but the relation is one of frustration and defeat.

A more sensible procedure for those willing to take the time is to allow the relationship to establish itself gradually. After a few days well but quietly spent, one begins to lose the sense of unreality and to come to terms with a scale of magnitude and of distance which could not at first be taken in. And it is only then that the spectacle, even as mere spectacle, makes its full impression or that one begins to have some dim sense of what the geologists mean when they talk of the millions of years during which the Canyon was cut and of the billions during which the rocks were prepared for the cutting. The Canyon requires what we call in the lingo of our day "a double take." Only that way does its size, its antiquity or the grandioseness of the forces which made it become real. Moreover, as I have learned from many visits, the process has to be repeated every time. First there is the impression of some sort of man-made diorama trying to fool the eye. Only later comes the gradual acceptance of the unbelievable fact.

Hendrik van Loon once remarked—I have not checked his figures—that the entire human population of the earth could be packed in a box only a mile wide, deep, and high. He then went on to add that if such a box were dropped into the middle of Grand Canyon, it would just about reach the rim but be not much more conspicuous than many of the mesas which here and there rise almost as high. Only a confirmed misanthropist will feel that the experiment would be worth making, but the visitor is soon struck by a more benign demonstration. This is that man—even hordes of men—cannot fill the Canyon sufficiently to detract from the sense of vast emptiness.

This is, after all, one of the most visited spots on the face of the earth. As the Swiss hotel is said to have boasted, "Thousands come here from all parts of the world seeking solitude." But at Grand Canyon at least they can find it. They form their little knot, of course, around the hotel and its terrace. But one can lose them very easily and then literally have a whole landscape to oneself. Even from the terrace of Bright Angel Lodge the Canyon itself is so empty that a little flurry of excitement arises when someone spots through his binoculars a speck moving up the side or across a plateau and when it can be assumed, though not actually seen, that the speck is a man or perhaps a man and a mule. The rim itself, except for the short stretch on either side of the main tourist area, is equally deserted. A few miles away—indeed within easy walking distance—one finds without looking a hundred perches where one may sit in absolute solitude, looking across a vista of many miles in which there is neither a human being nor any sign that any human being was ever there. And it is from such a perch that those who wish to take the Canyon in should begin to make its acquaintance.

Actually, of course, there are many areas in the Southwest a great deal farther from the conveniences and inconveniences of civilization—places hundreds of miles from a railroad and scores from a paved or even graded road; places where no man may come for months or even years. One knows that this is so and when one visits such a region the knowledge has its effect upon the imagination. But I cannot say that I ever looked upon any scene which, on the basis of what the eye could see, appeared to be more completely out of the world of man and modernity, although actually my perch was perhaps half a mile from a paved highway along which cars were passing at the rate of a hundred an hour, and only two or three miles from a crowded resort hotel. It is a pity—or perhaps it isn't—that so few visitors realize how close they are to an experience not elsewhere easy to have in the twentieth century, and the fact that one can have it so easily here reminds one again of the scale of this landscape. If, as Mr. van Loon said, the entire population of the earth could be all but lost in the Canyon, it is no wonder that a few thousands leave lots of unoccupied space.

Not very long ago, and after an absence of several years, I again took up my position on one of the little promontories which jut out from the rim. It was past the middle of June, and in the thin air of seven thousand feet even visitors from the southern Arizona desert are burned one tone deeper. But in the shade of a piñon pine the air still hints of the nights which can be almost cold, even at that season.

I looked across the ten miles to the opposite rim, down the successive terraces to the inner gorge at whose invisible bottom the great river still runs after having cut through a mile of stone, and then at the wall of an opposite promontory on my own side. I checked where I could the dividing lines between the successive formations of the geological ages—the Permian limestone on which I sat, the hundreds of feet of sandstone below it, the great Redwall of the Carboniferous age, the resisting plateau of Cambrian sediments, and finally the black wall of Archean schist. I made, in other words, a brief attempt at adjustment to the world of time as well as of space. But for the moment I was less interested in what the Canyon had been than in what it is at this moment and has been able to remain. It is not often that twentieth-century man has so much space to himself.

Here and there near the rim and below its edge there are scattered evidences that Indians inhabited the area—as one tribe still inhabits a section of the Canyon itself. But no evidence of even long past occupation was visible from where I sat, and indeed it nowhere appears that many men ever lived very long or very well here. This is dry country with thin soil or none, and also, perhaps, as one may at least fancy, a little too disconcerting in the immensities of its vistas. Yet it is by no means lifeless and now, as in the past, various small creatures find it very much to their liking. Violet green swallows dip and swerve, now above, now below the rim. Ravens soar above, nonchalantly putting another few hundred feet between them and the bottom a mile below where I sit. And if they seem to take the abyss with the casualness inspired by confidence in their strong wings and the solidity of the air for those who know how to navigate it, there are many other creatures obviously unaware of the terrible chasm open at their feet. Chipmunks and rock squirrels scamper a few feet below the edge; lizards dart here and there; a small gopher snake, apparently stalking some game, wiggles slowly across a piece of crumbling stone which a slight push would send hurtling below. Little junipers anchored at the very edge dangle bare roots over the side. And there, two feet below the rim, a pentstemon waves a red wand over nothingness.

Despite all these living things so obviously at home here, there is absolutely no sign from which I would be able to deduce that any man besides myself had ever been here or, for that matter, that he had ever existed at all. This scene, I say to myself, would be exactly what it is if he never had. It is not quite the world before man came, because too many other living things have disappeared since then. But otherwise it is still the world as though man had never been.

At least there is absolutely nothing to remind me of all that he has done in (and to) the globe he lives on. The tamer of fire and the inventor of the wheel might never have existed—to say nothing of Newton and Watt and Faraday. Neither is there anything to remind me of the less dubious human achievements with which I have been concerned for most of my life. Plato and Shakespeare and Mozart also might never have existed, and if I had never come in contact with anything not visible here, I can hardly imagine what my life would have been like or what the character of my consciousness would be.

Here, so I am tempted to say, are the eternal hills without the eternal thoughts with which we have clothed them. Yet actually the hills are not eternal, whether the thoughts are or are not. In a half a dozen places I can see the still visible evidences of recent rockfalls where great slabs of stone have broken loose and gone hurtling down. The widening of the Canyon is going on visibly, its deepening invisibly and no doubt much more slowly. One does not have to think in terms of geological time to realize that even the Canyon is changing. It is wider than it was a century ago and will inevitably be wider still after another has passed.

LENGTH: 2010 WORDS

Name ____ Class ____ Date ____

27 Where Solitude Is Easy to Find

SCORING: Reading time: ____	Rate from chart: ____ W.P.M.		
RETENTION	number right ____	× 2 equals ____	points
MAIN POINT	number right ____	× 4 equals ____	points
AUTHOR'S ATTITUDE	number right ____	× 2 equals ____	points
COMPLETION	number right ____	× 4 equals ____	points
VOCABULARY	number right ____	× 2 equals ____	points
	(Total points: 100)	**Total** ____	points

RETENTION Based on the passage, which of the following statements is True (T), False (F), or Not answerable (N)?

1. ____ In a century the canyon will be no wider than it is now.
2. ____ Krutch has never taken the mule down into the canyon.
3. ____ From Bright Angel Lodge the visitor actually cannot see the canyon's bottom.
4. ____ There is virtually no wildlife at the rim of the canyon.
5. ____ At first the canyon seems an optical illusion.
6. ____ Krutch implies he visited the canyon only twice.
7. ____ The first European to see the canyon came in the sixteenth century.
8. ____ Krutch's first visit was ten years before he wrote this.
9. ____ There are mesas, but no plateaus in the canyon.
10. ____ The entire population of the earth could fit into the canyon.
11. ____ Schist is black.
12. ____ Hendrik van Loon wrote a book on the Grand Canyon.
13. ____ The first sight of the canyon is a shock for many people.
14. ____ Solitude can be, or could be, sought in Switzerland.
15. ____ It is unusual to see a person actually moving about in the canyon.
16. ____ There are no other places in the Southwest to find solitude.
17. ____ Promontories jut out from the rim.

18. ____ The sides of the canyon reveal its "past."

19. ____ There is a river at the bottom of the canyon.

20. ____ The land around the canyon is arid.

MAIN POINT Which of the following statements best represents the main point of the passage? ____

1. There are still some places where people can "get away from it all."
2. It was a wise decision to create Grand Canyon National Park.
3. Nature does not need mankind in order to be spectacular.
4. Nature is, in its own way, something of a profound psychologist.
5. Spending time in the Grand Canyon is the best way to appreciate it.

AUTHOR'S ATTITUDE Which of the following statements best describe the author's attitude? ____; ____; and ____

1. The Grand Canyon is really worth seeing.
2. People ought to experience the descent and ascent beneath the rim.
3. It is impossible to get a sense of the scope of the canyon.
4. Solitude can be a very positive value.
5. Being a scientist is the best way to appreciate the canyon.
6. Unspoiled nature nourishes people's spirits.

COMPLETION Choose the best answer for each question:

1. ____ One group unawed by the canyon's depths is: (a) New Yorkers. (b) the Swiss tourist. (c) birds. (d) those who do not see it.

2. ____ A "pentstemon" with a "red wand" is probably a: (a) magician. (b) flower. (c) tourist with a red handkerchief. (d) prairie dog.

3. ____ Within three miles of Krutch's perch there was: (a) nothing but dry soil. (b) a car and a tent. (c) a crowded resort hotel. (d) a ranger station.

4. ____ For Krutch, no other scene is as: (a) awing (b) significant (c) basically exhausting (d) out of the world of man as the Grand Canyon.

5. ____ Still living within the Canyon itself is: (a) an Indian tribe. (b) only wildlife. (c) a "lost" gold miner. (d) a group of investigators.

VOCABULARY Choose the word or phrase from Column B that best defines the vocabulary entry in Column A:

	Column A	*Column B*
1.	____ pry loose	a. good
2.	____ brink	b. fated; unavoidable
3.	____ abyss	c. panoramic view
4.	____ benign	d. obvious
5.	____ vista	e. obliquity
6.	____ illusory	f. trained; experienced
7.	____ inevitable	g. people hater
8.	____ misanthropist	h. distant past
9.	____ grandiose	i. casually
10.	____ conspicuous	j. huge
11.	____ seasoned	k. observably
12.	____ nonchalantly	l. lived in
13.	____ visibly	m. release
14.	____ inhabited	n. eluctable
15.	____ antiquity	o. chasm
		p. edge
		q. arid; dry
		r. unreal

28

Patterns

Amy Lowell

Amy Lowell, a modern poet, describes a situation set in the past. A noble lady, in her formal garden, observes the strictly ordered patterns of her life and society. Although our own culture is far less rigid and mannered, we too are restricted, and sometimes controlled, by our own patterns.

I walk down the garden paths,
And all the daffodils
Are blowing, and the bright blue squills.
I walk down the patterned garden paths
In my stiff, brocaded gown.
With my powdered hair and jewelled fan,
I too am a rare
Pattern. As I wander down
The garden paths.

My dress is richly figured,
And the train
Makes a pink and silver stain
On the gravel, and the thrift
Of the borders.
Just a plate of current fashion,
Tripping by in high-heeled, ribboned shoes.

Not a softness anywhere about me,
Only whalebone and brocade.
And I sink on a seat in the shade
Of a lime tree. For my passion
Wars against the stiff brocade.
The daffodils and squills
Flutter in the breeze
As they please.
And I weep;
For the lime tree is in blossom
And one small flower has dropped upon my bosom.

And the plashing of waterdrops
In the marble fountain
Comes down the garden paths.
The dripping never stops.
Underneath my stiffened gown
Is the softness of a woman bathing in a marble basin,
A basin in the midst of hedges grown
So thick, she cannot see her lover hiding,
But she guesses he is near,
And the sliding of the water
Seems the stroking of a dear
Hand upon her.
What is summer in a fine brocaded gown!
I should like to see it lying in a heap upon the ground.
All the pink and silver crumpled up on the ground.

I would be the pink and silver as I ran along the paths,
And he would stumble after,
Bewildered by my laughter.
I should see the sun flashing from his sword-hilt and the buckles on his
 shoes.
I would choose
To lead him in a maze along the patterned paths,
A bright and laughing maze for my heavy-booted lover.
Till he caught me in the shade,
And the buttons of his waistcoat bruised my body as he clasped me,
Aching, melting, unafraid.
With the shadows of the leaves and the sundrops,
And the plopping of the waterdrops,
All about us in the open afternoon–
I am very like to swoon
With the weight of this brocade,
For the sun sifts through the shade.

Underneath the fallen blossom
In my bosom,
Is a letter I have hid.
It was brought to me this morning by a rider from the Duke.
"Madam, we regret to inform you that Lord Hartwell
Died in action Thursday se'nnight."
As I read it in the white, morning sunlight,
The letters squirmed like snakes.
"Any answer, Madam," said my footman.
"No," I told him.
"See that the messenger takes some refreshment.
No, no answer."
And I walked into the garden,
Up and down the patterned paths,
In my stiff, correct brocade.
The blue and yellow flowers stood up proudly in the sun,
Each one.
I stood upright too,
Held rigid to the pattern
By the stiffness of my gown.
Up and down I walked,
Up and down.

In a month he would have been my husband.
In a month, here, underneath this lime,
We would have broke the pattern;
He for me, and I for him,
He as Colonel, I as Lady,
On this shady seat.
He had a whim
That sunlight carried blessing.
And I answered, "It shall be as you have said."
Now he is dead.

In summer and in winter I shall walk
Up and down
The patterned garden paths
In my stiff, brocaded gown.
The squills and daffodils
Will give place to pillared roses, and to asters, and to snow.
I shall go
Up and down,
In my gown.
Gorgeously arrayed,
Boned and stayed.

And the softness of my body will be guarded from embrace
By each button, hook, and lace.
For the man who should loose me is dead,
Fighting with the Duke in Flanders,
In a pattern called a war.
Christ! What are patterns for?

Name Class Date

28 Patterns

SCORING: Reading time: ____ Rate from chart: ____ W.P.M.		
RETENTION	number right ____ × 2 equals ____ points	
MAIN POINT	number right ____ × 4 equals ____ points	
AUTHOR'S ATTITUDE	number right ____ × 2 equals ____ points	
COMPLETION	number right ____ × 4 equals ____ points	
VOCABULARY	number right ____ × 2 equals ____ points	
	(Total points: 100) **Total** ____ points	

RETENTION Based on the passage, which of the following statements is True (T), False (F), or Not answerable (N)?

1. ____ Flanders is modern Belgium.
2. ____ Lord Hartwell was a Colonel.
3. ____ Lord Hartwell died fighting against the Duke.
4. ____ The Lady's brocade gown was stiff.
5. ____ Whalebone and brocade are not soft.
6. ____ The Lady's gown is blue, like the squills.
7. ____ The patterning of the garden is like the patterning of her life.
8. ____ Even though he is dead, the Lady guesses her lover is near.
9. ____ The Lady betrayed intense emotion upon learning of her lover's death.
10. ____ The lime tree was in leaf, but not in blossom.
11. ____ The Lady received the bad news in the bright sunlit morning.
12. ____ Lord Hartwell associated sunshine with blessing.
13. ____ When he and the Lady married they would have broken the pattern.
14. ____ The Lady thought herself quite correct in her behavior.
15. ____ The Lady's lover wore boots and a sword.
16. ____ The pattern held the Lady upright.
17. ____ The Duke and Lord Hartwell died in the siege, though not at once.

18. ____ Now that the lover is dead, the Lady will break the pattern herself.

19. ____ War is a kind of pattern, too.

20. ____ The Lady will change all the patterns in the garden because Hartwell died.

MAIN POINT Which of the following statements best represents the main point of the passage? ____

1. Patterns are the restrictions society places on our lives.
2. If they really want to, people can break out of life's patterns.
3. When people live by patterns their environment shows it.
4. Patterns can be extremely useful when we are under severe stress.
5. No one has any choices about the patterns they must live by.

AUTHOR'S ATTITUDE Which of the following statements best describe the author's attitude? ____; ____; and ____

1. No one has the right to invoke patterns in a life.
2. The pattern restrains the Lady's passions.
3. Lord Hartwell understood fully the patterns of nature, life, and war.
4. Patterns have killed Hartwell and imprisoned the Lady.
5. The rigidity of the patterns is not a good thing.
6. Without patterns, unfortunately, society would fall apart.

COMPLETION Choose the best answer for each question:

1. ____ Lord Hartwell would have been the Lady's husband: (a) in a month. (b) when the Duke returned. (c) if the war were won. (d) in the pattern.

2. ____ A fine brocaded gown seems particularly inappropriate: (a) now that Hartwell is dead. (b) when it is the same color as the flowers in the garden. (c) in summertime. (d) for a woman who was almost a widow.

3. ____ The "bright and laughing maze": (a) represents nonpatterning. (b) is a kind of lover's game. (c) does not count now. (d) is in Flanders.

4. ____ The marble fountain is associated with: (a) taking a bath. (b) the Lady's weeping. (c) the waters of life. (d) the flowers' nourishment.

5. ____ The Lady "will be guarded from embrace" because: (a) the pattern dictates otherwise. (b) Hartwell's death means an end to her hopes for marriage. (c) her friends will now come to protect her from the curious. (d) she is sick at heart and wants to plant "pillared roses" and asters.

VOCABULARY Choose the word or phrase from Column B that best defines the vocabulary entry in Column A:

Column A	*Column B*
1. ____ whim	a. uncertain
2. ____ arrayed	b. exacting; proper
3. ____ stayed	c. blooming
4. ____ maze	d. center of
5. ____ bewildered	e. carefully done
6. ____ blowing	f. faint; collapse
7. ____ rare	g. wish
8. ____ figured	h. sounding
9. ____ train	i. restrained
10. ____ plashing	j. segment trailing behind
11. ____ swoon	k. set out; ordered
12. ____ correct	l. embroidered
13. ____ thrift	m. falling gently
14. ____ midst	n. cheap; wheezy
15. ____ fine	o. spareness
	p. extraordinary
	q. puzzling pattern
	r. tight

SECTION 5

Vocabulary Preview

The following words come from the eight reading selections in Section 5. Study the list carefully, pronouncing the words aloud if possible. Conceal the definitions with a card or your hand and test your command of the meanings of the words.

aboriginal, *adj.* native; primitive
accrue, *verb* to grow by periodic increases, as interest on money
accumulate, *verb* to amass; increase
acquiescence, *noun* acceptance without opposition
affable, *adj.* pleasant; agreeable
alleviation, *noun* anything that makes something easier to bear
ambiguous, *adj.* obscure; could be understood in two ways
anthropomorphize, *verb* to attribute human form or qualities to
apprehensive, *adj.* fearful
assimilate, *verb* to absorb
atherosclerosis, *noun* a loss of elasticity in the inner walls of the arteries
audacity, *noun* boldness
auxiliary, *adj.* providing help; supplementary
behaviorism, *noun* the theory that regards observable behavior as the proper subject for psychological study
Caliban, *noun* ugly, beastlike person
caste, *noun* rank in society
chemotherapy, *noun* the treatment of disease with chemical agents
circumlocution, *noun* a lengthy way of explaining things
cognizant, *adj.* being aware or informed of something
confer, *verb* to grant or bestow; compare views
contemplate, *verb* to ponder or carefully consider
cultivator, *noun* one who encourages the growth of someone or something
cuneiform, *noun* wedge-shaped writing
cynically, *adv.* distrusting human nature or motives
decipher, *verb* to figure out something obscure; decode
degenerative, *adj.* causing deterioration or decline
deities, *noun* gods
determinatives, *noun* factors that resolve or settle an issue
devastating, *verb* wasting; destroying

disconcerted, *adj.* confused
discretion, *noun* cautious reserve in speech; ability to make responsible decisions
egalitarian, *adj.* believing in human equality
espouse, *verb* to marry; support a cause
evangelist, *noun* one who preaches
feasibility, *noun* the quality of being possible to carry out
figurative, *adj.* pertaining to symbols or imagery
gerontology, *noun* the study of elderly people
hieratic, *adj.* priestly; of an early sacred Egyptian form of writing
hieroglyphic, *noun* a symbol used by the Egyptians in writing
howitzer, *noun* a type of cannon
hyperbaric, *adj.* having a pressure greater than that within the body tissues or fluids.
hypothalamus, *noun* part of the brain that controls body temperature and other autonomic functions
immortalize, *verb* to give eternal existence or lasting fame
increments, *noun* increases in quantity or value
insinuate, *verb* to imply or hint subtly
longevity, *noun* a long life; length of life
lustrous, *adj.* shining; bright
lysosome, *noun* a particle, found in a cell, which is capable of dissolving living matter
mandate, *noun* an authoritative command
mattock, *noun* a tool used for digging and grubbing
medium, *noun* a means of communication
metabolic, *adj.* relating to metabolism, the processes by which energy is provided for the body's functioning
microtechnology, *noun* the science of miniaturization
miniscule, *adj.* very small
mutilation, *noun* maiming or crippling
nonremunerative, *adj.* nonpaying
opiate, *noun* a narcotic
organically, *adv.* wholly; with parts interrelated
palette, *noun* board used by a painter to mix paints on
palisades, *noun* cliffs
pogroms, *noun* organized massacres
postmortem, *noun* examination after death
practitioner, *noun* one who practices a profession
prehominid, *noun* preprimate; prehuman
quash, *verb* to suppress
regimen, *noun* a systematic course of therapy

rejuvenate, *verb* to make young or youthful again
repositories, *noun* places of storage
rubric, *noun* a rule usually for the conduct of a religious service; a saying
scenario, *noun* an outline of a play
seminal, *adj.* having potential for development
staunch, *adj.* firm; strong
stimulus, *noun* something which excites or rouses to activity
systematize, *verb* arrange methodically
tainted, *adj.* contaminated; spoiled
teredo worms, *noun* shipworms
therapeutic, *adj.* having to do with healing; medicinal
tonnage, *noun* a duty on ships based on cargo capacity
unprecedented, *adj.* never before heard of; novel
unwieldy, *adj.* awkward; not easily managed
viable, *adj.* workable
visage, *noun* face; appearance
visceral, *adj.* instinctive; earthy

Choose the word or phrase that best defines the vocabulary item:

1. ____ hieratic: (a) uppermost (b) downright (c) priestly (d) organized (e) uncertain

2. ____ acquiescence: (a) agreeing (b) subservience (c) clumsiness (d) sloth (e) fury

3. ____ unprecedented: (a) novel (b) important (c) unimportant (d) trying (e) without hope

4. ____ scenario: (a) loose (b) plan of action (c) trouble (d) standards (e) worms

5. ____ circumlocution: (a) long windedness (b) quickness (c) around (d) imprisoned (e) bright

6. ____ regimen: (a) military group (b) health (c) plan (d) systematic (e) correct

7. ____ espouse: (a) marry (b) frighten (c) hurt (d) sidle (e) befriend

8. ____ audacity: (a) surprise (b) impatience (c) struggle (d) boldness (e) ambiguity

9. ____ unwieldy: (a) unused (b) hurriedly (c) not present (d) grandiose (e) clumsy

10. ____ pogroms: (a) scenarios (b) plans (c) massacres (d) preparations (e) deities

11. ____ accumulate: (a) amass (b) earn (c) slight (d) beguile (e) make

12. ____ nonremunerative: (a) free (b) moneymaking (c) unprofitable (d) not useful (e) struggling

13. ____ viable: (a) cynical (b) tough (c) helpful (d) workable (e) truthful

14. ____ caste: (a) hierarchy (b) social rank (c) throw (d) boxed (e) fielded

15. ____ prehominid: (a) previous (b) early man (c) prehuman (d) donkey (e) fool

16. ____ hyperbaric: (a) pressureful (b) excitable (c) too active (d) momentary (e) slight

17. ____ mandate: (a) field (b) boyfriend (c) authorization (d) course (e) personable

18. ____ cognizant: (a) small element (b) knowledgeable (c) fraud (d) function (e) confused

19. ____ increments: (a) increase (b) solid (c) prayers (d) cannons (e) commands

20. ____ systematize: (a) spoil (b) give rubrics (c) hopes (d) order (e) heal; repair

21. ____ alleviation: (a) making a joke (b) relieving (c) slighting (d) calibration (e) coruscation

22. ____ visceral: (a) instinctive (b) insignificant (c) striking (d) causative (e) fresh

23 ____ cynically: (a) evilly (b) without grace (c) distrustfully (d) coyly (e) toughly

24. ____ insinuate: (a) try (b) hint (c) lead astray (d) replete (e) medicate

25. ____ apprehensive: (a) uncertain (b) mean (c) humorless (d) abrupt (e) still

29

The Invention of Writing

V. Gordon Childe

In the earliest stages of writing, its purpose was to help governments administer more efficiently. Because of its enormous complexity, writing was a skill practiced solely by a select class of scribes. And only a privileged few could read what they wrote. Although writing was not invented to preserve great ideas or increase knowledge, the ancients respected the "magic" inherent in language preserved which would lead to later advances.

The invention of writing (as here defined) really marks an epoch in human progress. For us moderns it seems significant primarily because it offers an opportunity of penetrating to the very thoughts of our cultural ancestors, instead of trying to deduce those thoughts from their imperfect embodiments in deeds. But the true significance of writing is that it was destined to revolutionize the transmission of human knowledge. By its means a man can immortalize his experience and transmit it directly to contemporaries living far off and to generations yet unborn. It is the first step to raising science above the limits of space and time.

The utility of early scripts for this high mission must not be exaggerated. Writing was not invented as a medium of publication, but for the practical needs of administrative corporations. The earlier Sumerian and Egyptian scripts were distinctly clumsy instruments for expressing ideas. Even after a process of simplification lasting over 2000 years the cuneiform script employed between 600 and 1000 distinct characters. Before one could read or write, one had to memorize this formidable array of symbols and learn the complex rules for their combination.

THE INVENTION OF WRITING From *Man Makes Himself* by V. Gordon Childe. Reprinted by permission of Pitman Publishing Limited, London.

Egyptian hieroglyphic and hieratic scripts, despite their alphabetic elements, remained cumbered with a bewildering multitude of ideograms and determinatives, so that the number of characters required ran to about 500.

Under these conditions writing was inevitably a really difficult and specialized art that had to be learned by a long apprenticeship. Reading remained a mystery initiation into which was obtainable only by a prolonged schooling. Few possessed either the leisure or the talent to penetrate into the secrets of literature. Scribes were a comparatively restricted class in Oriental antiquity, like clerks in the Middle Ages. This class, it is true, never became a caste. Admission to the schools did not depend upon birth, though quite how scholars were selected is uncertain. But the "reading public" must have been a small minority in a vast population of illiterates.

Writing was, in fact, a profession, rather like metallurgy or weaving or war. But it was a profession that enjoyed a privileged position and offered prospects of advancement to office, power, and wealth. Literacy came thus to be valued not as a key to knowledge, but as a stepping-stone to prosperity and social rank. A rather hackneyed quotation from later Egyptian literature will illustrate an attitude that can hardly have been peculiar to the Nile Valley or the period of the texts.

An amusing group of Egyptian documents dating from the New Kingdom contrasts the prestige and privileges of a scribe with the hardships of a craftsman or a cultivator. They take the form of paternal admonitions, but embody sentiments that might be expressed today by a farmer or small shopkeeper writing to a son who has to choose between proceeding to higher education or entering industrial employment.

> "Put writing in your heart that you may protect yourself from hard labor of any kind and be a magistrate of high repute. The scribe is released from manual tasks; it is he who commands. . . . Do you not hold the scribe's palette? That is what makes the difference between you and the man who handles an oar.
>
> "I have seen the metal-worker at his task at the mouth of his furnace with fingers like a crocodile's. He stank worse than fish-spawn. Every workman who holds a chisel suffers more than the men who hack the ground; wood is his field and the chisel his mattock. At night when he is free, he toils more than his arms can do (? at overtime work); even at night he lights (his lamp to work by). The stonecutter seeks work in every hard stone; when he has done the great part of his labor his arms are exhausted, he is tired out . . . The weaver in a workshop is worse off than a woman; (he squats) with his knees to his belly and does not taste (fresh) air. He must give loaves to the porters to see the light."

The prospects of social advancement implied in these admonitions may not have been so bright or definite at earlier periods or in other countries. But the general attitude towards clerical employments and theoretical science as contrasted to manual labor and applied sciences probably goes back to the earliest phases of urban life, and was the same in Sumer as in Egypt. The foregoing quotations accordingly recall the fact that the second revolution had produced or accentuated a division of society into classes. In practice kings, priests, nobles, and generals stand opposed to peasants, fishermen, artisans, and laborers. And in this class division the scribes belong to the former class; writing is a "respectable" profession.

Now material progress in prehistoric times had been due mainly to improvements in technique, made presumably by the craftsmen and husbandmen themselves. But in the class division of urban society scribes belong to the "upper classes," in contrast to the working artisans and farmers; writing is a respectable profession while farming, metallurgy, and carpentry are not. The practical applied science of botany, chemistry, and geology were not accordingly embraced in the literary tradition whose exponents looked down upon manual labor; craft lore was not reduced to writing nor handed on in book form.

On the other hand, certain sciences and pseudo-sciences—mathematics, surgery, medicine, astrology, alchemy, haruspicy—were made the subjects of written treatises. They thus formed a body of learned sciences, accessible only to those who had been initiated into the mysteries of reading and writing. But by this very fact the disciplines in question were liable to be divorced from practical life. In entering the school the pupil turned his back on the plow and the bench; he had no desire to return to them.

Inevitably, too, words written with such difficulty and deciphered so laboriously must seem to possess an authority of their own. The immortalization of a word in writing must have seemed a supernatural process; it was surely magical that a man long vanished from the land of the living could still speak from a clay tablet or a papyrus roll. Words thus spoken must possess a kind of *mana*. Thus learned men in the East, like schoolmen in our own Middle Ages, were apt to turn to books in preference to Nature. In Egypt books on mathematics, surgery, and medicine, composed under the Old Kingdom (before 2400 B.C.) were slavishly, and often very incompetently, copied after 2000. Between 800 and 600 B.C. the upstart kings of Assyria were at pains to acquire for their libraries copies of texts going back to the time of Hammurabi (about 1800 B.C.) or of Sargon of Agade (2350).

Instead of demanding that a book should be up to date and embody the latest discoveries, the Egyptian or Babylonian student valued it for its antiquity. A publisher would then advertise his wares not as a "new and revised edition," but as a faithful copy of a fabulously old text. And so the "jacket" of the Rhind Mathematical Papyrus runs: "Rules for enquiring into nature and for knowing all that exists. The roll was written in the thirty-third year of King Aauserre in the likeness of a writing of antiquity made in the time of king Nemare (1880–1850 B.C.). It was the scribe Ahmose who made this copy." One of the treatises included in the Ebers Medical Papyrus is entitled "The Book of Healing Illnesses found in ancient writing in a chest at the feet of Anubis in the time of King Usaphaïs'' (a monarch of Dynasty I).

Nevertheless the schools for scribes did actually function as what we should call research institutes. Even for the purposes of teaching it was necessary to organize and systematize the knowledge to be imparted. The post of instructor gave opportunities and inducements for addition to knowledge by a sort of ''theoretical research.''

LENGTH: 1350 WORDS

Name Class Date

29 The Invention of Writing

SCORING: Reading time: ____ Rate from chart: ____ W.P.M.			
RETENTION	number right ____	× 2 equals ____	points
MAIN POINT	number right ____	× 4 equals ____	points
AUTHOR'S ATTITUDE	number right ____	× 3 equals ____	points
CONCLUSION	number right ____	× 3 equals ____	points
COMPLETION	number right ____	× 4 equals ____	points
VOCABULARY	number right ____	× 2 equals ____	points
	(Total points: 100)	**Total** ____	points

RETENTION Based on the passage, which of the following statements is True (T), False (F), or Not answerable (N)?

1. ____ Hieratic scripts have no alphabetic components.
2. ____ The invention of writing does not really mark an epoch in human progress.
3. ____ There are no Egyptian documents dating from the New Kingdom.
4. ____ The Egyptians had no stonemasons or stonecutters.
5. ____ Scribes were a relatively restricted class in Egypt.
6. ____ There were no members of royalty in scribal castes.
7. ____ The cuneiform script had up to 1000 separate characters.
8. ____ Cuneiform script lasted only 1000 to 1500 years.
9. ____ Only the highborn were admitted to ancient Egyptian scribal schools.
10. ____ Writing revolutionized the transmission of human knowledge.
11. ____ The scribes in Egypt were protected from hard labor.
12. ____ Writing was not thought of in Egypt as a "respectable" profession.
13. ____ Assyrian kings had libraries in 800 B.C.
14. ____ Haruspicy is fortune-telling by means of animal entrails.
15. ____ The ancients wrote books on pseudosciences.
16. ____ Writing and reading were like mysteries requiring initiation.
17. ____ Mana is a kind of magic.

18. ____ The Old Kingdom was before 2400 B.C.

19. ____ The scribal schools were never research institutes.

20. ____ Ahmose was a scribe.

MAIN POINT Which of the following statements best represents the main point of the passage? ____

1. Writing has always been important to civilization.
2. If you want to get a good job, you have to learn to write.
3. It's not whether you can write well, but whether you can write at all.
4. Writing is an important milestone in human civilization.
5. The Middle Ages actually shares a great deal with ancient Egypt.

AUTHOR'S ATTITUDE Which of the following statements best describes the author's attitude? ____

1. If you can write, you can work.
2. The invention of writing is of major importance in science.
3. Scribes were unfair to those who could not write as they did.
4. Writing is important, but religious mysteries are more important.
5. Science would have survived even if mankind had never learned writing.

CONCLUSION Which of the following statements is the best conclusion that can be drawn from the passage? ____

1. Society progresses on the back of the laborer.
2. Book learning still has a kind of mystery attached to it.
3. Nuclear physicists could inherit the earth.
4. Poverty is implied in caste systems unless education is free.
5. Social systems could not survive without educated specialists.

COMPLETION Choose the best answer for each question:

1. ____ One function of the scribal schools was to: (a) organize and systematize (b) codify (c) elaborate and censure (d) clarify knowledge to be imparted.

2. ____ Egyptian and Babylonian students valued books for their: (a) integrity. (b) antiquity. (c) covers. (d) modernity.

3. ____ Apparently, urban Egyptian society had clear: (a) violations of ethics. (b) overlaps of authority. (c) consciences. (d) class divisions.

4. ____ Writing permits a person to: (a) control thousands. (b) communicate after death. (c) change social status. (d) find a niche in the community.

5. ____ Grammar for the Egyptians was probably: (a) much more difficult than (b) about the same as (c) easier than (d) nonexistent in the sense it is for us.

VOCABULARY Choose the word or phrase from Column B that best defines the vocabulary entry in Column A:

Column A	*Column B*
1. ____ deduce	a. usefulness
2. ____ caste	b. interpreters
3. ____ hackneyed	c. things which encourage
4. ____ admonition	d. worn out
5. ____ embody	e. figured out
6. ____ inducements	f. not well done
7. ____ imparted	g. figure out
8. ____ exponents	h. warning
9. ____ deciphered	i. fatherly
10. ____ slavishly	j. body of information
11. ____ incompetently	k. social class
12. ____ theoretical	l. personify; represent
13. ____ lore	m. plausibly
14. ____ paternal	n. abstract; hypothetical
15. ____ utility	o. given
	p. stolidly; like a drudge
	q. all-purpose
	r. cut up; marred

30

The Whale Fishery

Albert Cook Church

One hundred years ago, New Englanders enjoyed extraordinary commercial success hunting for whales. Sturdy whaleships—built in New England and manned by its sailors—plied the Arctic and the Pacific. At home, there was a lively market for the oil and bone collected on these journeys. Towns like New Bedford and Nantucket have never been as prosperous as in the days of the whale fishery which will never return.

Whaleships of the eighteenth century were hardly equal in model or build to the vessels that came afterward when merchants and whalemen had accumulated more wealth and experience. They were short, bluff-bowed craft, averaging 250 tons; slow and unwieldy under most favorable conditions. They were sent to sea uncoppered, and cruised nearly their entire voyages in warm latitudes where marine growth and barnacles form quickly on uncoppered hulls, an easy prey to teredo worms. The wonder is that these clumsy old craft ever managed to drift back to Nantucket.

It was customary to call at the convenient islands in the Pacific to overhaul hull and gear, replenish stores with vegetables and tropical fruits, and ship home from foreign ports oil and whalebone taken on the outward cruise to enable them to carry more on the return voyage. Larger ships were built and coppered. New Bedford soon took the lead, outstripping Nantucket both in number of vessels and tonnage. The shoal waters about the harbor entrance at Nantucket made it nearly impossible for ships of heavy tonnage to enter without lightering cargo, if deeply

---

laden, and floating pontoons called "camels" were built to overcome this inconvenience. Doubtless these handicaps were at least partially responsible for the fact that most of the large type whaleships built after this period hailed from mainland ports.

The War of 1812 and the British practice of impressing crews of American ships created serious damage to the whaling industry, and many whalers fell prey to British privateers before they had heard of the war. This wholesale destruction by the British proved their undoing, however, for upon learning they were seizing American whaleships in the South Pacific, the U.S. frigate *Essex* recaptured the prizes and destroyed whaleships of the enemy. The *Essex* practically swept British whaleships from the seas, and their Pacific fishery never recovered.

After the treaty was signed in 1814 the impressment ceased, and whaling began to pick up lost ground. The three decades following 1820 were the golden age of American whalemen. Voyages were carried to greater extremes and became correspondingly more profitable. Three- and four-year voyages were the rule, and even longer in many instances.

New grounds were located where whales seemed to exist in unlimited number, and in 1835 the ship *Ganges* of Nantucket opened the northwest coast right whale fishery. Pushing farther into the frozen north, the ships *Hercules* and *Janus* of New Bedford captured the first bowhead whales off the coast of Kamchatka in 1843, and five years later the Sag Harbor bark *Superior* sailed through Bering Strait to attack the bowheads in the Arctic.

The fishery reached its highest development and prosperity about 1857, the New Bedford fleet numbering 329 whaleships at that time. But with the Civil War came new disasters that doomed the fishery.

The Confederate cruiser *Shenandoah* caught the Arctic whaling fleet unawares in 1865, captured and burned twenty-five ships—mostly large ones—and bonded four others. Rebel cruisers destroyed fifty whaleships, of which twenty-eight were owned in New Bedford. Many whalers were sold and others transferred to the merchant service. The United States government purchased forty to furnish the larger portion of the so-called "Stone fleet," sunk off Savannah and Charleston harbors to prevent entrance of blockade runners, and this shipping was seldom replaced save by building an occasional vessel.

Following, but six years later, in September 1871, thirty-three whaleships were abandoned in the Arctic, hopelessly crushed in the ice; in 1876 twelve more were lost in a similar manner. Again, in August 1888, five whaleships were lost, this time by a terrific gale off Point Barrow in the Arctic Ocean. Scarcely a season went by without several such disasters, although these were the most notable. Many a staunch ship left her bones to bleach on some distant shore, while the perilous ice fields, sunken coral reefs and tropical hurricanes claimed occasional victims from the steadily diminishing fleet.

Although the fishery made a feeble effort to regain its prestige, the discovery of mineral oil and the relative cheapness of petroleum further reduced the demand for sperm and whale oil to such a degree that there was no longer any profit in conducting that part of the industry, and ships were constantly withdrawn from service and dismantled in port upon completion of their voyages. About 1880, most of the larger vessels, fitted with steam as auxiliary power, engaged in the Arctic fishery where the heavy catches of whalebone were still a source of profit. The steam whalers, as they were called, were handier to navigate among the ice pack than the exclusively sail-propelled craft, and for several years proved very successful. They made voyages during the season when the ice pack separated, sometimes wintering in the Arctic, but otherwise returning to San Francisco, where they refitted.

The last sailing whaleship abandoned the Arctic fishery years ago, and one by one the small fleet of steam whalers disappeared. Some were lost battling the treacherous ice floes that hemmed them in on all sides; others limped slowly back to San Francisco and were condemned as unfit for further service. The surviving few ships hailing from New Bedford, that for twenty years or more had been in the Arctic fishery, turned their prows homeward, around the Horn, and after a brief pause in port were again returned to sperm whaling in the Atlantic.

The most famous of the remaining fleet was the splendid old whaleship *Charles W. Morgan,* built at New Bedford in 1841, and named after one of the most successful and representative whaling merchants of his time. This grand old ship, ninety-seven years old and still in existence today as these lines are written, has a most remarkable record.

During the eighty years the *Morgan* was in active service as a whaler she made thirty-seven voyages, cruising in the Arctic and Antarctic, the Atlantic and Pacific, Japan and Okhotsk Seas, and the Indian Ocean. Her trail covered every known sea where whales were found, and her log books reveal that she covered more miles and took more whales than any other whaleship.

The log books also show the *Morgan* had her share of the trials and tribulations apt to occur to any vessel engaged in the whale fishery. She had been ashore, had a few mutinies at sea, and was set on fire once by the crew. She weathered two hurricanes and was struck by lightning three times. A blazing passenger steamer drifted across New Bedford harbor while the *Morgan* was in port and sank alongside, a flaming torch; but the *Morgan* escaped with no further damage than blistered paint on a few of her scorched oaken planks.

On her final whaling voyage, September 9, 1920, the *Charles W. Morgan* sailed from New Bedford, returning to port the following year, May 28, 1921, with a catch of seven hundred barrels of sperm oil.

Originally rigged as a ship, the *Morgan* was known as a single topsail full-rigged whaleship until 1876, when she was altered into a bark rig with double topsails. During 1925 she was again rigged as a ship and placed in a sand berth at South Dartmouth, Massachusetts. In 1941 she was moved to the Marine Historical

Association at Mystic, Connecticut, where she is now permanently berthed. Everything practical has been done to preserve this wonderful old whaleship.

While the *Morgan* remains an outstanding example of her type, it was by no means uncommon for whaleships to reach a ripe old age during service: in fact the bark *Rousseau* was in commission eighty-seven years, and the ship *Maria* was broken up in 1872 after being in service ninety years. Bark *Canton* was lost in her seventy-sixth year off the Azores, and when fitting for that voyage on the railway her keel was found to be straight as a gunbarrel.

No wonder they reached such a ripe old age, for better ships were never built. Live oak and copper fastened. Before leaving port they were repaired from keel to truck to withstand the terrific strains to which a whaleship was subjected. Not only did they have to contend with severe storms and hurricanes at sea, with no possible hope for shelter, as did other deep-water ships, but there were the unusual strains of cutting-in huge whales alongside, wrenching at their fluke chains in plunging seas. Master shipwrights, and riggers who wove the intricate maze of hemp and manila from deadeye to to'gallant truck, all took pride in the calling they knew so well, and did the best they knew.

The American whale fishery had passed into history. The *Morgan* alone remains, a monument to the industry and the American whalemen that brought its fame.

LENGTH: 1340 WORDS

Name _______________ Class _______________ Date _______________

30 The Whale Fishery

SCORING: Reading time: _____	Rate from chart: _____ W.P.M.	
RETENTION	number right ____ × 2 equals ____	points
MAIN POINT	number right ____ × 4 equals ____	points
AUTHOR'S ATTITUDE	number right ____ × 3 equals ____	points
CONCLUSION	number right ____ × 3 equals ____	points
COMPLETION	number right ____ × 4 equals ____	points
VOCABULARY	number right ____ × 2 equals ____	points
	(Total points: 100) **Total** ____	points

RETENTION Based on the passage, which of the following statements is True (T), False (F), or Not answerable (N)?

1. ____ Teredo worms never got the Charles W. Morgan.
2. ____ The Morgan remains the only surviving whale fishery.
3. ____ The Morgan can be seen in its sand berth in Nantucket.
4. ____ The Morgan last sailed as a whale fishery in 1921.
5. ____ Another whale fishery, the Rousseau, sailed for eighty-seven years.
6. ____ Most whaling ships averaged thirty-seven years in service.
7. ____ Petroleum supplanted sperm oil.
8. ____ The Morgan was built with oak planks.
9. ____ The Confederacy had a navy, but with no cruisers.
10. ____ The Ganges was a Confederate sloop.
11. ____ Bowheads were found in the Arctic.
12. ____ Whale fisheries averaged more than 2000 tons in weight.
13. ____ There were no catchable whales in the Atlantic.
14. ____ The Essex had a serious effect on British whaling industries.
15. ____ Ships of heavy tonnage were not built in Nantucket.
16. ____ The War of 1812 was fought over whaling rights.
17. ____ The Confederacy destroyed at least fifty Union whaling ships.

18. ____ Ice claimed at least forty-five whaling ships after the Civil War.

19. ____ There were as many as three hundred whaling ships in service at one time.

20. ____ The highest period of the fisheries' development was the 1890's.

MAIN POINT Which of the following statements best represents the main point of the passage? ____

1. Yankee ingenuity was invented in part by the whaling imagination.
2. Industries like whaling represent a glorious aspect of our history.
3. Industry tends to exploit its resources right up to exhaustion.
4. Regional industries can cause regional tension, even in America.
5. Whaling reveals America's capacity for internationalism.

AUTHOR'S ATTITUDE Which of the following statements best describes the author's attitude? ____

1. The whales had a terrible disadvantage against the whale fisheries.
2. The Nantucketers should have urged preservation of the whales forever.
3. The whaling men are deserving of our sympathies.
4. Whalers overreached themselves when they attempted the Arctic whales.
5. Government support would have been beneficial to whaling.

CONCLUSION Which of the following statements is the best conclusion that can be drawn from the passage? ____

1. If whalers had been moderate, Nantucket would be a major city today.
2. Industry should be aware of the possibilities of obsolescence.
3. Excitement and adventure are not the best bases for major industry.
4. New England destroyed itself in its anxiety to fish out whale fields.
5. Intervention by foreign governments can destroy domestic industry.

COMPLETION Choose the best answer for each question:

1. ____ Mystic, Connecticut, contains: (a) the Marine Historical Association. (b) simulated whaling rides. (c) the log books of all the whalers. (d) the remains of more than seventy-two whales.

2. ____ Log books show that the Charles W. Morgan: (a) never fought a battle. (b) caught more whales than any other whaler. (c) berthed into Savannah and Charleston during the Civil War. (d) evaded capture in two wars.

3. ____ The Charles W. Morgan was built in: (a) 1880. (b) San Francisco. (c) both Nantucket and Savannah. (d) New Bedford.

4. ____ The average whaling voyage lasted: (a) eighteen months. (b) until the catch was made. (c) almost four years. (d) upward of seven full years.

5. ____ Whaling was made unprofitable by the development of petroleum and the discovery of: (a) steam power. (b) mineral oil. (c) margarine. (d) new applications for electricity and hydroelectric power.

VOCABULARY Choose the word or phrase from Column B that best defines the vocabulary entry in Column A:

Column A	*Column B*
1. ____ auxiliary	a. seize
2. ____ dismantled	b. difficulties
3. ____ tribulations	c. dominated; controlled
4. ____ staunch	d. weak
5. ____ unwieldy	e. outmoding
6. ____ accumulate	f. firm
7. ____ replenish	g. complication
8. ____ laden	h. permit
9. ____ impress	i. perquisites
10. ____ obsolescence	j. heap up
11. ____ enable	k. stock anew
12. ____ contend	l. assert
13. ____ subjected	m. clumsy
14. ____ maze	n. weighted down
15. ____ feeble	o. taken apart
	p. supplant; take over
	q. supplemental
	r. berate

31

Who Invented Scalping?

James Axtell

Scalping is commonly associated with American Indians. Recently, however, some theories have been developed suggesting that Europeans introduced this warlike behavior as they conquered the New World. James Axtell examines the evidence surrounding the practice and reaches a conclusion. In the process, he offers considerable information about the relations among Indians and their contacts with Europeans.

Americans have always assumed that scalping and Indians were synonymous. Cutting the crown of hair from a fallen adversary has traditionally been viewed as an ancient Indian custom, performed to obtain tangible proof of the warrior's valor. But in recent years many voices—Indian and white—have seriously questioned whether the Indians did in fact invent scalping. The latest suggestion is that the white colonists, in establishing bounties for enemy hair, introduced scalping to Indian allies innocent of the practice.

This theory presupposes two facts: one, that the white colonists who settled America in the seventeenth century knew how to scalp before they left Europe; and two, that the Indians did not know how to scalp before the white men arrived. But are these facts? And if they are not, who *did* invent scalping in America?

Total silence from both participants and historians casts doubt on the first proposition. For no one has ever insinuated, much less proved, that the European armies who fought so ruthlessly the Crusades, the Hundred Years' War, and the Wars of Religion ever scalped their victims. Even when they were combating a

WHO INVENTED SCALPING? From *American Heritage,* April 1977. © 1977 by American Heritage Publishing Co., Inc. Reprinted by permission of the publisher.

European form of "savagery" in Ireland, Queen Elizabeth's forces were never scalped or ever took scalps. The grim, gray visages of severed heads lining the path to a commander's tent were more terrible than impersonal shocks of hair and skin.

Nor does the second proposition fare much better. For there is abundant evidence from various sources that the Indians practiced scalping long before the white man arrived and that they continued to do so without the incentive of colonial cash.

The first and most familiar source of evidence is the written descriptions of the earliest European observers, who presumably saw the Indian cultures of the eastern seaboard in something like an aboriginal condition. When Jacques Cartier sailed down the St. Lawrence to what is now Quebec City in 1535, he met the Stadaconans, who showed him "the scalps of five Indians, stretched on hoops like parchment." His host, Donnacona, told him they were from "Toudamans from the south, who waged war continually against his people."

Twenty-nine years later, another Frenchman, artist Jacques le Moyne, witnessed the Timucuans' practice of scalping on the St. Johns River in Florida:

> They carried slips of reeds, sharper than any steel blade . . . they cut the skin of the head down to the bone from front to back and all the way around and pulled it off while the hair, more than a foot and a half long, was still attached to it. When they had done this, they dug a hole in the ground and made a fire, kindling it with a piece of smoldering ember. . . . Over the fire they dried the scalps until they looked like parchment. . . . They hung the bones and the scalps at the ends of their spears, carrying them home in triumph.

When they arrived at their village, they held a victory ceremony in which the legs, arms, and scalps of the vanquished were attached to poles with "great solemnities."

The French were not alone in witnessing the Indian custom of scalping. When the English brazenly set themselves down amid the powerful Powhatan Confederacy in Virginia, the Indians used an old tactic to try to quash their audacity. In 1608 Powhatan launched a surprise attack on a village of "neare neighbours and subjects," killing twenty-four men. When the victors retired from the scene of battle, they brought away "the long haire of the one side of their heades [the other being shaved] with the skinne cased off with shels or reeds." The prisoners and scalps were then presented to the chief, who hung "the lockes of haire with their skinnes" on a line between two trees. "And thus," wrote Captain John Smith, "he made ostentation . . . , shewing them to the English men that then came unto him, at his appointment."

The first Dutchmen to penetrate the Iroquois country of upstate New York also found evidence of native scalping. When the surgeon of Fort Orange (Albany) journeyed into Mohawk and Oneida territory in the winter of 1634–35, he saw atop a gate of the old Oneida castle on Oriskany Creek "three wooden images carved like men, and with them . . . three scalps fluttering in the wind." On a smaller gate at the east end of the castle a scalp was also hanging, no doubt to impress white visitors as well as hostile neighbors.

The list of Europeans who upon first meeting the eastern Indians found scalping prevalent is a long one. The first characteristic their descriptions share is an expression of surprise at the discovery of such a novel custom. The nearly universal highlighting of the custom in early accounts, the search for meaningful comparisons (such as parchment), the detailed anatomical descriptions of the act itself, and the total absence of any suggestion of white familiarity with the practice all suggest that their surprise was not disingenuous.

The second theme of these descriptions is that scalping was surrounded by a number of rituals and customs that could hardly have been borrowed from the freebooting European traders and fishermen who may have preceded the earliest authors. The elaborate preparation of the scalps by drying, stretching on hoops, painting, and decorating; scalp yells when a scalp was taken and later when it was borne home on raised spears or poles; occasional nude female custodianship of the prizes; scalp dances and body decorations; scalps as nonremunerative trophies of war to be publicly displayed on canoes, cabins, and palisades; and the substitution of a scalp for a living captive to be adopted in the place of a deceased member of the family—all these appear too ritualized and too widespread throughout eastern America to have been recent introductions by Europeans.

The final characteristic of the early accounts is an obvious search for words to describe scalping to a European audience. The older English word *scalp* did not acquire its distinctly American meaning until 1675 when King Philip's War brought the object renewed prominence in New England. Until then, the best expressions were compounds such as "hair-scalp" and "head-skin," phrases such as "the skin and hair of the scalp of the head," or the simple but ambiguous word "head." Likewise, the only meaning of the verb *to scalp* meant "to carve, engrave, scrape, or scratch." Consequently, English writers were forced to use "skin," "flay," or "excoriate" until 1676 when the American meaning became popular. French, Dutch, German, and Swedish speakers were also forced to resort to circumlocutions until they borrowed the English words in the eighteenth century.

On the other hand, the languages of the eastern Indians contained many words to describe the scalp, the act of scalping, and the victim of scalping. A Catholic priest among the Hurons in 1623 learned that an *onontsira* was a war trophy consisting of "the skin of the head with its hair." The five languages of the Iroquois were especially rich in words to describe the act that has earned them, however unjustly, an enduring reputation for inhuman ferocity. To the Mohawks and Oneidas, the scalp was *onnonra;* the act of taking it, *kannonrackwan*. Their western brothers at Onondaga spoke of *hononksera,* a variation of the Huron word. And although they were recorded after initial contact with the Europeans, the vocabularies of the other Iroquois nations and of the Delaware, Algonquin, Malecite, Micmac, and Montagnais all contained words for scalp, scalping, and the scalped that are closely related to the native words for hair, head, skull, and skin. That these words were obviously not borrowed from European languages lends further support to the notion that they were native to America and deeply rooted in Indian life.

Understandably, words have done the most to fix the image of Indian scalping on the historical record, but paintings and drawings reinforce that image. The single most important picture in this regard is Théodore de Bry's engraving of Le Moyne's drawing of "How Ourina's Men Treated the Enemy Dead." Based on Le Moyne's observations in 1564–65, the 1591 engraving was the first pictorial representation of Indian scalping, one faithful to Le Moyne's verbal description and to subsequent accounts from other regions of eastern America. The details—sharp reeds to extract the scalp, drying the green skin over a fire, displaying the trophies on long poles, and later celebrating the victory with established rituals by the sorcerer—lend authenticity to De Bry's rendering and support to the argument for the Indian invention of scalping.

Drawings reveal yet another piece of evidence damaging to the new theory of scalping, namely scalp locks. A small braid of hair on the crown, often decorated with paint or jewelry, the scalp lock was worn widely in both eastern and western America. Contrary to the notion of scalping as a recent and mercenary introduction, the scalp lock originally possessed ancient religious meaning in most tribes, symbolizing the warrior's life-force. For anyone to touch it even lightly was regarded as a grave insult. If the white man had taught the Indians to scalp one another for money, it is highly unlikely that the Indians were also hoodwinked into making it easier for their enemies by growing hairy handles. Something far deeper in native culture and history must account for the practice.

The final and most conclusive evidence of scalping in pre-Columbian America comes from archaeology. Since Indian skulls of the requisite age can be found to show distinct and unambiguous marks made by the scalping knife, the Indians must have known of scalping before the arrival of the white man. A wealth of evidence, particularly from prehistoric sites along the Mississippi and Missouri rivers and in the Southeast, indicates just such a conclusion.

Two kinds of evidence of scalping have been unearthed by archaeologists armed with trowels and carbon-14 dating. The first is cuts or scratches on the skulls of victims who had been previously killed. These cuts are of course subject to various interpretations, given the existence of post-mortem ritual mutilations in many Indian cultures. The trophy skulls found in several Hopewellian burial mounds in Ohio, for example, frequently exhibit superficial cuts, apparently made by flint knives in the process of removing the flesh.

But the second kind of evidence is more conclusive. In a number of prehistoric sites, circular lesions have been found on the skulls of victims who survived scalping long enough to allow the bone tissue to regenerate partially, leaving a telltale scar. Contrary to popular belief, scalping itself was not a fatal operation, and American history is full of survivors. Scalping is the only possible explanation for these lesions, which appear exactly where eyewitness descriptions and drawings indicate the scalp was traditionally cut.

In the light of such evidence, it is clear that Indians, not white men, introduced scalping to the New World. At the same time, it cannot be denied that the colonists encouraged the spread of scalping to many tribes unfamiliar with the practice by posting scalp bounties. Nor can it be forgotten that Americans of every stripe—from frontiersmen to ministers—were tainted by participating in the bloody market for human hair. Yet in the end, the American stereotype of scalping must stand as historical fact, whether we are comfortable with it or not.

LENGTH: 1712 WORDS

Name Class Date

31 Who Invented Scalping?

SCORING: Reading time: _____ Rate from chart: _____ W.P.M.		
RETENTION	number right _____ × 2 equals _____ points	
MAIN POINT	number right _____ × 4 equals _____ points	
AUTHOR'S ATTITUDE	number right _____ × 3 equals _____ points	
CONCLUSION	number right _____ × 3 equals _____ points	
COMPLETION	number right _____ × 4 equals _____ points	
VOCABULARY	number right _____ × 2 equals _____ points	
	(Total points: 100) **Total** _____ points	

RETENTION Based on the passage, which of the following statements is True (T), False (F), or Not answerable (N)?

1. _____ Archaeology provides the final and conclusive evidence of scalping.
2. _____ There are no eyewitness accounts of scalping.
3. _____ Americans have assumed scalping and Indians are synonymous.
4. _____ The first illustrations of scalping date from the sixteenth century.
5. _____ Scalping leaves circular lesions on the skull.
6. _____ The Hopewellian burial mounds are in Ohio.
7. _____ Axtell is himself part Indian.
8. _____ Some scalping victims survive the experience.
9. _____ The European colonists offered cash for Indian scalps.
10. _____ Indians grew scalp locks to make scalping more efficient.
11. _____ Touching scalp locks was quite common, but only for women.
12. _____ Queen Elizabeth's forces fought in Ireland.
13. _____ Cartier sailed the St. Lawrence to Quebec.
14. _____ Early European settlers are curiously silent about scalping.
15. _____ King Philip's Wars were in Canada.
16. _____ Reeds can be used as knives.
17. _____ The Iroquois invented the scalpel.

18. ____ Scalping locks did not possess religious meaning.

19. ____ The upstate New York Iroquois practiced scalping when the Dutch arrived.

20. ____ The Powhatan Confederacy was a Dutch settlement in New Jersey.

MAIN POINT Which of the following statements best represents the main point of the passage? ____

1. More than one kind of evidence is necessary to establish a theory.
2. The Indians had become well organized by the time the English arrived.
3. Aboriginal practices can be strongly influenced by invaders.
4. Scalping was something for which no pre-existent tradition had a word.
5. Research into the ways of Indian life is essential for American history.

AUTHOR'S ATTITUDE Which of the following statements best describes the author's attitude? ____

1. Indians are really just like the Europeans.
2. Those who scalp their enemies are to be condemned.
3. The Indians were ruthless, but the Europeans were much worse.
4. The Europeans were ruthless, but the Indians were much worse.
5. Scalping is brutal, but it is a fact of history.

CONCLUSION Which of the following statements is the best conclusion that can be drawn from the passage? ____

1. Anthropology unites mankind across time and across cultures.
2. Europeans taught the Indians to take scalps for cash bounties.
3. The Indians took scalps long before any Europeans came to America.
4. There is not enough conclusive evidence to decide who invented scalping.
5. Scalping was probably not really "invented" by anyone.

COMPLETION Choose the best answer for each question:

1. ____ When a scalp was taken, Indians had a ritual: (a) poem spoken. (b) yell. (c) spear contest. (d) haircut.

2. ____ This article was written in part because people thought: (a) nothing was known about scalping. (b) John Smith had scalped Massasoit after he ceased to be useful. (c) Europeans invented scalping. (d) Indians had no scalpels.

3. ____ Early Europeans saw that not only did Indians display scalps, but also: (a) occasional nude females. (b) bones and body parts. (c) their prowess. (d) their disingenuousness.

4. ____ In 1608 Powhatan: (a) had already been scalped. (b) set sail for England with John Smith. (c) retreated further inland. (d) suddenly attacked the English.

5. ____ Apparently, before they left Europe, colonial settlers did not: (a) like the Indians. (b) have the sense to protect themselves well. (c) know how to take a scalp. (d) prepare carefully for the extreme weather conditions.

VOCABULARY Choose the word or phrase from Column B that best defines the vocabulary entry in Column A:

Column A	*Column B*
1. ____ visage	a. daring
2. ____ valor	b. succeed
3. ____ adversary	c. put a stop to
4. ____ aboriginal	d. prize
5. ____ fare well	e. face
6. ____ prevalent	f. widespread
7. ____ disingenuous	g. spoiled; corrupted
8. ____ audacity	h. primitive
9. ____ quash	i. courage
10. ____ sorceror	j. knave
11. ____ requisite	k. goodbye
12. ____ tainted	l. wounds; cuts
13. ____ lesions	m. enemy
14. ____ post-mortem	n. shaman; medicine man

15. ____ bounty

o. needed

p. examination after death

q. shrewd; experienced

r. not an imitation

32

The Trojan Horse

Arthur Koestler

Japan is one of the world's most resourceful and ingenious nations. It was cloistered from foreign visitors and influences for over two hundred years. When the nation was suddenly "opened" to foreigners in 1868, Japan made a commitment to "catch up" with the West. Its success is legendary. But in this passage Arthur Koestler also explores the deeper structures and problems beneath the changes.

This unique quality of contemporary Japan derives from the uniqueness of Japanese history. No nation has suffered such earthquakes both in the literal and the figurative sense as the Japanese have in the course of the last century. When, after two hundred and fifty years of hermetic isolation and mental inbreeding, the Meiji Restoration of 1868 suddenly threw the islands open to the world, the results were as explosive as if the windows of a pressurized cabin had been broken. Nothing similar had in fact happened to any race in recorded history. Within a single generation, the pent-up energies of the nation exploded in a frantic effort to catch up with everything that the West had accomplished in half a millennium. They succeeded to a spectacular degree; at the beginning of the twentieth century, Japan had become one of the leading military and industrial powers of the world.

By the force of circumstances, this result could only be achieved through learning-by-imitation. The Industrial Revolution of the eighteenth and nineteenth centuries in the West had grown organically out of the Scientific Revolution of the seventeenth century, whose roots reach back to the revival of Greek learning between the twelfth and sixteenth centuries. The Japanese could not be expected to duplicate the whole process, to produce their own Roger Bacons, Isaac Newtons and James Watts'. They had to proceed in reverse; starting with the mechanical copying of the end-products of the applied sciences, they had to work their way back to the theoretical foundations—from Edison to Galileo.

The starting point of this evolution in reverse gear is a bronze howitzer which Commodore Perry, after forcing his entry into Tokyo Bay, had presented as a gift to the Japanese authorities. A year or two later, they fired a salute to the American fleet from a battery of 'handsome bronze howitzers, exactly copied in every respect from the one Commodore Perry gave them; every appointment about the gun, down to the smallest particular, was exactly copied: percussion locks, drag ropes, powder or cartridge holder and all'. They had to begin by copying mechanically, since they were not yet able to understand the exact purpose of the various parts of the gun; their eagerness to copy was not due to any inherent imitative tendency in the Japanese character, but to the hunger for knowledge of a people just emerging from two hundred and fifty years of solitary confinement.

Before that long period of segregation imposed by the Tokugawa Shogunate, whatever the Japanese imported from abroad—Chinese philosophy and art, Indian Yoga, Mongolian cooking—they transformed and adapted to their special needs and tastes, until only a remote resemblance to the original remained. They even created a specific Japanese way of using, or abusing, the English language. But the spectacular success of that first experiment in imitating the West was a dangerous precedent. It created a breach in their intellectual and spiritual defences, in their loyalty to a great and singular tradition. Western science and technology acted as a Trojan Horse; out of its belly poured alien philosophies, fashions, political concepts, attitudes to life. They could not be copied like Perry's bronze howitzers, and they did not blend with the traditional culture.

Perhaps Japan would have been able either to assimilate, or to discard these alien imports, had it not suffered a series of further shocks, which shattered its social structure. The Meiji Restoration of 1868, which opened up the country to the world, had started as a *coup d'état* with exactly the opposite programme; its slogans had been: 'Honour the Emperor—expel the Barbarians'. Yet within a few years, the Barbarian influence was victorious all along the line, and the country had caught the 'European fever'. It was one of the symptoms brought on by the Government's radical reforms, which were like a surgical operation on the body social. Within a span of five years, the feudal system had ceased to exist. The legal inequality between the four traditional castes—warriors, peasants, artisans and merchants—was abolished. The daimyos, great feudal lords, lost their fiefs and privileges; the samurai lost their two swords, were paid off with a pension, and replaced by a people's army. Nobody was allowed to wear the dress and insignia of his former caste, and the eta—the sweepers, scavengers and tanners—

ceased to be untouchables. A nation-wide network of schools was set up; a minimum of six years of schooling became compulsory for all boys and girls in the land, and generous provisions were made for Secondary schools and Universities. A Code of Laws was drawn up, following partly the French, partly the English example; for that purpose a new word had to be coined, for 'civic rights', which previously had not existed in the Japanese language. To put it briefly: 'Japan, just emerging from mediaevalism in the last half of the nineteenth century and as weak then as Siam is today, produced leaders able to conceive and carry out one of the most statesmanlike and successful jobs ever attempted in any nation.'

But—and this is a decisive but—these pressure-cooker reforms failed to create a socially and ideologically stable society. The upheavals continued. A Japanese who lived for four score years, from 1865 to 1945, would have witnessed developments which, in European history, occupy several centuries: Absolute Monarchy, Constitutional Monarchy, Liberalism, Imperialist Expansion, Military Dictatorship, Totalitarian Fascism, Foreign Occupation. He would also have witnessed the disestablishment of Buddhism, the proclamation of Shinto as the State Religion, and the subsequent disestablishment of Shinto—changes which struck at the very root of ethical beliefs. Furthermore, he would have watched a remarkable transformation in the physique of his younger compatriots, from the average height of five feet one inch of conscripts at the turn of the century to five feet two inches in 1914 and five feet four inches in 1952—an increase of three inches in fifty years.*

As if to dramatize these developments, Nature contributed tremors and flames. There were disastrous earthquakes in 1892 and 1894, the Imperial Palace burnt down in 1873, most of the Capital was destroyed by the Great Earthquake and Fire of 1923, which claimed 150,000 victims. The 700,000 houses which had gone up in flames were re-built in a hurry—and destroyed again twenty years later, in 1945. That was the year in which the two man-made suns descended on Hiroshima and Nagasaki—but the two conventional fire-raids on Tokyo, earlier in the same year, had claimed another 100,000 victims, and reduced the Capital to charred rubble, for the second time within a generation.

In the course of the next five years, the first conquering invader whom the Japanese had known in history, imposed a revolution which transformed the nation even more radically than the Meiji reform. That had come from within; the new régime was enforced by the Occupation Authority. The State religion was abolished, the school textbooks of history and geography were burnt, the Prime Minister was hanged. The Emperor was no longer a god, the Army and Navy no longer existed. Forty per cent of the total area under cultivation was confiscated from the absentee

Encyclopædia Britannica 12/900. The average stature of women is nearly two inches less, but the difference is rapidly decreasing. The change in physique is attributed to dietary reasons, medical care, sports, etc. The only comparable phenomenon was the increase in average height in the offspring of Eastern European immigrants to the United States. But the Japanese keep getting taller at home.

landlords and distributed among the tenants; a new constitution established Western-style Parliamentary rule; women were given the vote and legal status equal to men; compulsory education was extended to nine years, and the number of universities mushroomed from forty-odd to nearly five hundred.

The Japanese, dazed by fire and brimstone, by the wholesale collapse of their houses, leaders, gods and values, did not resist. Quite the contrary. Their attitude varied from enthusiastic collaboration with the foreign reformer—and this was the attitude of the overwhelming majority—to passive and polite acquiescence. If a small minority was cynically amused, they did not show it. The undefeated armies overseas, whose standing orders had been death before surrender, peacefully yielded up their arms at the Emperor's radioed order; there was no fighting on the beaches and no fighting in the streets, and no attempt to 'repel the Barbarian invader with bamboo spears'. The most ferociously warlike foe turned overnight into the most peaceful and affable population which an occupation army ever had to deal with.

The key to this almost unbelievable event is contained in a single syllable: chu—the absolute and unquestionable duty to obey the Emperor's command. The Emperor had spoken, and the war was over. That some were relieved and others would have preferred death; that they were disillusioned with their political leaders and that their towns were in shambles, was beside the point. Nor did it matter much whether a person believed that the Emperor was really a god and a descendant of the Sun, or whether he regarded these as symbolic statements. Chu was much older than State Shinto; it meant unconditional loyalty to the head of the social hierarchy, whether he was called Emperor or Shogun, whether of divine origin or not. Chu was the First Commandment of Japanese ethics, ko, the loyalty due to parents and ancestors, was the Second; all other rules of conduct came lower down in the list. The dramatic change which, on 14 August 1945, transformed the nation overnight from a tiger into a lamb was thus, paradoxically, a proof of its basically unchanged character; it showed that, in spite of revolutions and reforms, the traditional code of feudal ethics had never lost its hold; that the ancient pattern had survived underneath the imported, prefabricated superstructure.

LENGTH: 1680 WORDS

Name Class Date

32 The Trojan Horse

SCORING: Reading time: ____ Rate from chart: ____ W.P.M.		
RETENTION	number right ____ × 2 equals ____ points	
MAIN POINT	number right ____ × 4 equals ____ points	
AUTHOR'S ATTITUDE	number right ____ × 3 equals ____ points	
CONCLUSION	number right ____ × 3 equals ____ points	
COMPLETION	number right ____ × 4 equals ____ points	
VOCABULARY	number right ____ × 2 equals ____ points	
	(Total points: 100) **Total** ____ points	

RETENTION Based on the passage, which of the following statements is True (T), False (F), or Not answerable (N)?

1. ____ The Meiji Restoration was a reform movement.
2. ____ Admiral Perry saw the trade advantages in opening Japan.
3. ____ Conventional bombing of Tokyo killed 100,000 people.
4. ____ The Invasion of Japan cost many American lives.
5. ____ The Occupation of Japan caused much hostility against U.S. citizens.
6. ____ Japanese live for four score years.
7. ____ There were originally four traditional castes in Japan.
8. ____ Apparently, the eta—former untouchables—were not considered a caste.
9. ____ Feudalism had been part of Japanese traditional patterns.
10. ____ Japanese women were given the vote during U.S. Occupation.
11. ____ There were disastrous earthquakes in the 1890's.
12. ____ The Japanese are now healthier, but not taller, than fifty years ago.
13. ____ Despite earthquakes and fires, the Imperial Palace was never damaged.
14. ____ Shintoism was a Japanese official religion.
15. ____ Japan was never Fascistic.
16. ____ Until 1945 only six years of education were required in Japan.

17. ____ Today there are close to 500 universities in Japan.

18. ____ Imitation helped the Japanese develop a Western economy.

19. ____ The Tokugawa Shogunate welcomed foreigners to Japan.

20. ____ Sudden governmental take-overs are unknown in Japan.

MAIN POINT Which of the following statements best represents the main point of the passage? ____

1. A culture that can change with the times can grow with the times.
2. In 1850 Perry foretold the future of Japan's growth.
3. Japan is amazing for having survived cultural, military, and natural catastrophes.
4. The Western world could not have been held accountable for the affection Japan developed for its ways.
5. Any nation cut off from the rest of the world would have reacted as Japan did.

AUTHOR'S ATTITUDE Which of the following statements best describes the author's attitude? ____

1. The West took unfair advantage of an innocent people.
2. The cost of Japan's capacity to change was simply too great to justify it.
3. Cultural change is one of the most desirable qualities of any nation.
4. Nations which remain stable over the generations are the best to live in.
5. New concepts are more difficult to absorb than new industries or techniques.

CONCLUSION Which of the following statements is the best conclusion that can be drawn from the passage? ____

1. Despite superficial changes in society, the Japanese held to one firm idea, which in turn held the culture together.
2. No one can fully understand the culture of another people.
3. We must know about Japan so as to protect ourselves from similar "invasion," perhaps from outer space.
4. The more things change, the more they remain the same.
5. One should never look a gift horse, particularly a Trojan Horse, in the mouth.

COMPLETION Choose the best answer for each question.

1. ____ The Trojan Horse Koestler refers to is: (a) religion. (b) political change. (c) universal education. (d) Western science.

2. ____ The reforms of the nineteenth century failed to produce: (a) a sense of security. (b) ideological stability. (c) changes of any sort. (d) new approaches to science and technology.

3. ____ Shintoism supplanted: (a) Feudalism. (b) Liberalism. (c) Buddhism. (d) Absolutism.

4. ____ Japanese history is described as: (a) millennial. (b) unique. (c) a Shogun heritage. (d) unstable and precarious.

5. ____ Because Japanese technology began by imitation, it had to wait for the development of: (a) Western acceptance of new ideas. (b) a society that could consume its own products. (c) original products. (d) solid theoretical foundations.

VOCABULARY Choose the word or phrase from Column B that best defines the vocabulary entry in Column A:

	Column A		*Column B*
1. ____	confiscated	a.	basic; built-in
2. ____	hermetic isolation	b.	excited; wild
3. ____	mental inbreeding	c.	adopt; absorb
4. ____	radical reforms	d.	hazardous example
5. ____	ethical beliefs	e.	foreign ideologies
6. ____	assimilate	f.	easy-going
7. ____	inherent	g.	far-reaching changes
8. ____	dangerous precedent	h.	moral concepts
9. ____	frantic	i.	submitting quietly
10. ____	traditional castes	j.	completely cut off
11. ____	alien imports	k.	seized
12. ____	Chu	l.	obedience of one's parents
13. ____	polite acquiescence	m.	limited thinking

14. ____ affable

15. ____ Ko

n. established classes

o. insanity

p. threatened

q. well-mannered sneering

r. obedience to the Emperor

33

A Third Force Arises in Psychology

James Moriarty

Psychology, although it was discussed by Aristotle and other ancient philosophers, is quite young as a science. Freud created psychoanalysis, which changed the world's view regarding the mind and its workings. Behaviorism, associated with experimental psychology, increased the scientific detachment of the disciple. Now a third movement, humanistic psychology, has risen to mediate between them.

Two major movements in psychology in this century have been psychoanalysis and behaviorism. The former, building on the insights and clinical experience of Freud, is based on a search for childhood experience and unconscious motivation as roots of behavior. The latter starts with the simple act of response to a stimulus, builds through the conditioning theory of B. F. Skinner to the picture of a man's current behavior as a variation of past learning and exposure to social models.

Another movement has arisen in part as a rejection of behaviorism. In the last two decades it has not only produced research but has also influenced psychotherapy, education and even business management techniques. This third force, as it was termed by the recently deceased Dr. Abraham Maslow, is grouped under the rubric of humanistic psychology.

The movement has also achieved some formal status as a separate discipline. The American Association for Humanistic Psychology, founded in 1962, holds its national meeting prior to the American Psychological Association convention, and

A THIRD FORCE ARISES IN PSYCHOLOGY Reprinted with permission from *Science News,* the weekly news magazine of science, September 19, 1970.

in August the first International Conference on Humanistic Psychology was held in Amsterdam.

Although born out of dissatisfaction with the behaviorists' "mechanomorphic view of man," as Dr. James Bugental of the Stanford Research Institute terms it, humanistic psychology on a more positive side has developed in an effort to help a healthy man to realize his full potentials. In this respect is expands the concerns of psychoanalysis. Although some theorists and ego-psychologists, such as Erik Erikson, have based their work on psychoanalytic foundations, most psychoanalysts are concerned more with pathological behavior and its treatment, as befits their medical background. In this process they search for what they consider normal behavior, which often turns out to be statistically average behavior.

This "psychopathology of the normal" is rejected by the humanists. Dr. Bugental, one of the early leaders of the movement, says he would like to see psychology spend less time studying "what man has done," and more time studying "what he might do."

Central to the interest in man's potential is the typical humanist fervor over the uniqueness of man. "Some humanistic psychologists hold a transcendental view of man," says Dr. Bugental. "For them, man is little less than a god. On the more pragmatic end of the spectrum, other humanistic psychologists view man as a very unique animal. Man is to be valued for his uniqueness in the animal kingdom."

The concept of examining man's uniqueness and exploring unknown potentials is employed at the Esalen Institute of Big Sur, Calif., one of the 100 or so so-called "growth centers" that have developed in the last decade. These humanistically oriented centers are interested in developing the potential of normal people who are no more unhealthy than those who experience life as the psychopathology of the average. "Our workshops regularly bring out new states, new ways of feeling and relating," says Michael Murphy, director of Esalen. "In this sense we are part of humanistic psychology as opposed to psychoanalysis or behaviorism."

The growth centers use various processes to explore human potential and expand consciousness. Efforts are made, for example, to increase sensitivity to interpersonal relationships. Psychosomatic techniques are employed to create awareness of visceral senses. And meditation is utilized to explore intrapsychic processes such as altered states of consciousness.

An exercise that is commonly used to make people aware of alternate forms of relating is to place two persons together but not allow them to communicate with words or hands. A highly verbal person is then forced to explore alternate methods of communication and in the process becomes aware of alternate senses.

Encounter group exercises are used to create an atmosphere where people can express raw aggression, or reveal their inner fears and sense of isolation. Participants in the exercises who do not normally experience such phenomena, or commonly suppress such feelings, are invited to explore the atypical feelings. These experiences often give them insights into the lifestyles of other persons. At places such as the Quest Center for Human Growth in Washington, D.C., exercises like these are used to bring about increased emotional intimacy and honest confrontation.

Because of its beliefs and techniques, the humanistic approach differs dramatically from both psychoanalysis and behaviorism in the relations between practitioner and subject.

"The humanistic therapeutic situation is a person-to-person relationship, instead of a transference relationship as in psychoanalysis," says Dr. Charlotte Buhler, one of the founders of the AAHP. The client thus perceives the therapist as another person in a trusting relationship, and not as an emotional figure from the past. Understanding present interpersonal relationships is emphasized, rather than delving into past relationships and analyzing their effects on present relations.

The patient and the therapist together examine values and beliefs in the process of exploring what Dr. Buhler terms "the meaningfulness of life." In contrast to more traditional therapy, the therapist reveals his own values and enters the process whereby the patient develops his values.

On the other hand, the humanistic approach rejects the behaviorist concept of scientific objectivity and an impersonal attitude on the part of the researcher toward his experimental subjects. Dr. Sidney Jourard of the University of Florida at Gainesville believes that the data subjects reveal to this impersonal model of the experimenter are qualitatively different from information that can be gathered in a trusting experimenter-subject relationship. Some exploratory research supports Dr. Jourard's hypothesis.

W. J. Powell Jr., a student of Dr. Jourard, conducted interviews with college students asking them to make themselves as fully known to him as they cared to. He compared the amounts of self-disclosure under three conditions. In one, the interviewer responded to the students' disclosure with authentic disclosures of his own; in another the interviewer responded with expressions of approval and support; in the third the interviewer responded with reflection and restatement of the students' disclosures.

Powell found that approving and supporting did not increase the students' responses at all. The process of reflection and restatement increased disclosure of negative self-statements, such as, "I sometimes have doubts about my abilities." However it did not affect positive, self-enhancing expressions. On the other hand, authentic self-disclosure on the part of the interviewer resulted in significant increases in the subjects' disclosures of both positive and negative references to themselves.

"If the aim of the research is to get the subject to disclose himself, the experimenter should show himself trustworthy," says Dr. Jourard. "If the experimenter is trustworthy, the subject will not be afraid to show himself and will be helped to explore other hidden possibilities."

Dr. Jourard points out that this process converges with the social modeling processes that social learning theorists have been examining. The experimenter or therapist is in effect showing a viable way of exerting one's being. The effect may be: "See, I am not afraid to reveal myself. In the process of throwing off suppression I am exploring new potentialities in myself."

Dr. Jourard has come to define his clients not as patients but as "fellow-seekers." He feels that such an approach can be broadened to humanize teacher-pupil, therapist-patient and experimenter-subject relationships.

LENGTH: 1248 WORDS

Name Class Date

33 A Third Force Arises in Psychology

SCORING: Reading time: _____ Rate from chart: _____ W.P.M.			
RETENTION	number right _____	× 2 equals _____	points
MAIN POINT	number right _____	× 4 equals _____	points
AUTHOR'S ATTITUDE	number right _____	× 3 equals _____	points
CONCLUSION	number right _____	× 3 equals _____	points
COMPLETION	number right _____	× 4 equals _____	points
VOCABULARY	number right _____	× 2 equals _____	points
	(Total points: 100)	**Total** _____	points

RETENTION Based on the passage, which of the following statements is True (T), False (F), or Not answerable (N)?

1. _____ The behaviorist approach stresses scientific procedure.
2. _____ Dr. Charlotte Buhler opposes the humanist psychology group.
3. _____ The humanist psychologist treats subjects as patients.
4. _____ Humanist psychology rejects behaviorist attitudes toward objectivity.
5. _____ In large measure, objectivity was rejected by Freud.
6. _____ Conditioning theory belongs to behaviorist psychology.
7. _____ Humanistic psychology has produced controversy, but no research.
8. _____ Humanistic psychology has not yet achieved status as a formal discipline.
9. _____ Freud had clinical experience in psychology.
10. _____ Amsterdam saw the first international conference of humanist psychology.
11. _____ Humanist psychology helps the ill, but is not useful for the healthy.
12. _____ The behaviorist regularly reveals his own feelings to his subjects.
13. _____ B. F. Skinner was a converted Freudian.
14. _____ The Freudians have a "mechanomorphic view of man," says James Bugental.
15. _____ Psychoanalysts are concerned with pathological behavior.

16. ____ Normal behavior often turns out to be statistically average behavior.

17. ____ The Esalen Institute favors humanistic psychology.

18. ____ It is unusual for the humanist psychologist to favor the uniqueness of man.

19. ____ Meditation is useless for exploring altered states of consciousness.

20. ____ A transcendental view of man is typical of humanist psychology.

MAIN POINT Which of the following statements best represents the main point of the passage? ____

1. Until recently there were no alternatives between Freudianism and behaviorism.
2. Humanist psychology offers a legitimate nonscientific approach.
3. Scientific approaches are profoundly limiting to psychology.
4. A new psychological approach has developed to benefit normal people.
5. It is too early to tell whether the new approach will be as effective as former approaches, but it is interesting.

AUTHOR'S ATTITUDE Which of the following statements best describes the author's attitude? ____

1. Behaviorism is effective, but potentially dangerous.
2. It has been a long wait, but humanist psychology is worth it.
3. Freud was a genius, but warped by his emphasis on pathology.
4. Humanistic psychology is interesting, but clearly a bit quirky.
5. It is not certain if humanist psychology will survive, but it should.

CONCLUSION Which of the following statements is the best conclusion that can be drawn from the passage? ____

1. Freud would have condemned this new movement in psychology.
2. A third movement seems to have been long awaited and well greeted.
3. Any dehumanizing approach to psychology must be damaging in the long run.

4. Strict scientific approaches are the most valid in modern psychology.

5. Any true humanistic approach must compromise scientific objectivity.

COMPLETION Choose the best answer for each question:

1. ____ Encounter group exercises are useful for: (a) behaviorist experimentation. (b) failed Freudians. (c) expressing raw emotion. (d) learning to think.

2. ____ Restriction of verbal communication helps develop: (a) more frustration. (b) the humanist hypothesis, as distinct from Freudianism. (c) patterns of behavior for the therapist. (d) awareness of alternate senses.

3. ____ The humanistic therapeutic situation stresses: (a) a one-on-one relationship. (b) clearheadedness and patience. (c) the point that much behavior is normal behavior. (d) meditation and confrontation.

4. ____ Authentic self disclosure on the part of the therapist increases: (a) patient awareness. (b) self-confidence and ease. (c) patient disclosure. (d) humanist content.

5. ____ One early humanist psychologist suggested that psychology should spend less time examining what man has done and more examining: (a) what man ought to do. (b) what man will do. (c) what man might do. (d) what everyone is already doing.

VOCABULARY Choose the word or phrase from Column B that best defines the vocabulary item in Column A:

Column A	*Column B*
1. ____ atypical	a. hide
2. ____ pragmatic	b. gut feelings
3. ____ fervor	c. feverish
4. ____ visceral senses	d. digging into
5. ____ suppress	e. effective means
6. ____ response to a stimulus	f. unusual
7. ____ pathological behavior	g. events
8. ____ therapeutic	h. intensity; excitement
9. ____ delving	i. sense; understand

10. ____ hypothesis

11. ____ converge

12. ____ viable way

13. ____ perceive

14. ____ transcendental

15. ____ phenomena

j. practical; utilitarian

k. meet

l. capable of overcoming limits

m. theory

n. related to treatment

o. unhealthy actions

p. inform; transmit

q. remarkable; amazing

r. behavioral reaction

34

Are We Afraid of Living Longer?

Albert Rosenfeld

The biological aging process is the subject of some of our most sophisticated scientific research. Albert Rosenfeld gives us a close look at the scientific problems encountered in laboratories around the country. But there are social as well as scientific consequences of such research. He questions whether we are willing to face the consequences of our research.

In his new novel, *Paradise I,* Alan Harrington envisions a time, only a few decades hence, when injections of "T-minus serum" rejuvenate the old and confer an indefinitely extended life-span on the lucky few who are chosen by computer lottery. Those rejected by the computer, the masses who have no access to the precious serum, grow increasingly restive and resentful. Finally: "Pogroms . . . against the favored people . . . in New York, Boston, Chicago, Cincinnati, Atlanta. . . . Bounty hunters hire themselves out. . . . and the hunt is on."

In an earlier short story, by Stephen Leacock, the characters no longer die of old age; they die only because of physical accidents. As a consequence, they spend most of their time and attention being very careful *not* to have an accident. In yet another story, by Alan Nourse, the long-lived heroes have so much time that they take all the time they have. They never get a project off the drawing board.

Do such literary imaginings accurately reflect the ways in which people would behave if antiaging substances were available to them? None among us can say for

---

ARE WE AFRAID OF LIVING LONGER? From *Saturday Review,* May 27, 1978.

sure, of course. But the young among us may get the chance to find out at first-hand.

For we in this century may well have the capacity for the first time in human history to do something about the process of aging—to hold back, even to *turn* back, its ravages.

Yet we are not leaping at the opportunity.

Why not?

Partly because we fear the consequences of success. But mostly because of a large credibility gap: We still can't really believe in the sudden science-factual feasibility of an outcome that we had assumed would always remain purely science-fictional.

It is important that we close this credibility gap because our government is right now, at various levels, discussing research on aging and its future consequences. If the scenarios being envisioned do not incorporate into their considerations the very real possibility that we may discover the basic biological mechanisms of the aging process and thus acquire the long-dreamed-of possibility of extending significantly the good years of human life, then to that extent those scenarios will be seriously defective—if not useless.

These thoughts resurfaced in my mind recently when I was invited to testify before a congressional subcommittee on aging. This was a "futures" hearing, and the topic was "Life Extension and Tomorrow's Elderly." Such discussions are going on in many places outside the government as well. The trouble with most of them—though less so outside the government—is that people tend to think of life extension as being modest gains of another few years and as continuing increments of more of the same. These would come about by virtue of the alleviation or cure of specific degenerative diseases such as late-onset cancer, heart disease, and stroke. The result would be an ever larger population of elderly people facing social, economic, and ethical problems similar to today's, only aggravated and a bit more complex.

"In any attempt at futurology," said Dr. Leonard Hayflick, a distinguished gerontologist, at a Chicago conference last year, "it is wisest to base predictions on similar events that have happened in the past." But what if there are no similar events to be found in the past? Some events are unprecedented, such as our capability of recombining DNA molecules and of manipulating genes. On which past events may we base our predictions of the consequences? In all likelihood, the outcome of successful research on aging would generate conditions radically different from those we now face—especially as the merely old chronologically became less and less elderly and aged physically. We talk and write glibly about "the graying of America," but I for one wouldn't place any bets that gray will be the predominant hair color of future old folks. And nursing homes as we now know them could become as rare as TB sanatoriums already have.

We cannot be certain that this increase in longevity will happen, but to rule it out of our future considerations as if it could not happen is simply foolish. It not only could happen, it could probably happen much sooner if we deliberately choose to bring it about rather than wait passively for the knowledge to accrue. In a study conducted by the RAND Corporation, a sampling of scientific forecasters guessed that a 50-year increase in human longevity could be attained by the year 2020. Other surveys have come up with more conservative predictions, but they still indicate that many experts consider such ideas anything but preposterous.

Late in 1977, the Academic Press brought out a new and completely revised edition of *Time, Cells and Aging,* a seminal book first published in 1962 by Dr. Bernard L. Strehler, of the University of Southern California. Strehler was amazed at the quantity of new knowledge that had accumulated in the 15-year interim, allowing him to be much more optimistic in this edition about the prospects of conquering old age and extending the human life-span. Strehler has indeed been among the more outspoken—at times even evangelistic—of those gerontologists trying to close the credibility gap, and his own scholarly book is one of the better arguments in that direction.

If Strehler is surprised at how much has come to pass in the decade and a half since the first edition of *Time, Cells and Aging,* I am doubly so as I contemplate what has occurred in only a year and a half since the publication of *Prolongevity,* my own book on the subject. Some random examples:

I wrote of Dr. Denham Harman, of the University of Nebraska, who, among others, has succeeded in substantially extending the life expectancy of mice by the use of antioxidants such as 2-MEA (2-mercaptoethylamine), BHT (butylated hydroxytoluene), vitamin E, and a quinoline derivative called Santoquin. Now Harman has noted an unexpected effect in the next generation: Those mice whose mothers were fed antioxidants and thus lived longer—though they themselves are fed standard laboratory diets with no antioxidants added—also seem to be living longer, the apparent beneficiaries of their mothers' improved condition!

I wrote about a series of classic experiments that began more than 40 years ago with Dr. Clive M. McCay, of Cornell, in which laboratory rats were deliberately underfed while their nutritious, well-balanced diet was maintained. This regimen resulted in extending their life-span by a third, a half, or even another full lifetime. The trouble is that to be effective, such a dietary plan has to begin very early in life—before puberty, in fact—which virtually eliminates the method as possibly transferrable to human beings—since no one would undertake such an experiment, of such doubtful outcome, over such a long period of time, on children. But now Dr. Charles H. Barrows, Jr., of the National Institute on Aging, has been conducting experiments and collecting data from others that strongly suggest that antiaging benefits may still be gained even if the dietary regimen is started much later in life. In one series of studies, life-spans of rats were increased by 25 percent to 33 percent by cutting protein levels in half starting at the age of sixteen months—equivalent according to Barrows's calculations to age forty-five on the human scale. Thus new hope suddenly emerges for adding to the life-span by simple dietary controls.

I wrote too of thymosin, a hormone believed to have the capacity to boost the body's faulty or failing immune system. Developed most energetically at the University of Texas Medical Branch at Galveston by Dr. Allan L. Goldstein and his associates, thymosin has already shown promise when used experimentally against some of the inherited immune deficiency diseases. In recent studies by Dr. Paul B. Chretien, at the National Cancer Institute, thymosin was used in addition to standard chemotherapy. The combination enabled victims of one form of lung cancer to survive significantly longer than a control group of patients—presumably by boosting their failing immune system, thought this is not yet regarded as proved. We know that our immune system declines with advancing age, rendering us more susceptible to every variety of infection and stress. Though thymosin is not a specifically antiaging hormone, if it does indeed bring a failing immune system back up to optimal level, it should improve the quality of our later years considerably. (No experiments have yet been done on human subjects, and the hormone will be in short supply for some time, though a pharmaceutical house, Hoffmann-LaRoche, has enough faith in the hormone's potential to be working on methods for speeding up its production.)

Antioxidants and thymic hormones are only two of the many substances being evaluated on animals for their potential antiaging effects. Others include temperature-lowering drugs; L-dopa (originally developed as a treatment for Parkinsonism); and such categories of agents as cross-link inhibitors, lysosome-membrane stabilizers, and lipofuscin scavengers—all of which seem to hold real promise of dealing with specific "wear and tear" aspects of aging.

But one of the major themes of *Prolongevity* was that wear-and-tear phenomena are not necessarily the keys to aging. Rather, it seems probable that aging is genetically programmed, that we have ticking away within us a genetic "clock of aging" (perhaps more than one) that appears to dictate the sequence and roughly the rate at which our organisms will deteriorate. More and more gerontologists, though still probably a minority of them, share this conviction.

It may be that only a small number of genes are involved in our programmed aging. A strong argument for this has been put forth by Dr. Richard G. Cutler, of the National Institute on Aging, and Dr. George A. Sacher, of the Argonne National Laboratory, and concurred in by Strehler. The argument, based on evolutionary theory, goes something like this: The present longevity of our species—two or three times greater than that of our prehominid ancestors—came about in a spectacularly short period of time evolutionarily speaking, perhaps in no more than a few million years. During this same brief period, what has been termed the "explosive growth" of our brain took place and we also acquired a prolonged period of infantile helplessness. The one development enabled us to evolve culture and the other, to pass it along to our offspring, thus allowing us to become creatures of both cultural and biological evolution. Cutler, Sacher, and Strehler all argue convincingly that for all this to have occurred in so short a time, only a very small number of mutant genes could have been involved.

It does make sense that a few gene changes could have remarkably widespread consequences. We know for instance that even a single gene defect causing a single cell abnormality can have devastating effects throughout an entire organism. It is not unreasonable then to imagine that a relatively few genes could program us to live longer and that a relatively few are involved in our present programmed aging.

For those who believe that the clock of aging is located in the DNA in each cell's nucleus (Hayflick is among those who espouse this view), it would thus appear possible to alter the clock by altering a few critical genes or gene clusters. Dr. Roy L. Walford, of UCLA, who favors the theory that aging is somehow bound to the decline of the immune system, has suggested that a likely candidate as a key control site of aging is the main histocompatibility complex (MHC), a gene system that regulates a number of immune functions and is located on a short stretch of a single chromosome. Indeed, several studies—published in *Nature,* in late 1977—indicate that Walford may well be right. And if it turns out that only a few gene sites are involved in dictating the aging process, the genetic engineers are learning so rapidly to transfer specific genes from one cell to another and from one organism to another that it is not absurd to speculate that they could one day reset our genetic clock of aging.

There is however another major theory about the clock of aging: that it is hormonal in nature and is located in the brain—specifically in that tiny region that houses the hypothalamus and pituitary, which govern the release of all hormones. If the clock is hormonal, the hormones still must act on individual cells of course, but it is now known that hormones are perfectly capable of triggering the turn-on and turn-off of genes in the nuclear DNA. And if the clock is hormonal, it can still be a genetic clock, since the cells that release the hormones must be programmed by their genes to do so—as is true of all cellular functions.

As one example of a hormonal clock of aging, we know that the Pacific salmon begins to age and die almost instantaneously after spawning. We also know that the process is triggered by a massive release of corticosteroid hormones. It has now been demonstrated that removing the adrenal gland keeps the salmon from aging and dying on schedule.

The octopus is another sea creature that deteriorates and dies soon after spawning. In this case, the hormone is released by the optic gland. By removing the gland, Dr. Jerome Wodinsky, of Brandeis University, has been able to double the life-span of the female octopus.

In the case of the steelhead trout, which undergoes a similar fate, Dr. Edwin W. House, of Idaho State University, has zeroed in on the region of the hypothalamus and pituitary as the activation site of the fish's aging process. Could the same be true for mammals, including human beings—though aging occurs at a much statelier pace? A number of scientists think so.

The boldest theorist and researcher of this lot is Dr. W. Donner Denckla, who did most of his work at the Roche Institute of Molecular Biology before moving recently to Harvard's Thorndike Laboratories (from whence he must soon move again, alas, for lack of space). Denckla theorizes, based on logic as well as on experiment, that the deteriorative changes of aging are actuated by a hormone (or family of hormones) that begins to be released by the pituitary at puberty. Others have characterized this as yet unfound hormone as the "aging" or "death" hormone, but Denckla prefers the more cautious, descriptive designation DECO (decreasing oxygen consumption). It has also been called the thyroid-blocking hormone, since it appears to work by preventing the cells' intake of thyroid hormone. Denckla has recently discovered that DECO also blocks the intake of the growth hormone. Working along these lines, he has brought up to a dozen the number of biochemical, metabolic, and immune functions he has been able to "restore to juvenile competence" in old rats.

Just as others have removed the adrenal gland of a salmon and the optic gland of an octopus, Denckla removes the pituitary of an older rat, thus theoretically preventing the release of any more DECO; he then supplies thyroid and other necessary hormones that the rat's body, in the absence of the pituitary, can no longer manufacture for itself. As a result, a host of functions, all the way from antibody production to fur growth, return to their youthful peak rate. Denckla believes he is also coming closer to extracting and purifying DECO—which would be the first concrete evidence of its existence—by the use of newly-worked-out techniques.

If Denckla does isolate, purify, and synthesize DECO and if it does turn out to be the clock-controlling hormone, what then?

One would look for a way to inhibit its release. Fanciful speculation? Of course. For now. But look at what happened in the case of the human growth hormone:

After it was isolated and synthesized, another related brain hormone, somatostatin, was discovered—which, among its other activities, inhibits the release of the growth hormone! Other scientists then proceeded, in record time, to synthesize the gene that contains the instructions for making somatostatin and now, as their latest feat, to transfer that gene to a laboratory bacterium so that somatostatin can be "manufactured" in tissue culture. In fact, about two gallons of the bacterial culture have produced a quantity of somatostatin that would formerly have required half a million sheep brains for its extraction! Few would have predicted a year and a half ago that we would have such powerful techniques in our hands so soon.

None of this means that the solution to aging will be found easily or that it will occur overnight. The same is true, as we know, of the cancer problem. Yet we proceed in the faith that the latter can be solved, that we can discover the cause of the malignant process and interfere with it, that we can successfully treat—and someday cure and prevent—cancer. There is no good reason why we should not take the same attitude toward aging; not death, mind you—since we would still die sooner or later—but aging. In fact, if we were to arrive at a solution to aging, it might well contain within it solutions to the problems of cancer and of the major degenerative diseases of old age—heart disease, atherosclerosis, stroke, diabetes, arthritis, senile dementia. Aging research could turn out to be the shortest route to these other solutions. Since we are far from certain that this is true, however, research on aging should in no sense replace the separate, ongoing quests for the individual answers.

Besides, we may need both kinds of answers. Diseases, just because they have similar symptoms and go by the same names, may not be the same entities in the young as in the old. There are early and late forms of heart disease, cancer, diabetes, arthritis, and dementia, and the therapies for the earlier occurring varieties may not prevent those that may show themselves as part of the organism's overall deterioration. Since we don't know these answers, we are well advised not to abandon any promising lines of research.

Many of our current life-prolonging (or rather, death-postponing) techniques are fantastically expensive—in time, money, personnel resources, and physical and emotional anguish. They represent what the noted biologist Dr. Lewis Thomas has characterized as "halfway technology": the intensive care units; the complex heart surgery; the kidney dialysis machines; the cobalt bombs; the artificial respirators; the heart-lung machines; the hyperbaric chambers; the transplantation of organs; the implantation of artificial parts; the sophisticated, computerized, round-the-clock monitoring that seems to begin prenatally and that sometimes cannot even end postmortally without an ethical debate. If we are to overleap this no-win impasse, we need to push ahead to the "high technolgoy" of cure and prevention.

Not the least important of the pertinent happenings in gerontology in the past year and a half is that our new National Institute on Aging (NIA), officially established in 1974, has finally moved into high gear under the able directorship of Dr. Robert N. Butler. Though Butler is a behavioral rather than a biological gerontologist, he is fully cognizant of the biological potential. The NIA is unfortunately grossly underfunded for its task, which I suppose is to be expected for a "new baby." But its appropriation should be at least doubled before long if Butler is to carry out the NIA's research mandate without at the same time slighting the needs of those who are elderly now and entitled to the best we can do for them. Basic research in other fields will be equally important of course, since much of the relevant progress that will emerge will come from fields not specifically labeled "aging."

Which brings us back to where we began: to the question of the consequences of success. If aging research succeeds in even its more modest goal of adding many more high-quality years to the present life-span, the consequences will be profound. They will be economic, social, political, psychological, ethical, moral, philosophical, religious; they will be potentially good and bad; they will be far-reaching, and hardly any areas of our lives will remain unaffected. More and more people staying around for longer and longer periods of time immediately raises questions about pollution, overpopulation, and our planet's dwindling resources. Even a cursory look at the economic consequences evokes dilemmas in regard to retirement programs, insurance policies, social security benefits—all predicated on current life expectancy. However, things do not have to turn out as badly as they always seem to in the science-fiction scenarios.

When the credibility gap in regard to aging research has been bridged, when a reasonable understanding of the capabilities and the potential consequences is in hand, we can then decide which way to move. And move we must, of course, since the one decision we are not free to make in this dynamic life is to stand still.

LENGTH: 4028 WORDS

Name Class Date

34 Are We Afraid of Living Longer?

SCORING: Reading time: _____ Rate from chart: _____ W.P.M.

RETENTION	number right _____	× 2 equals _____	points
MAIN POINT	number right _____	× 4 equals _____	points
AUTHOR'S ATTITUDE	number right _____	× 3 equals _____	points
CONCLUSION	number right _____	× 3 equals _____	points
COMPLETION	number right _____	× 4 equals _____	points
VOCABULARY	number right _____	× 2 equals _____	points
	(Total points: 100)	**Total** _____	points

RETENTION Based on the passage, which of the following statements is True (T), False (F), or Not answerable (N)?

1. _____ Genes can now be "manufactured" in laboratory bacteria.
2. _____ DECO is released by the rat's pituitary gland.
3. _____ As of yet, there is no identifiable human growth hormone.
4. _____ Two sources for the human "clock of aging" have been definitely validated.
5. _____ The human "clock of aging" could be genetic, hormonal, or both.
6. _____ Aging in salmon, octopus, and trout is particularly slow and stately.
7. _____ Because of the credibility gap, there is no current research on aging.
8. _____ Science fiction treats the problems of prolongevity in detail.
9. _____ Alan Harrington did research before becoming a novelist.
10. _____ Spawning is a critical aging period in the life of many fish.
11. _____ There is reason for being optimistic about aging, according to Strehler.
12. _____ We can now recombine DNA molecules.
13. _____ Rosenfeld has not yet published his book on aging.
14. _____ Books on aging have largely been ignored by scientists.
15. _____ Future predictions are best based, if possible, on past events.
16. _____ We are not leaping at the opportunity to retard aging.

17. ____ No one reading this article could benefit from the research described.

18. ____ Wear and tear phenomena are not necessarily the keys to aging.

19. ____ The National Institute on Aging does not yet officially exist.

20. ____ "Half-way technology" refers to current methods of prolonging life.

MAIN POINT Which of the following statements best represents the main point of the passage? ____

1. Science fiction creates problems when it become science fact.
2. There is a real gap between technology and our capacity to use it.
3. Aging is a vastly more complex phenomenon than we had thought.
4. Someone must mediate between scientists and politicians.
5. We must decide that we want people to live longer before this can be achieved.

AUTHOR'S ATTITUDE Which of the following statements best describes the author's attitude? ____

1. It is easy to see why research on aging is so slow.
2. In a sense, science is more understanding than sociology.
3. The patience of scientists is usually well rewarded.
4. Since the young will benefit, the young should decide about aging.
5. The fact that no one is raising a row about aging is very surprising.

CONCLUSION Which of the following statements is the best conclusion that can be drawn from the passage? ____

1. Unless policies are made now, advances in gerontology may cause sudden problems.
2. Until only a few years ago, prolongevity was just science fiction.
3. A national agency should establish priorities for prolongevity.
4. The question of a prolongevity lottery could be very beneficial.
5. Science is best directed into nonsociological areas.

COMPLETION Choose the best answer for each question:

1. ____ One kind of substance quite effective in combatting aging is: (a) BHT. (b) the B-complex vitamin. (c) simple dope. (d) progesterone.

2. ____ Apparently, the congressional subcommittees have: (a) aging problems of their own. (b) abnormal life spans. (c) "futures" hearings. (d) established aging as one of their more important priorities for legislation.

3. ____ In comparison with conditions now, the problems engendered by greater life expectancy will be: (a) quite different from anything we know now. (b) much like those we now experience. (c) very exciting. (d) simply more intense than those we now experience, but not conspicuously different.

4. ____ Apparently, laboratory rats lived much longer when: (a) they were permitted to stay in nuclear families. (b) their protein intake was halved. (c) parts of their stomach were replaced. (d) lysosomes were not involved.

5. ____ The present longevity of our species is approximately: (a) the same as (b) two to three times greater than (c) half as much as (d) eleven times greater than our prehominid ancestors.

VOCABULARY Choose the word or phrase from Column B that best defines the vocabulary entry in Column A:

Column A	*Column B*
1. ____ malignant	a. retardant
2. ____ chromosome	b. relief
3. ____ evangelistic	c. increases
4. ____ unprecedented	d. achievability
5. ____ increments	e. harmful; possibly fatal
6. ____ alleviation	f. applicability
7. ____ degenerative	g. without previous example
8. ____ cursory	h. part of a gene
9. ____ feasibility	i. before birth; after death
10. ____ rejuvenate	j. with a preacher's zeal

11. ____ mandate

12. ____ prenatally; postmortally

13. ____ impasse

14. ____ cognizant

15. ____ inhibitor

k. breaking down; wearing out

l. brief; not extensive

m. restore youthfulness

n. redolently; not redolently

o. impossible impediment

p. knowledgeable; aware

q. demand

r. asymptomatic of

35

The Age of Miracle Chips

Editors of Time

Our age is witnessing a number of scientific and social revolutions. Among the most familiar, and yet most amazing, is the computer revolution. Only a few years ago, the ordinary handheld logarithmic computer cost a fortune and was housed in a full-sized room. We have almost come to take such advances in technology for granted. Yet we do not know where they are leading us.

It is tiny, only about a quarter of an inch square, and quite flat. Under a microscope, it resembles a stylized Navaho rug or the aerial view of a railroad switching yard. Like the grains of sand on a beach, it is made mostly of silicon, next to oxygen the most abundant element on the surface of the earth.

Yet this inert fleck—still unfamiliar to the vast majority of Americans—has astonishing powers that are already transforming society. For the so-called miracle chip has a calculating capability equal to that of a room-size computer of only 25 years ago. Unlike the hulking Calibans of vacuum tubes and tangled wires from which it evolved, it is cheap, easy to mass produce, fast, infinitely versatile and convenient.

The miracle chip represents a quantum leap in the technology of mankind, a development that over the past few years has acquired the force and significance associated with the development of hand tools or the discovery of the steam engine. Just as the Industrial Revolution took over an immense range of tasks from men's muscles and enormously expanded productivity, so the microcomputer is rapidly assuming huge burdens of drudgery from the human brain and thereby expanding the mind's capacities in ways that man has only begun to grasp. With the chip, amazing feats of memory and execution become possible in everything from automobile engines to universities and hospitals, from farms to banks and corporate offices, from outer space to a baby's nursery.

Those outside the electronic priesthood often have trouble grasping the principles of the new microtechnology or comprehending the accomplishments of the minuscule computers. The usual human sense of scale, the proportion between size and capability, the time ratio assumed between thought and action, are swept into a new and surreal terrain. Consequently, people tend to anthropomorphize the computer; they are superstitious about it. In *2001: A Space Odyssey,* the companionable computer HAL turns rogue in outer space and methodically begins assassinating its masters. In a B-movie called *Demon Seed,* the world's most advanced computer actually impregnates a scientist's wife, played by Julie Christie; it is so smart that it yearns to be alive—and scarily succeeds. Some manufacturers of computer games have discovered that people are disconcerted when the computer responds instantly after the human has made his move. So the computers have been programmed to wait a little while before making countermoves, as if scratching their heads in contemplation.

A fear of intellectual inadequacy, of powerlessness before the tireless electronic wizards, has given rise to dozens of science-fiction fantasies of computer takeovers. In *The Tale of the Big Computer,* by Swedish Physicist Hannes Alfvén, written under the pen name Olof Johannesson, the human beings of today become the horses of tomorrow. The world runs not for man but for the existence and welfare of computers.

Other scientists too are apprehensive. D. Raj Reddy, a computer scientist at Pittsburgh's Carnegie-Mellon University, fears that universally available microcomputers could turn into formidable weapons. Among other things, says Reddy, sophisticated computers in the wrong hands could begin subverting a society by tampering with people's relationships with their own computers—instructing the other computers to cut off telephone, bank and other services, for example. The danger lies in the fast-expanding computer data banks, with their concentration of information about people and governments, and in the possibility of access to those repositories. Already, computer theft is a growth industry, so much so that the FBI has a special program to train agents to cope with the electronic cutpurses.

Dartmouth College President John G. Kemeny, an eminent mathematician, envisions great benefits from the computer, but in his worst-case imaginings he sees a government that would possess one immense, interconnecting computer system: Big Brother. The alternative is obviously to isolate government computers from one other, to decentralize them, to prevent them from possibly becoming dictatorial. But that would require considerable foresight, sophistication—and possibly a tough new variety of civil rights legislation.

Some of the most informed apprehensions about computers are expressed by Professor Joseph Weizenbaum of M.I.T.'s Laboratory for Computer Science. Human dependence on computers, Weizenbaum argues, has already become irreversible, and in that dependence resides a frightening vulnerability. It is not just that the systems might break down; the remedy for that could eventually be provided by a number of back-up systems. Besides, industrialized man is already vulnerable to serious dislocations by breakdowns—when the electrical power of New York City goes out, for example. Perhaps a greater danger, says Weizenbaum, lies in the fact that "a computer will do what you tell it to do, but that may be much different from what you had in mind." The machines can break loose from human intentions. Computers, he argues, are infinitely literal-minded; they exercise no judgments, have no values. Fed a program that was mistaken, a military computer might send off missiles in the wrong direction or fire them at the wrong time. Several years ago, Admiral Thomas Moorer, then Chairman of the Joint Chiefs of Staff, told a Senate committee: "It is unfortunate that we have become slaves to these damned computers."

Some social critics are worried that a democratization of computers, making them as common as television sets are today, may eventually cause human intellectual powers to atrophy. Even now, students equipped with pocket calculators have been relieved of having to do their figuring on paper; will they eventually forget how to do it, just as urban man has lost so many crafts of survival? Possibly. But the steam engine did not destroy men's muscles, and the typewriter has not ruined the ability to write longhand.

Certain pre-computer skills should be taught so that they do not vanish. But as Leibniz observed in 1671: "It is unworthy of excellent men to lose hours like slaves in the labor of calculation which could safely be relegated to anyone else if machines were used." Einstein had to have help with his calculations; they are drone's work anyway. Says Author Martin Gardner (*Mathematical Carnival*): "There is no reason why a person should have to sit down and compute the square root of seven. The computer is freeing the individual for more interesting tasks."

The rapid proliferation of microcomputers will doubtless cause many social dislocations. But the hope is that the burgeoning technology will create an almost limitless range of new products and services and therefore a great new job market. Though one expert estimates that it would take the entire U.S. female population between ages 18 and 45 to run the nation's telephone system if it were not computerized, Ma Bell now employs more people than it did when its first automatic switching service was introduced.

All of the prodigies of technology leave many people not only nostalgic for simpler times but alarmed by the unknown dangers that "progress" may bring with it. Those who first used fire must have terrified their generation. Practically any breakthrough in knowledge carries with it the possibility that it will be used for evil. But with microcomputers, the optimists can argue an extremely persuasive case. The Industrial Revolution had the effect of standardizing and routinizing life. Microtechnology, with its nearly infinite capacities and adaptability, tends on the contrary toward individualization; with computers, people can design their lives far more in line with their own wishes. They can work at terminals at home instead of in offices, educate themselves in a variety of subjects at precisely the speed they wish, shop electronically with the widest possible discretion. Among other things, microtechnology will make the mechanism of supply and demand operate more responsively; customers' wishes will be registered at the speed of light.

Some, like Sociologist Seymour Martin Lipset, envision a "more egalitarian society" because of the computer. Transferring so much work to the machines, thinks Lipset, may produce something like Athenian democracy; Athenians could be equal because they had slaves to do their work for them.

Says Isaac Asimov, the prolific author and futuristic polymath: "We are reaching the stage where the problems that we must solve are going to become insoluble without computers. I do not fear computers. I fear the lack of them." Many people have great expectations and doubts about the new technology, especially in a century when they have felt themselves enslaved and terrorized by the works of science. Stewart Brand, creator of the *Whole Earth Catalog,* argues for a longer perspective: "This is a story that goes back to the beginning of tool-using animals, back to the rocks the earliest man picked up in Africa. As soon as he started picking up rocks, his hands started changing, his brain started changing. Computers are simply a quantum jump in the same co-evolutionary process."

LENGTH: 1410 WORDS

35 The Age of Miracle Chips

SCORING: Reading time: _____ Rate from chart: _____ W.P.M.		
RETENTION	number right____ × 2 equals____	points
MAIN POINT	number right____ × 4 equals____	points
AUTHOR'S ATTITUDE	number right____ × 3 equals____	points
CONCLUSION	number right____ × 3 equals____	points
COMPLETION	number right____ × 4 equals____	points
VOCABULARY	number right____ × 2 equals____	points
	(Total points: 100) **Total** ____	points

RETENTION Based on the passage, which of the following statements is True (T), False (F), or Not answerable (N)?

1. ____ The miracle chip is a single square inch in size.
2. ____ Movies and fiction have been "starring" computers.
3. ____ One fear is that computers could become sophisticated weapons.
4. ____ Terrorists have already attacked one data bank center.
5. ____ Computer theft is a growth industry.
6. ____ There is no fear that computers will cause people to lose math skills.
7. ____ Apparently, early tools may have affected man's biology.
8. ____ The FBI has special courses in computer crime control.
9. ____ Dartmouth's president has no fear that computers will turn tyrants.
10. ____ Fortunately computers will cause no social dislocations.
11. ____ The Bell Telephone Company employs more people now than before it used computers.
12. ____ Shopping by computer may become a reality.
13. ____ Isaac Azimov is worried about a shortage of computers.
14. ____ Stewart Brand of the *Whole Earth Catalog* sees no connection between computers and simple hand tools.
15. ____ The computer's greatest impact will be in education.

16. ____ Computers may actually produce a more egalitarian society.

17. ____ The Industrial Revolution standardized life for most people.

18. ____ Computers could not, in all likelihood, produce new job markets.

19. ____ The future may see the distinction between man and computer blur.

20. ____ Einstein did all his calculations himself.

MAIN POINT Which of the following statements best represents the main point of the passage? ____

1. Computers are going to make life simpler for modern man.
2. No one knows exactly what effect computers will have on modern life.
3. Whatever happens computers will be a serious threat to personal freedoms.
4. There is probably no cause to be frightened about the prospect of computers.
5. Computer technology is one of the most important of recent years.

AUTHOR'S ATTITUDE Which of the following statements best describes the author's attitude? ____

1. Computers are a good thing, and we shouldn't be afraid of them.
2. Computers are dangerous, and we ought to legislate against them.
3. Computers are neither good nor bad.
4. Computers ought to hurry up and "free" mankind from drudgery.
5. Drudgery is itself a positive force.

CONCLUSION Which of the following statements is the best conclusion that can be drawn from the passage? ____

1. We must plan now if we want to be part of the computer technology.
2. New legislation is almost certainly in the offing to govern computers.
3. We should be doing as much social planning as technical planning for computer technology.
4. Controlling our fear of computers is probably as important as controlling our production of them.
5. This is not the time to be nostalgic about the slide rule and simple math.

COMPLETION Choose the best answer for each question:

1. ____ The miracle chip represents: (a) an insignificant change (b) a major change (c) a minor change (d) an unnoticeable change in the technology of mankind.

2. ____ In one film, Julie Christie is: (a) made pregnant (b) killed (c) held for an unbelievable ransom (d) completely enslaved by a computer.

3. ____ One way of subverting society would be to: (a) steal their computers. (b) alter people's relationship with their computers. (c) make people totally dependent on computers. (d) make people ignorant and computers smart.

4. ____ Computers: (a) are best when they are small and unobtrusive. (b) have no values; they are literal-"thinking." (c) will be the drones of the "new hive." (d) are likely to be the playthings of rich people.

5. ____ Both the steam engine and the typewriter were: (a) never thought to be portable. (b) threats to progress. (c) a threat to people's skills. (d) blessings in disguise.

VOCABULARY Choose the word or phrase from Column B that best defines the vocabulary entry in Column A:

Column A	*Column B*
1. ____ atrophy	a. extremely small
2. ____ vulnerability	b. humanize
3. ____ quantum leap	c. prize
4. ____ inert	d. desire
5. ____ miniscule	e. uncombining; stable
6. ____ anthropomorphize	f. lazy
7. ____ subvert	g. weakness
8. ____ surreal terrain	h. fruitful
9. ____ yearn	i. redirect or overthrow
10. ____ burgeoning	j. huge move
11. ____ recondite	k. judgment
12. ____ prolific	l. dry up; wither

13. ____ discretion

14. ____ prodigies

15. ____ dislocations

m. growing

n. profound; abstruse

o. make more real; realize

p. upsets

q. bizarre locale

r. wonders

36

Bloody Monday: The Trauma of College Admissions

Herbert S. Sacks

Applying to colleges has become an American ritual, an important milepost in the development of young people. In this article, Sacks discussed the emotional pain involved in the procedure, as well as its effects on parent-child relations. He also looks at the overall implications of college admission and how it has taken precedence in young people's thoughts about education. While offering some alternatives, he admits they all contain problems of their own.

On Monday, the 17th of April, 19–, hundreds of thousands of American high school seniors will stream to mailboxes and post offices to intercept the morning mail and learn which colleges and universities will admit them to the class of 19–. "Bloody Monday," as it is called, kaleidoscopically reveals the fears, struggles, and aspirations of late adolescents. What are the issues involved in this awesome moment—a time to be savored by some, for others a moment of humiliation and embarrassment?

The present system of college admissions tends to disregard educational principles and is often insensitive to what we know of adolescent development. Normal adolescent development is tumultuous, never straight-line, with dramatic regressions and progressions. Admissions judgments are intolerant of these peaks and nadirs in the students' mental lives that encumber academic performance. The system rewards those fortunate young people whose learning experiences occur in a relatively conflict-free sphere, away from the ongoing *Sturm und Drang,* or those whose excessive defenses against their adolescent drives permit them to repress conflict.

The normal late adolescent is naturally preoccupied with thoughts of emancipation from parents and home, with the strengthening of autonomous strivings, the achievement of mastery over impulses and capacities, with a firming of sexual identities, the evolution of love relationships, and the early moves toward a vocational choice. The knowledge of impending departure from home is a pressure cooker that, over a period of months, leads toward a coalescence of emerging identity fragments, the residues and precipitates from other life crises experienced since infancy. The admissions process becomes a lightning rod for more intrinsic normative issues in human development, and the distortions that result often lead us to ignore the harsh realities of the process itself.

Eager American parents, having regard for intelligence and respect for scholarship and spurred by economic and social considerations, have set the stage for the college matriculation process. Even at the junior high school level, educators assist in laying down the foundations of the admissions crisis by subtle coercion and threats about the necessity of making a good record for the future.

A chorus of concern about college admissions begins to be heard by the tenth grade, when many schools, especially the private ones, urge their students to take the Preliminary Scholastic Aptitude Tests (PSATs) in a trial run before October of their junior year when the test really counts. These test results will be used to derive National Merit Scholarship Qualifying Scores, which publicly identify high performers. Students are well apprised of the necessity of performing well in the junior year and in the first half of the senior year. With the SATs and achievement tests taken more than once, the preliminaries are over and the crunch is on.

In the fall of the senior year, applications and catalogs must be secured, visits and interviews arranged, and an estimate made of how many and what quality colleges the students ought to consider. Parental clamor urging children forward as if they were racehorses is often greeted with agreement but with no follow-through action by late adolescents. The stubbornness of youth is a good match for the chivying behavior of parents. The awareness of seniors that they have not sent for applications is counterpoint to their rich fantasies of crisp autumn days in sought-after colleges.

After irritable confrontations with parents, marked by children's claims of usurpation of their independence, and painful sessions with low-keyed but insistent school guidance personnel, the applications begin to appear in the mail. Their deadlines are noted by the students, and then brochures and application forms are swiftly put away in desk drawers.

After a period of quiescence the skirmishes are renewed, with provocative contributions from uncomfortable parents dismayed by their own periodic loss of control. In the seesawing arguments, the reluctance of the seniors to fill out the applications, combined with parental intensities and irrationalities, stirs up a recapitulation of earlier childhood struggles. Questions of trust, responsibility, duty, and the students' ability to govern themselves flood the dialogue between old and young. It often seems that the joint regression of parents and children is necessary in order for the participants to begin to appreciate the roots of the brouhaha and to discover a little more about each other before they can disengage and move forward, together and separately.

The Application Form. Finally, the applications are carefully read by the senior. Most of them are composed of straightforward biographical questions followed by an exploratory essay focused upon an autobiographical theme designed to gain a simple grasp of the applicant's beliefs and life experience. The autobiographical statement unsettles many students who are concerned with how much to tell, how to decide which vignettes show growth rather than vulnerability, and how to sort out passing moral positions and social posture without appearing to be on an ego trip.

Another often troublesome section of the application is a career-choice question which permits some colleges in the private sector to admit applicants with identifiable interests without excessively inflating the teaching loads of those departments weakened by budgetary strains. For most late adolescents, probing questions about career choice present unreasonable demands for a decision that they obviously are not ready to make. Career-choice questions are seen by some as accusations of how incompetent they are to handle the personal and academic requirements of college, because the colleges explicitly want to know in which majors and departments the matriculants will spend most of their time.

In 1977, 83 private colleges from Columbia to Colorado recognized a new six-page common application form in order to simplify the admissions process. Some colleges will require both the new form and their own application form in the beginning years, with the expectation that the latter will ultimately be dropped. The clearinghouse psychology implied by the new system may deprive many colleges of particular information they require to serve their entrants better, to change recruitment policies, and to rough out a profile of expectable departmental needs. The common form not so subtly suggests to students that there are few differences among participating schools in terms of philosophy, goals, quality of student body, and approaches to settling institutional conflicts. If separation from home carries with it the desired goals of achieving sustained autonomous advances and enhanced self-regard, then, paradoxically, a large number of selective private colleges are intimating that the candidate's uniqueness and distinction will not be treated with sensitivity. Like those student applicants aspiring to public-sector institutions, often admitted by computer determination, the private-sector students will have to accommodate themselves to increased anonymity.

Actual work on the application becomes an endurance feat with the expectation of injury to the narcissistic ego. As one young woman explained it: "I feel like I'm being asked to stand naked before a gallery of judges all wearing their academic robes, with my family and friends being kept from me in the background." She was sure that bodily defects, common to all humans, would be recognized by the impersonal judges and found unacceptable. This fantasy of exposure to critical judgment without the protection of loving and caring people speaks to the larger ambivalence of this time in the student's life—the wish to be nurtured at home versus the urgency of breaking old attachments in order to advance to a new level of self-realization.

The Interview. Even though most state universities do not offer interviews, and an increasing number of private colleges are granting group interviews for orientation purposes rather than admissions judgments, the individual interview is still a factor in the most selective colleges—though it is decreasing in importance. A discerning satire called *College Entrance,* written and published by a young man interviewed at Yale, takes into account the myriad impressions and fantasies experienced by many applicants each year. A little dulled, Mark comes to the interview, his eighth, before time, dressed in his interview garb, carefully chosen to reflect his view of himself. Anxiously he surveys his competition sunken into leather couches around him, hating their 800 SAT scores and their apparent equanimity. A beautiful woman dean invites him into her office. "Things were not going well. While I spoke of my time in Exeter she admired my jacket; the summer in Chile, 'You have a very nice tan, Mark,' she cooed; working for Common Cause, 'You certainly seem very mature.' " His story accelerates as the beautiful older woman seduces him under the watchful eye of a portrait of Elihu Yale. He responds to her moves by becoming sexually active. She cries out, "You're in! You're in! Oh my God, this is the first time, never before, what fine credentials!" The fantasy, put to print, reveals Mark's inner feelings of awkwardness, inadequacy, and hopelessness in this unwanted competition. His tension is expressed through a regression to an earlier epoch in his life history with a fantasied revival of the Oedipal triangle in his family. Thus he has an unacceptable sexual connection with Mother Yale acted out under the gaze of a stern, punishing father. The passive submission, an older conflict for Mark, is turned into its opposite through talents not identifiable by the most perspicacious college application form. In the real world, Mark was turned down by Yale.

College Recruitment. A brilliant black female senior at an urban high school was invited by an Afro-American student group supported by the admissions office to spend the weekend at a New England college. The black experience at this institution was presented to the student guests in a carefully orchestrated program. The camaraderie and sophistication of the approach suffused the young woman's judgment, and she began to think of this college as her first choice. A few weeks passed and she visited the school once again at the behest of a former high school classmate who wished to renew an old tie. In the absence of the tightly organized program of the preceding month, she was discouraged to find depressed students, beset by inordinate work obligations, who were threatening to transfer to other, less demanding institutions. Complaints of dormitory overcrowding, poor food, and uninspired teaching were aired by the same students who had been part of the earlier charade. It was impossible for her either to validate or ignore allusions to racial problems badly handled by the college administration. The young woman realized that the students' dour view of college life might be overcast by their worries over imminent examinations, but the undeniably deceptive treatment she had received earlier from her first choice college left her skeptical about the standards and ethics of the higher educational system she had been so eager to enter.

Upon closer scrutiny, the young woman would have discovered that the selling job expressly designed for highly able black candidates also operates in different ways for desirable white candidates. As the fervor mounts for the achievement of specific recruitment goals by college admissions offices, misunderstandings, overstatements, mild deceptions, and abuses of the truth contaminate exchanges with qualified applicants. Colleges with shaky financial underpinnings have developed sleazy marketing techniques publicly exposed in college fairs. The Department of Health, Education, and Welfare has, in fact, threatened increased federal intervention unless postsecondary institutions intensify efforts to assure that the student consumer is not hoodwinked. In the next few years, undergraduate colleges are going to have to give more accurate data about themselves, acknowledge their shortcomings, and indicate steps taken to improve themselves. They will have to tell applicants about the quality of academic departments, progress made in implementing affirmative action programs, dropout rates, job placement of recent graduates, and the success rates of college seniors applying to graduate and professional schools. The National Center for Educational Statistics of HEW and educational administrators suggest that the colleges' misrepresentation of themselves to high school juniors and seniors figures largely in their dropout and transfer rates. Fifty percent of entering college students do not graduate because they drop out or transfer.

The Winter Months. Among many students there is a brittle kind of industriousness in their pursuit of high marks in the first semester of the senior year. Cajoling of teachers and grade bargaining contribute to an atmosphere unconducive to eduational inquiry. In the second semester, when the interim reports have been made by the secondary schools to colleges, a general collapse of educational objectives is widely recognized. (The same phenomenon is observable in preprofessional college seniors after they submit their applications to medical and law schools.) To deal with the expectable, many secondary schools have made it possible for qualified students to graduate at midyear and others have planned independent projects that are ostensibly a bridge to college-level efforts. Some students who are gifted but discouraged by the high school experience have been admitted to fine colleges after skipping the twelfth grade. Indeed, since 1972, Johns Hopkins University has not required the high school diploma for admission.

Yet another small and apparently declining number of high school graduates need more time to understand the critical events of the past few years and so take a moratorium by delaying matriculation at college by a year. The possibility of deferring admission appears in the Yale Introductory Bulletin and in the material sent with the admissions letter. There are no stumbling blocks or financial penalties (except through annual tuition and board increments) for those who postpone, save the proviso that they not enroll in another institution. Hampshire College, a less structured institution whose student body is less competitive, encourages postponed entry in selected cases. They report, however, a 50 percent decline in student deferrals over the past three years, not because of an attitudinal shift on the part of the admissions office but for economic reasons. The cost of college escalates each year, even as inflation reduces the buying power of the parental dollar. There is a limited selection of job opportunities for the high school senior, and the work often pays poorly and has little educational value.

Let us now move from educational administrative issues to psychological matters. In March, with its dark mornings and wintry blasts, students tell of anxiety dreams. One accomplished senior girl dreamed that she had died, and letters from Yale, Harvard, Wellesley, and Wesleyan were lying unopened on a table in her home. After her death her parents had not withdrawn her applications. Her associations revealed that in the first semester of the senior year she had not worked well; and despite her pledges to herself and to her parents, her marks were undistinguished. She worried that this downturn in her performance would eliminate her from consideration by the colleges where she had submitted applications. Thus, in the dream, she was dead when the mail arrived from these admissions offices. But now that she was lost, everyone would be sorry—colleges and parents—because she was probably admitted everywhere. The fat letters from these colleges remained unopened to spare her parents further grief. The failure of her parents to notify the colleges of her demise was a measure of their inordinate investment in her gaining admission to enhance their own conceit, rather than as a fulfillment of a goal she had sought. In this light, her death served them right!

The excessive participation of parents in their children's experiences repeats critical unsettled events in their own life histories. In Erikson's terms, the admissions crisis becomes for the parents a matter of establishing generativity, which is primarily the need to found and guide the next generation. If the parental effort is unsuccessful, parents often feel a sense of impoverishment or stagnation. Thus for some parents and students, failure or relative failure at different points on the spectrum of the crisis may be perceived as a mutual tragedy.

Early Decision. Under the terms of most early decision programs, seniors may be notified of acceptance as early as December 1. The early filing of an application is already a distinguishing hallmark in the student's relationship with his peers and teachers. The interview experiences of early admission candidates are carefully examined by other seniors who surgically extract those aspects of the encounters which fit their own expectations, fears and wishes. Their special stature serves as a catalyst for the inevitable fragmentation of the senior class. A senior admitted to Amherst early in the year could not express his exhilaration at school because he did not want to injure his relationships with his closest friends. He felt forced out of his group, partly because he withdrew himself and partly because of the group members' resentment of his achievement, which intensified their own concerns about their incomplete applications. In order to regain his sense of belonging, the successful student began to deprecate Amherst silently. After all, if that vaunted institution accepted the likes of him with all of his deficits, could it really stand for excellence?

Anxieties and family pressures actually propel some seniors into a premature resolve to apply for an early decision. If accepted, however, a number of seniors begin to reconsider their positions and discover that they do not wish to attend the institutions that accepted them. One honorable young man of academic and athletic distinction, early admitted to Williams, was arrested in the shoplifting of a one-dollar toy. He clearly wanted to get caught, disgrace himself and his family and give Williams a chance to review his acceptance. His situation is repeated in many examples from this age group and others and was first classically described by Freud (1916) in a piece called "Those Wrecked by Success," which shed fresh light upon the psychology of crime.

Bloody Monday. Every year, following the April 15 mailing, seniors urgently look for the unmistakable sign of acceptance—the fat envelope. The secondary schools, because of their involvement with their students and their wish to evaluate their teaching effectiveness, the quality of their school's reputation, and the wisdom and influence of their student recommendations to the colleges, are eager, too, for the results. During this day the successful students' feelings of triumph and grandiosity are muted to preserve the sensitivities of friends who have been disappointed by the thin letter. In some communities, at night, students hold bittersweet parties with the eerie yet therapeutic quality of a wake. Subtle resentment and reluctant joy make for an ambience that many college students recall with more nostalgia than their high school graduation ceremonies. Here the stature of the young men and women is on public display and subject to more severe judgment than any admissions committee could visit upon them.

While both sexes suffer the pain of admissions rejection, why do so many young men (in contrast to young women) react with such anguish, for so long?

Certainly, reactions to injury occur in both sexes, but in young men they are often colored by maladaptive behavior. According to Matina Horner, women may be protected by societal proscriptions against their being successful and competitive with men. In the past, if a woman failed to reach her attempted goal, she could fall back upon a family-supported position and become a wife, mother, and volunteer. But this reasoning, perhaps valid for middle-class women 10 years ago, would seem to be outdated in light of the pervasive influence of the women's movement.

One answer may lie in the fact that the most blatant expressions of the competitive battle are heard from young men who have already made career choices and are driven by the fear of failure and its mortification. If they succeed, they often cannot enjoy the fruits of the victory because of their uneasiness about the degree of aggression mobilized and directed against their competitive peers in reaching their goal. Another answer, suggested by women, is that men translate their feelings about admissions judgments into assessments of their manhood and their capacity to become self-supporting in a respectable occupation.

Many college seniors awaiting admissions decisions for graduate and professional schools recapitulate the undergraduate admission ordeal. Old secondary school triumphs are weighed against the fantasy of impending defeat four years later. A male college senior recalled being sent around the world after high school graduation as a Presidential Scholar. Later, with a 3.2 GPA and 720 LSATs, he was rejected by seven law schools. Another college senior who had never written for college publications was dejected because a famous graduate school of journalism would not consider the merit of his secondary school editorial experience. A Yale woman, living near four competent male seniors awaiting Judgment Day, was perplexed because her men friends were openly mourning their rejections by Harvard College four years earlier. All had temporarily vacated any sense of the shape or meaning or history of their Yale experience.

The Senior Year Ends. In the last two months of secondary school there is further progress in attempting to give up some aspects of the loved other self of the past, with its backpack of doubts and infantile conflicts. The battle in which many have suffered during the past academic year begins to yield gently to enhanced self-regard, a renewed sense of direction, and a readiness to leave home for a summer job, which for many is clearly understood as the real departure. The continuing issues of late adolescence are not wholly relieved but, nonetheless, a profound shift in the ego structure gradually becomes recognizable with an increase in the youth's capacities for adaptation. Even for those who are disappointed by their college acceptances, the process of separation moves forward inexorably despite the fact that their diminished self-regard may not allow them to make full use of their adaptive capabilities until they embrace the freshman identity in the college they will attend.

Alternatives. There is heuristic opportunity in conducting national pilot projects to test modifications of the admissions practices that might reduce the intensity of the crisis and at the same time enrich educational prospects. But there is no proposal that I have studied that is not rife with major difficulties. Several alternative possibilities follow.

Student notification of college acceptance should be made on November 15 of the senior year. Colleges would have to either accept or reject, eliminating the "deferred" category. This proposal compels greater risk taking on the part of the colleges, since the earlier SAT and achievement test scores would be less reliable indicators and fall semester grades would not be available. Given the inexactness of the present system, however, it seems unlikely that there would be a significant diminution in the quality of the accepted candidate pool under this system. The rejected student, on the other hand, would have enough time to seek out another institution and could make an unhurried decision.

A drawback of this system is that it would militate against consideration of marginal applicants who have an extraordinarily successful fall semester in their senior year. But slots could be saved for these late-bloomers. There would also be serious problems for students who would have to file applications by May of the junior year as well as major disruptions of the admissions calendar in both secondary schools and colleges.

Student notification of college acceptance should be made on June 15 of the senior year. In this way, the educational virtues of the senior year would be preserved. It would mean, however, that the college admissions community would have to be beefed up with knowledgeable personnel to process the returns so as to guarantee the presence of a full complement in the entering class. Colleges in the private sector which are laboring under financial duress would be further strained by the hazard of a falloff of candidates who agree to matriculate. In addition, the rejected student would have less time to make other arrangements for the new academic year.

Colleges should have a rolling admissions program with the schools choosing different deadlines for submission of application forms and different notification dates. Thus, a given college might have deadlines of October 1 for application, with notification on November 15; November 15 for application, with notification on January 1, etc. The "deferred" category would be eliminated. Colleges seeking the best candidates would have to take greater risks in offering early acceptance to students because the same students might be applying the next month, for instance, to a similar level institution which might offer them places. The students would have the privilege of either securing acceptance upon notification or waiting until April. This process has the virtue of reducing shotgun applications to as many as a dozen institutions and offering both college and student a less ambivalent marriage.

A sizable percentage of high school graduates could defer application to college for two years. These students would apply to a national service program for work with social value in this country or overseas. Upon completion of this endeavor, supervisory reports of the students' performances would be submitted to the colleges considering them for admissions. The national service program would be an opportunity for the government to fund colleges based upon a GI Bill model of compensation.

Problems include the difficulties in assessing recommendations from field supervisors and evaluating the meaning of the two-year hiatus from high school. This proposal would place a heavy burden upon high school counselors to reconstruct salient features of a graduate's past performance and to integrate that impression with the developmental changes accruing from the field work with its opportunity for growth.

The emancipation experience mediated by the admissions crisis is a rite of passage. This developmental hurdle seems to be so necessary in our society today that if the institution of college did not exist, it would have to be invented. Parents can and should be helped to understand the character and dynamics of this crisis. With an improved grasp of the issues, they might better judge when to stand aside and when to provide support. More sensitively trained college advisors are needed to prepare the candidates for success or failure in their quest. The advisors would have the obligation of clarifying the perils of rejection to all candidates and of emphasizing to them the nature of the national lottery they are playing. And after Judgment Day, instead of investing time and energy only in those with no acceptances, consideration should also be given to the responses of those who failed to gain admission into their primary choice colleges—and of those who succeeded.

LENGTH: 4408 WORDS

Name Class Date

36 Bloody Monday: The Trauma of College Admissions

SCORING: Reading time: _____ Rate from chart: _____ W.P.M.

RETENTION	number right ____	× 2 equals ____	points
MAIN POINT	number right ____	× 4 equals ____	points
AUTHOR'S ATTITUDE	number right ____	× 3 equals ____	points
CONCLUSION	number right ____	× 3 equals ____	points
COMPLETION	number right ____	× 4 equals ____	points
VOCABULARY	number right ____	× 3 equals ____	points
	(Total points: 100)	**Total** ____	points

RETENTION Based on the passage, which of the following statements is True (T), False (F), or Not answerable (N)?

1. ____ Hundreds of thousands of students are admitted to college each year.
2. ____ College seniors sometimes relive the trauma of undergraduate admissions.
3. ____ Family pressure has no effect on the Early Admissions applications.
4. ____ Some colleges use unethical "selling" techniques.
5. ____ Women take rejection from their college choice more harshly than men do.
6. ____ November 15th marks the Early Decision acceptance deadline.
7. ____ About half of a freshman class graduates from its college four years later.
8. ____ High school academics are rarely affected by college admissions.
9. ____ Prep schools often have vested interests in which colleges admit their seniors.
10. ____ Middle-class families have the worst traumas over admissions.
11. ____ Admissions applications take into account adolescent insecurities.
12. ____ *College Entrance* is an Oedipal satire on admissions.
13. ____ Personal interviews are becoming more important in admissions procedures.

14. ____ Fortunately, the computer is playing a smaller role in public college admission procedures.

15. ____ The standardized application form underscores institutional differences.

16. ____ Current admissions practices disregard educational principles.

17. ____ Some PSAT scores do not "really count."

18. ____ Sacks describes "joint regression" of parents and children.

19. ____ Oddly enough, Sacks never went through the procedure himself.

20. ____ The autobiographical statement is mentioned as unsettling.

MAIN POINT Which of the following statements best represents the main point of the passage? ____

1. College Admissions procedures are here to stay.
2. Few people are unaffected by the trauma of college admissions.
3. The college admissions procedure has become a trauma of adolescence.
4. People seem outwardly concerned but inwardly pleased about admissions trauma.
5. A national review of admissions procedures is almost surely on the way.

AUTHOR'S ATTITUDE Which of the following statements best represents the author's attitude? ____

1. Present admissions procedures are harmful and contradictory; they must be changed.
2. Bad as they are, there are no real alternatives for the present procedures.
3. The college admissions trauma is building the nation's character.
4. Colleges really have no concern for the emotions of those they reject.
5. The college admissions trauma is better than the unemployment trauma.

CONCLUSION Which of the following statements is the best conclusion that can be drawn from the passage? ____

1. If changes come, they will come from protesting high schools.
2. Should changes come, high school parents will lead the way.

3. Colleges are likely to be the only sources of change of admissions procedures.

4. Admissions procedures will probably be developed by the testing people in Princeton.

5. In all likelihood no changes whatever will come in our time.

COMPLETION Choose the best answer for each question:

1. ____ Sacks suggests trying out: (a) no admissions procedure at all. (b) a series of pilot projects to modify procedures. (c) virtually anything that looks even half promising. (d) admissions procedures used in the 1880's.

2. ____ Parents pressure their children from intellectual and: (a) cultural (b) maternal (c) moral (d) social motives.

3. ____ Students with early admission often cannot: (a) face such success. (b) satisfy ambitious parents. (c) enjoy their success. (d) decide on a career.

4. ____ One example of college recruitment shows that some colleges: (a) act out elaborate charades. (b) have more room than they admit. (c) want students, but won't help them. (d) have very erratic admissions procedures.

5. ____ Sacks seems to assume that: (a) all students are equal in ability. (b) parents and students have serious conflicts. (c) colleges are careless of their policies. (d) high school students can easily handle the strain of admissions.

VOCABULARY Choose the word or phrase from Column B that best defines the vocabulary entry from Column A:

	Column A	*Column B*
1. ____	hiatus	a. force; pressure
2. ____	defer	b. thoughtful; shrewd
3. ____	diminution	c. calm spell
4. ____	well apprised	d. augmented
5. ____	period of quiescence	e. traumatic
6. ____	coercion	f. extraordinary
7. ____	matriculants	g. boosts

8. ____ enhanced
9. ____ perspicacious
10. ____ ambivalence
11. ____ inordinate
12. ____ increments
13. ____ pervasive
14. ____ recapitulate
15. ____ deprecate

h. widespread
i. reduction
j. entering students
k. under a spell
l. completely informed
m. uncertain feelings
n. put off
o. conspicuous
p. devalue
q. absence; break
r. summarize; go over

Charts for Measuring Speed of Reading

To find the speed at which you have read a given selection, divide the total number of words (given at the end of each passage and on the charts below) by the number of seconds it took you to read the passage. Then multiply that figure by 60 in order to get the speed in words per minute (W.P.M.). For example: if you read Passage 1 in 90 seconds, or 1.5 minutes, you could calculate your speed in this way:

$$1670 \div 90 = 18.5 \times 60 = 1110 \text{ W.P.M.}$$

The charts on pages 334–38 show how many words you read per minute depending on how long it takes to read the passage.

SECTION 1 **Selections**

Time in Mins.	1	2	3	4	5	6	7
1	1670	583	1985	2660	1790	1665	1020
1.5	1110	389	1323	1773	1193	1110	680
2	835	292	993	1330	895	833	510
2.5	668	233	794	1064	716	666	408
3	557	194	662	886	597	555	340
3.5	477	167	567	760	511	476	291
4	418	146	496	665	448	416	255
4.5	370	130	441	591	398	370	227
5	334	117	397	532	358	333	204
5.5	305	106	361	483	325	303	185
6	278	97	330	443	298	278	170
6.5	257	90	305	409	275	256	157
7	239	83	284	380	256	238	146
7.5	223	78	265	355	239	222	136
8	209	73	248	333	224	208	128
8.5	196	69	234	313	211	196	120
9	186	65	221	296	199	185	113
9.5	176	61	209	280	188	175	107
10	167	58	199	266	179	167	102
10.5	159		189	253	170	159	97
11	152		180	242	163	151	
11.5	145		172	231	156	145	
12	139		165	222	149	139	
12.5	134		159	213	143	133	
13	128		153	204	138	128	
13.5	123		147	197	133	123	
14	119		142	190	128	119	
14.5	115		137	183	123	115	
15	111		132	177	119	111	

Time in Mins.	8	9	10	11	12	13	14	15
1	1890		1107	2781	1440	1332	3735	2774
1.5	1260		738	1854	960	888	2490	1849
2	945		554	1391	720	666	1868	1387
2.5	756		443	1112	576	533	1494	1110
3	630		369	927	480	444	1245	925
3.5	540		316	795	411	381	1067	793
4	473		277	695	360	333	934	694
4.5	420		246	618	320	296	830	616
5	378		221	556	288	266	747	555
5.5	344		201	506	262	242	679	504
6	315		185	464	240	222	623	462
6.5	291		170	428	222	205	575	427
7	270		158	397	206	190	534	396
7.5	252		148	371	192	178	498	370
8	236		138	348	180	167	467	347
8.5	222		130	327	169	157	439	326
9	210		123	309	160	148	415	308
9.5	199		117	293	152	140	393	292
10	189		111	278	144	133	374	277
10.5	180		105	265	137	127	356	264
11	172		101	253	131	121	340	252
11.5	164		96	242	125	116	325	241
12	157		92	232	120	111	311	231
12.5	151		89	223	115	107	300	222
13	145		85	214	111	102	287	213
13.5	140		82	206	107	99	277	205
14	135		79	199	103	95	267	198
14.5	130			192	99	92	256	191
15	126			185	96	89	249	185
15.5	122			179			241	179
16	118			174			233	173
16.5	115			169			226	168
17	111			164			220	163

Time in Mins.	16	17	18	19	20	21	22
1	1560	1771	1320	1250	2054	1740	
1.5	1040	1181	880	833	1369	1160	
2	780	886	660	625	1027	870	
2.5	624	708	528	500	822	696	
3	520	590	440	417	685	580	
3.5	446	506	377	357	587	497	
4	390	443	330	313	514	435	
4.5	347	394	293	278	456	387	
5	312	354	264	250	411	348	
5.5	284	322	240	227	374	316	
6	260	295	220	208	342	290	
6.5	240	273	203	192	316	268	
7	223	253	189	179	293	249	
7.5	208	236	176	167	274	232	
8	195	221	165	156	257	218	
8.5	184	208	155	147	242	205	
9	173	198	147	139	228	193	
9.5	164	186	139	132	216	183	
10	156	177	132	125	205	174	
10.5	149	169	126	119	196	167	
11	142	161	120	114	187	158	
11.5	137	154	115	109	179	151	
12	130	148	110	104	171	145	
12.5	125	142	106	100	164	139	
13	120	136	102	96	158	134	
13.5	116	131	98	93	152	129	
14	111	127	94	89	147	124	
14.5	108	122			142	120	
15	104	118			137	116	
15.5	101	114			133	112	
16	98	111			128	109	
16.5	95	107			125	106	
17		104			121	102	
17.5		101			117	99	

SECTION 4 **Selections**

Time in Mins.	23	24	25	26	27	28
1	4833	1700	2563	1680	2010	
1.5	3222	1128	1709	1120	1370	
2	2417	852	1282	840	1005	
2.5	1933	678	1025	672	802	
3	1611	564	842	560	670	
3.5	1381	486	722	480	572	
4	1208	421	632	420	502	
4.5	1074	378	562	373	446	
5	967	342	506	336	402	
5.5	879	312	459	305	365	
6	806	282	422	280	334	
6.5	744	258	389	258	340	
7	690	240	362	240	286	
7.5	644	228	337	224	268	
8	604	210	316	210	250	
8.5	569	198	297	197	236	
9	537	186	281	187	222	
9.5	509	174	266	177	215	
10	483	168	256	168	201	
10.5	460	162	241	160	192	
11	439	156	229	153	184	
11.5	420	150	219	146	174	
12	403	144	211	140	167	
12.5	387	138	202	134	160	
13	372	132	194	129	154	
13.5	358	126	187	124	148	
14	345		180	120		
14.5	333		174	116		
15	322		168	112		
15.5	312		163	108		
16	302		158	105		
16.5	293		153	102		
17	284		148	99		
17.5	276		144			
18	269		140			

SECTION 5 **Selections**

Time in Mins.	29	30	31	32	33	34	35	36
1	1350	1340	1712	1680	1248	4028	1410	4408
1.5	900	895	1141	1120	832	2680	942	3000
2	675	670	856	840	624	2014	708	2204
2.5	540	535	685	672	499	1610	564	1790
3	450	446	571	560	415	1340	468	1490
3.5	386	383	489	480	357	1150	402	1280
4	338	335	428	420	312	1008	354	1122
4.5	300	298	380	373	277	896	312	1000
5	270	268	342	336	248	806	282	900
5.5	245	244	311	305	227	734	258	816
6	225	223	285	280	208	673	234	750
6.5	208	206	263	258	192	620	216	691
7	193	191	245	240	178	576	198	642
7.5	180	178	228	224	166	536	186	598
8	169	167	214	210	156	504	174	561
8.5	158	158	201	197	143	474	162	528
9	150	149	190	187	137	447	156	499
9.5	142	141	180	177	131	424	150	473
10	135	134	171	168	125	403	144	445
10.5			163	160		384	132	420
11			156	153		367	126	401
11.5			149	146		350	120	384
12			143	140		336		367
12.5			137	134		323		353
13			132	129		310		339
13.5				124		298		326
14				120		288		314
14.5						278		320
15						269		294
15.5						260		284
16						252		275
16.5						244		267
17						237		259
17.5						230		252
18						224		245

Reading Speed in Words per Minute

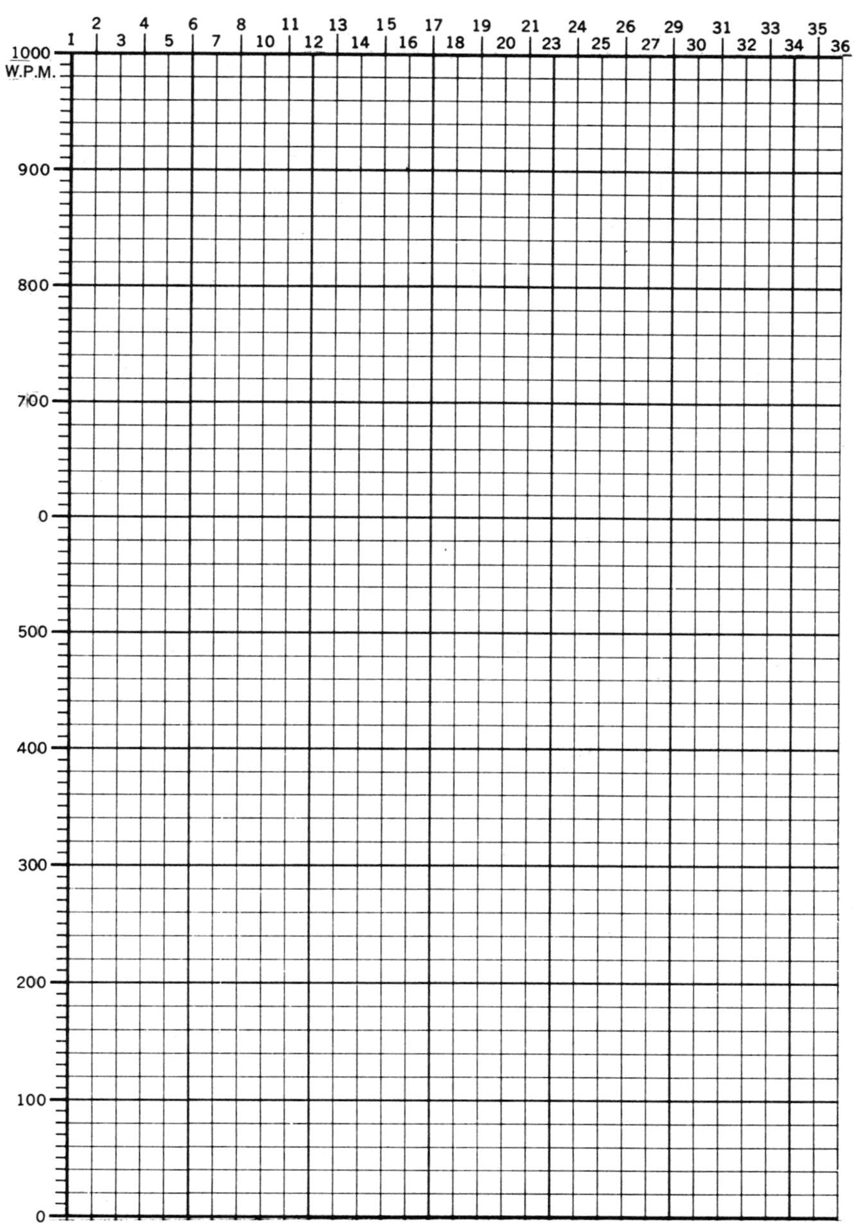

The numbers on the horizontal line refer to the selections; those on the vertical line refer to reading speed in words per minute. Make a dot at your speed for each selection and connect the dots with a line. (*Note:* The poetry selections, for which your reading speed was not measured, have been omitted from this chart.)

Retention Skill

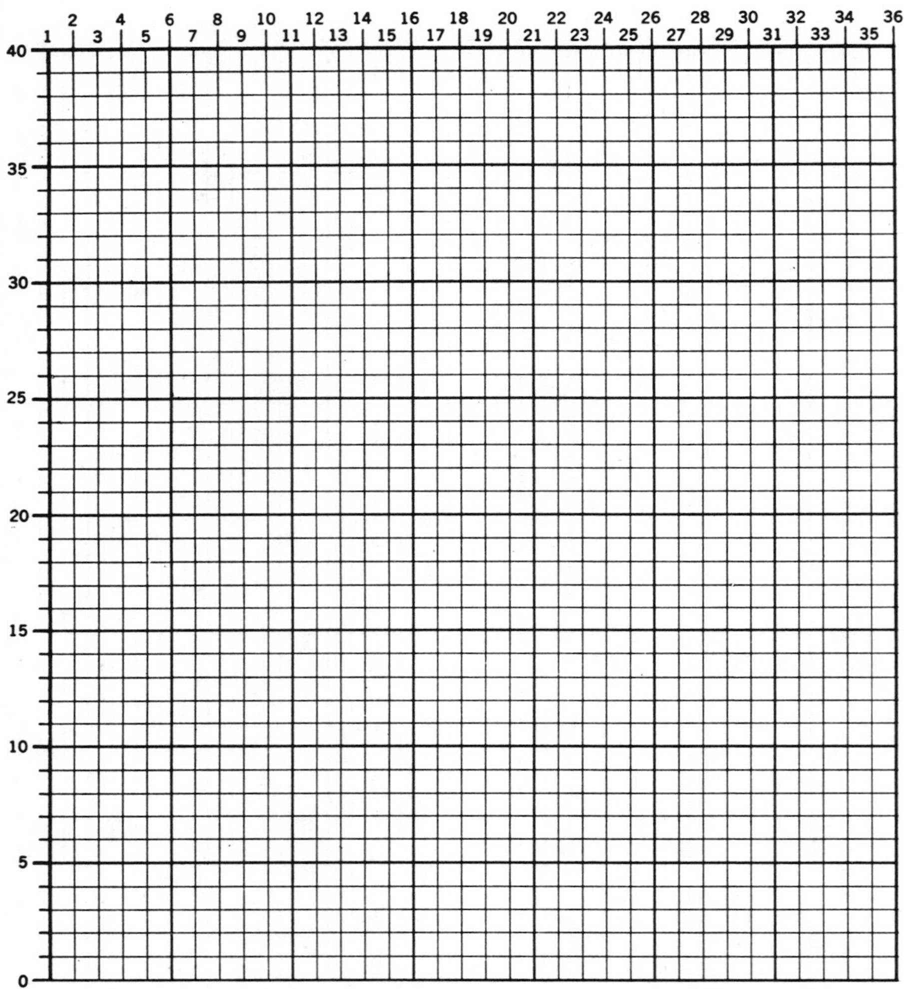

The numbers on the horizontal line refer to the selections; those on the vertical line refer to your point score for retention questions. Make a dot at your retention score for each selection and connect the dots with a line.

Vocabulary Skill

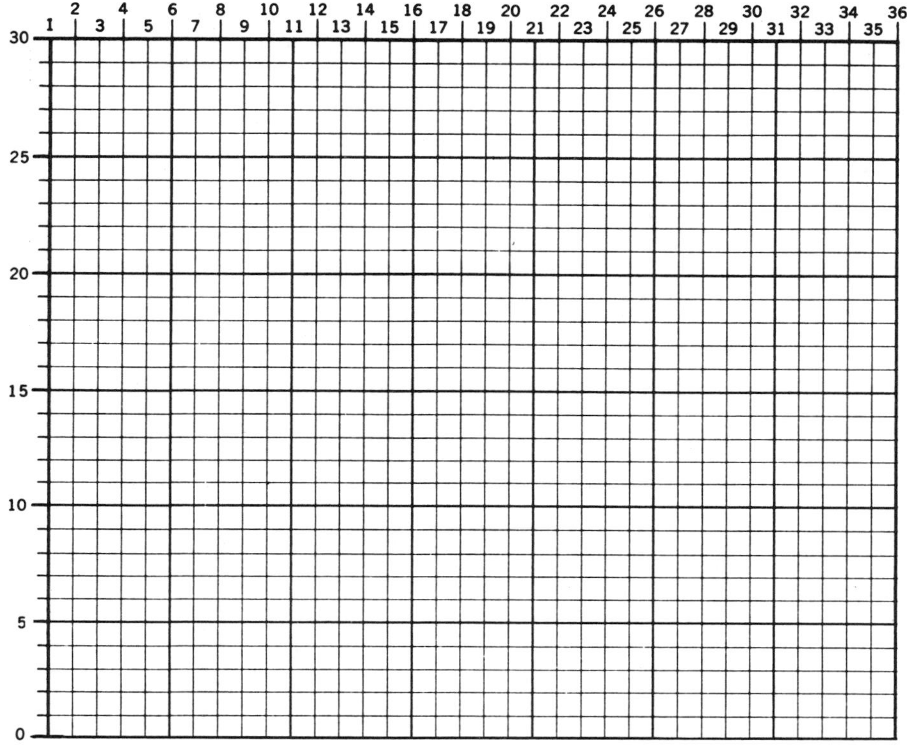

The numbers on the horizontal line refer to the selections; those on the vertical line refer to your point score for vocabulary questions. Make a dot at your vocabulary score for each selection and connect the dots with a line.

Inferential and Completion Skills

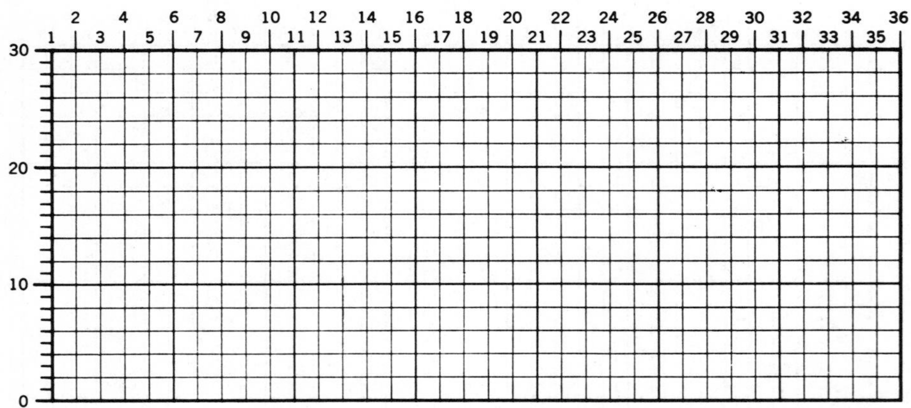

The numbers on the horizontal line refer to the selections; those on the vertical line refer to your point score. Add your scores for inference, completion, main point, author's attitude, and conclusion questions. Enter the total for each selection on the chart as a dot, and connect the dots with a line.

Progress Chart

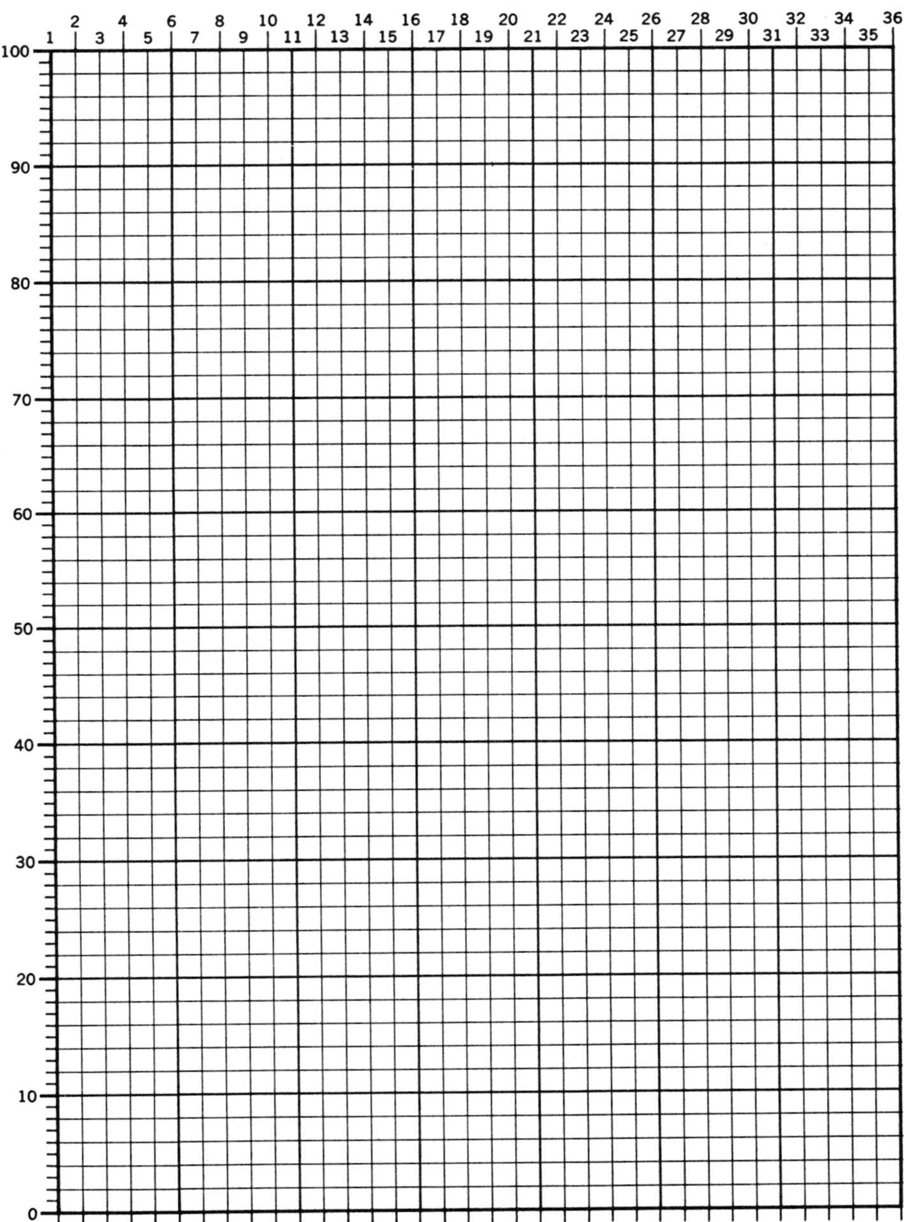

DATE

The numbers on the horizontal line refer to the selections; those on the vertical line refer to your total point score for each selection. Check your progress by graphing your scores. Enter the date of each exercise on the lower part of the chart.